A-Z RICHMOND UPON THAMES, KINGSTON UPON THAMES

CONTENTS

REFERENCE

Motorway	M4	Car Park	P
A Road	A3	Church or Chapel	†
B Road	B358	Fire Station	■
Dual Carriageway		Hospital	H
One-way Street		House Numbers (A & B Roads only)	2 — 33
Traffic flow on A roads is indicated by a heavy line on the drivers' left.	→		
Large Scale Page Only		Information Centre	i
Junction Names	KEW GREEN	National Grid Reference	525
Restricted Access		Park & Ride	Kingston upon Thames P+L
Pedestrianized Road		Police Station	▲
Track & Footpath		Post Office	★
Residential Walkway		Toilet:	
Railway Stations:	Tunnel / Level Crossing	without facilities for the Disabled	▽
National Rail Network	⇄	with facilities for the Disabled	▽
Underground	●	Disabled facilities only	▽
Croydon Tramlink	Tunnel / Stop	Educational Establishment	
The boarding of Tramlink trams at stops may be limited to a single direction, indicated by the arrow.		Hospital or Hospice	
Built-up Area		Industrial Building	
Local Authority Boundary	—·—·—	Leisure or Recreational Facility	
Posttown Boundary		Place of Interest	
Postcode Boundary (within posttown)	— — —	Public Building	
Map Continuation	14 / Large Scale Town Centre 36	Shopping Centre or Market	
		Other Selected Buildings	

SCALE

Map Pages 4-35	Map Page 36
1:19000 3.33 inches to 1 mile	1:9500 6.67 inches to 1 mile
0 ¼ ½ Mile	0 ⅛ ¼ Mile
0 250 500 750 Metres	0 100 200 300 Metres
5.26cm to 1km 8.47cm to 1 mile	10.53 cm to 1km 16.94 cm to 1 mile

Copyright of Geographers' A-Z Map Company Limited

Head Office :
Fairfield Road, Borough Green, Sevenoaks, Kent TN15 8PP
Telephone: 01732 781000 (Enquiries & Trade Sales)
01732 783422 (Retail Sales)
www.a-zmaps.co.uk

Copyright © Geographers' A-Z Map Co. Ltd.

EDITION 4   2005

KU-043-264

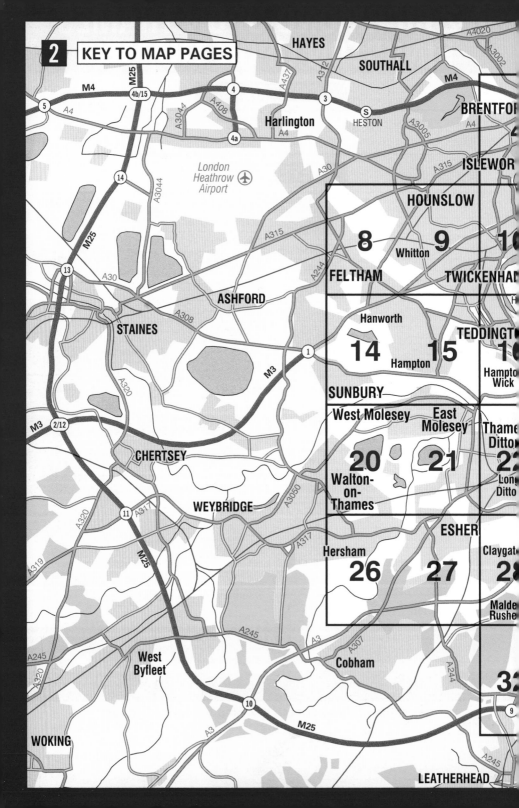

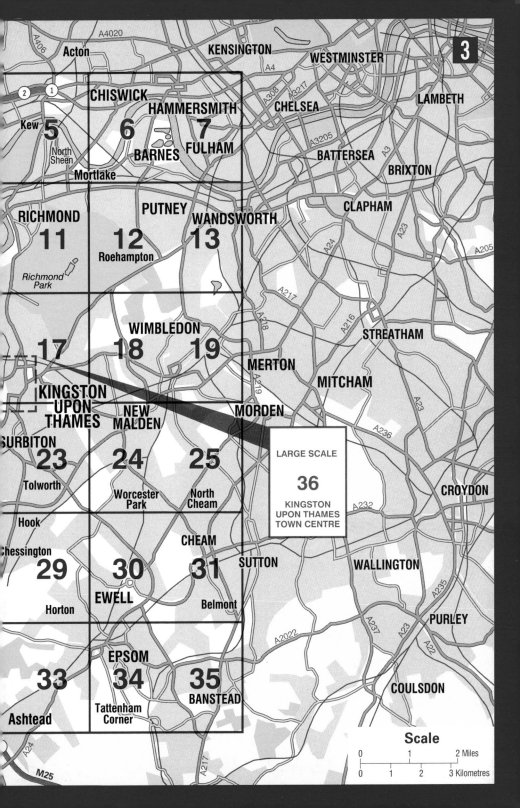

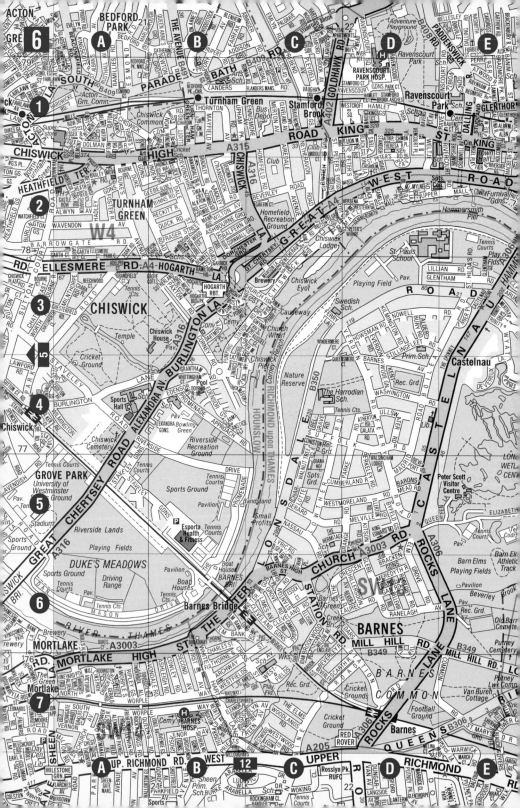

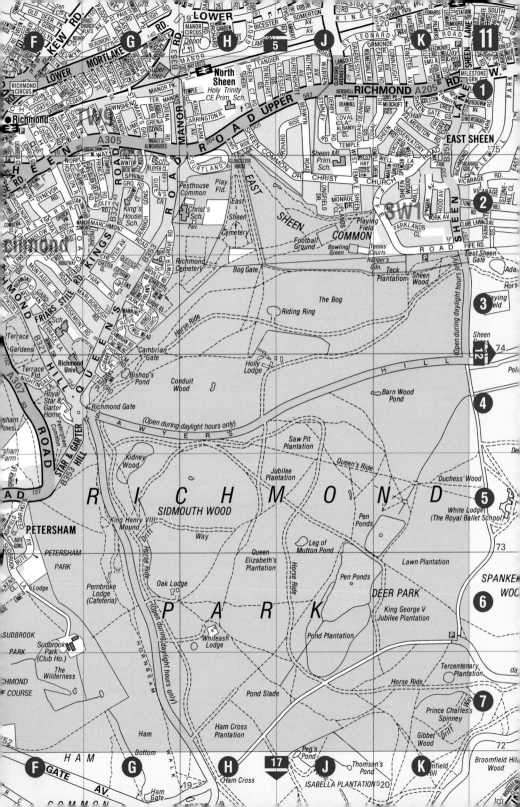

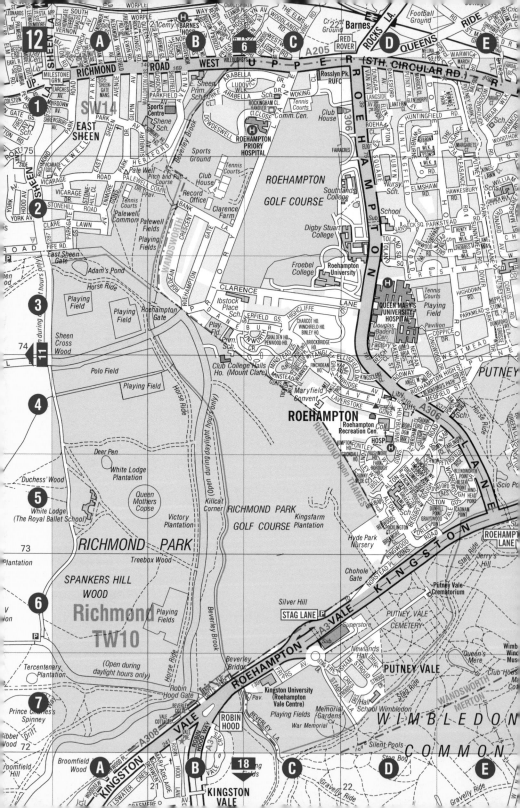

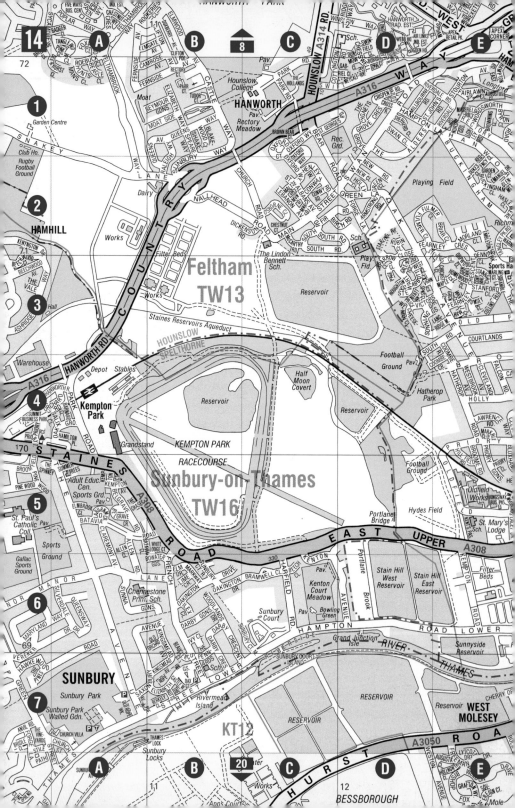

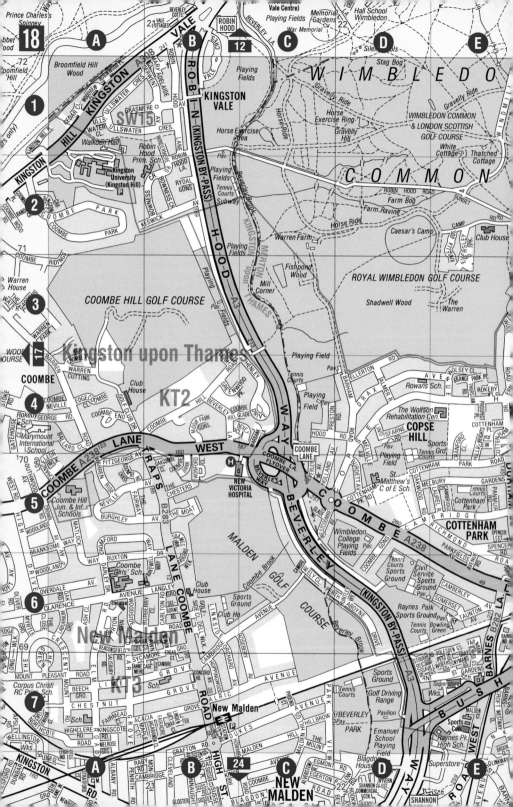

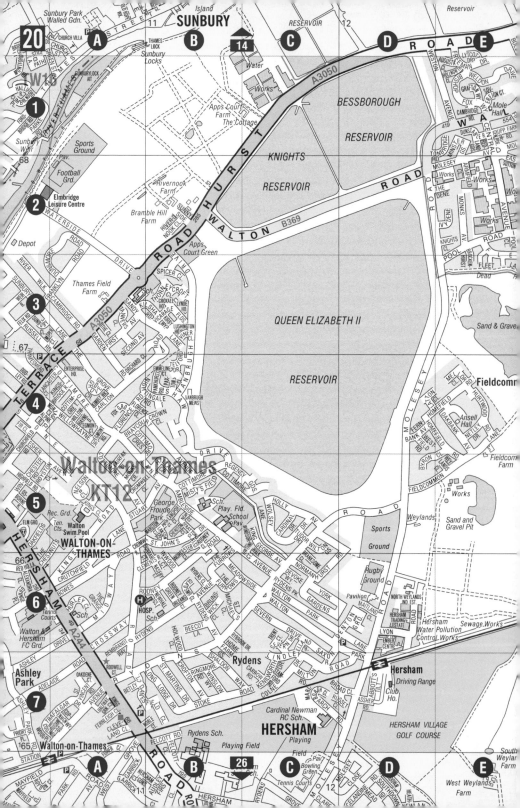

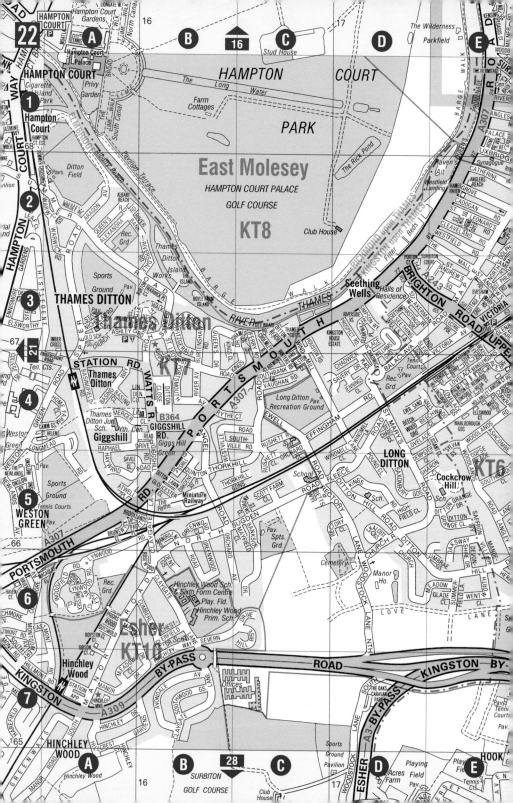

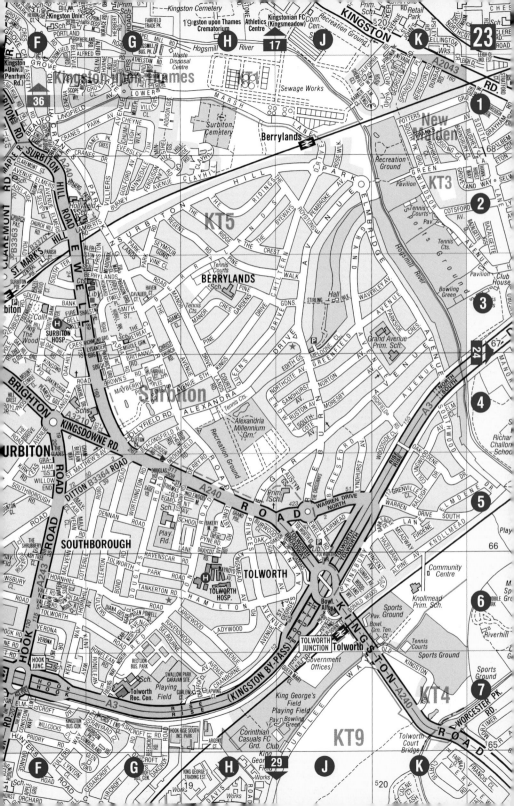

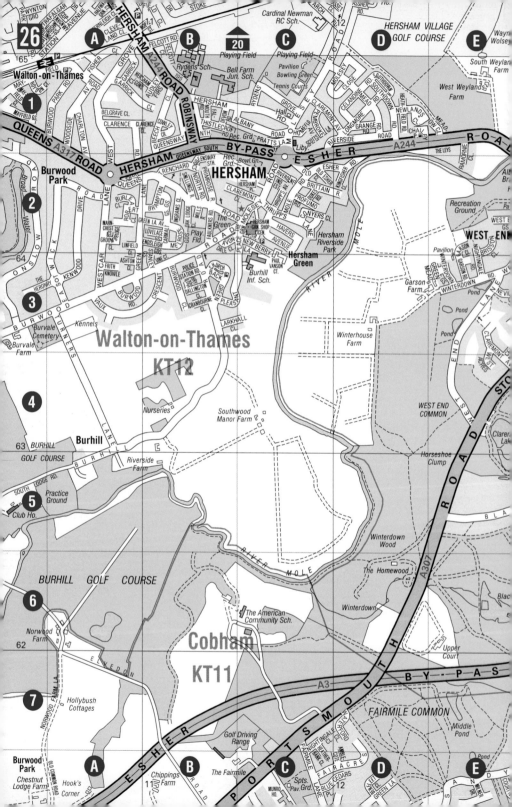

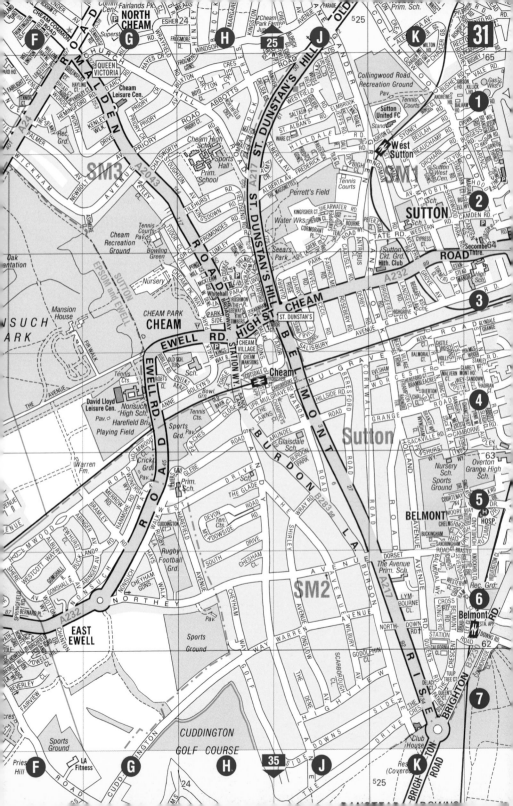

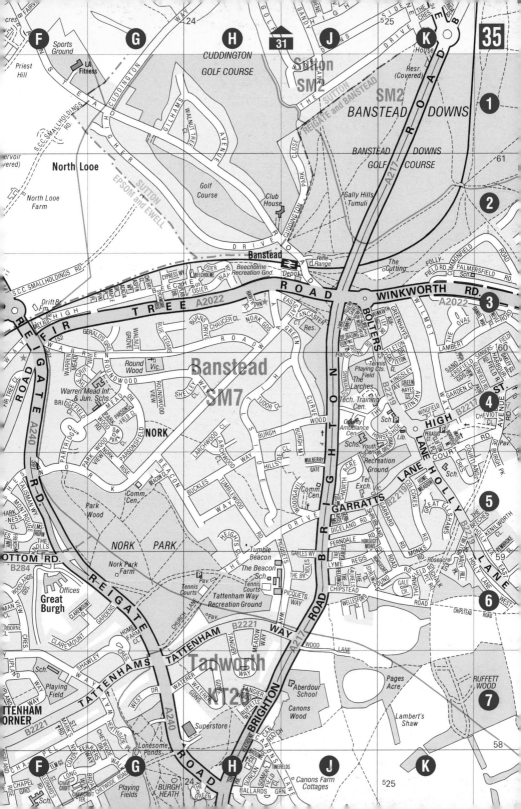

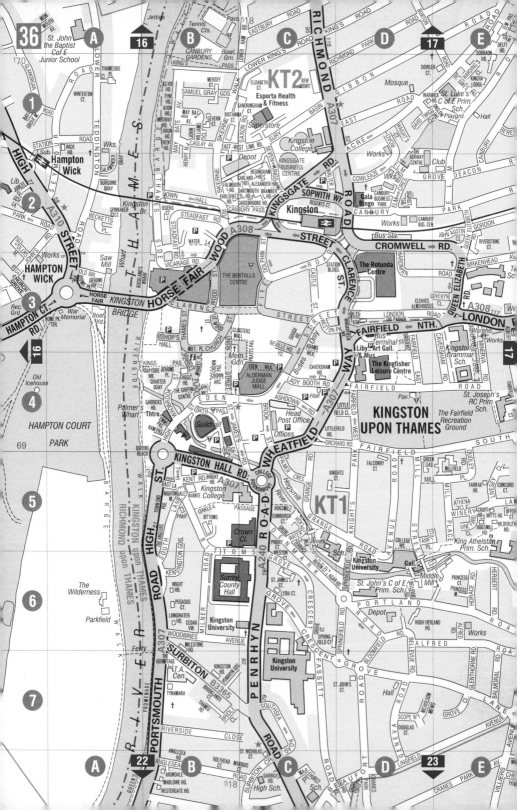

INDEX

Including Streets, Places & Areas, Hospitals & Hospices, Industrial Estates,
Selected Flats & Walkways, Junction Names and Selected Places of Interest.

HOW TO USE THIS INDEX

1. Each street name is followed by its Postcode District (or, if outside the London Postcodes, by its Locality Abbreviation(s)), and then by its map reference;
e.g. **Abbots Av.** KT19: Eps . . . .7H **29** is in the KT19 Postcode District and is to be found in square 7H on page **29**. The page number being shown in bold type.

2. A strict alphabetical order is followed in which Av., Rd., St., etc. (though abbreviated) are read in full and as part of the street name;
e.g. **Aldersbrook Dr.** appears after **Alders, The** but before **Alders Gro.**

3. Streets and a selection of flats and walkways too small to be shown on the maps, appear in the index in *Italics* with the thoroughfare to which it is connected shown in brackets; e.g. *Abbot's Ho.* W14 . . . .1J **7** (off St Mary Abbots Ter.)

4. Addresses that are in more than one part are referred to as not continuous.

5. Places and areas are shown in the index in **blue type** and the map reference is to the actual map square in which the town centre or area is located and not to the place name shown on the map; e.g. **BARNES** 6C **6**

6. An example of a selected place of interest is Boston Manor House 2C **4**

7. An example of a station is Ashtead Station (Rail) 6F **33**

8. An example of a hospital or hospice is BARNES HOSPITAL 7B **6**

9. Junction names are shown in the index in **BOLD CAPITAL TYPE**; e.g. **APEX CONRNER** 7E **8**

10. Map references for entries that appear on large scale page **36** are shown first, with small scale map references shown in brackets;
e.g. **Acre Rd.** KT2: King T 1D **36** (5F **17**)

GENERAL ABBREVIATIONS

All. : Alley	Cft. : Croft	Junc. : Junction	Ri. : Rise
App. : Approach	Dr. : Drive	La. : Lane	Rd. : Road
Arc. : Arcade	E. : East	Lit. : Little	Rdbt. : Roundabout
Av. : Avenue	Ent. : Enterprise	Lwr. : Lower	Shop. : Shopping
Bri. : Bridge	Est. : Estate	Mnr. : Manor	Sth. : South
B'way. : Broadway	Fld. : Field	Mans. : Mansions	Sq. : Square
Bldg. : Building	Flds. : Fields	Mkt. : Market	Sta. : Station
Bldgs. : Buildings	Gdns. : Gardens	Mdw. : Meadow	St. : Street
Bus. : Business	Gth. : Garth	Mdws. : Meadows	Ter. : Terrace
Cvn. : Caravan	Ga. : Gate	M. : Mews	Twr. : Tower
C'way. : Causeway	Gt. : Great	Mt. : Mount	Trad. : Trading
Cen. : Centre	Grn. : Green	Mus. : Museum	Up. : Upper
Chu. : Church	Gro. : Grove	Nth. : North	Va. : Vale
Cl. : Close	Hgts. : Heights	Pal. : Palace	Vw. : View
Comn. : Common	Ho. : House	Pde. : Parade	Vs. : Villas
Cnr. : Corner	Ho's. : Houses	Pas. : Passage	Vis. : Visitors
Cotts. : Cottages	Ind. : Industrial	Pl. : Place	Wlk. : Walk
Ct. : Court	Info. : Information	Prom. : Promenade	W. : West
Cres. : Crescent	Intl. : International		Yd. : Yard

POSTTOWN AND POSTAL LOCALITY ABBREVIATIONS

Asht : **Ashtead**	Ewe : **Ewell**	Kew : **Kew**	Tatt C : **Tattenham Corner**
Bans : **Banstead**	Felt : **Feltham**	King T : **Kingston upon Thames**	Tedd : **Teddington**
Bford : **Brentford**	Ham : **Ham**	Lea : **Leatherhead**	T Ditt : **Thames Ditton**
Cheam : **Cheam**	Hamp : **Hampton**	Mord : **Morden**	Twick : **Twickenham**
Chess : **Chessington**	Hamp H : **Hampton Hill**	N Mald : **New Malden**	Walt T : **Walton-on-Thames**
Clay : **Claygate**	Hamp W : **Hampton Wick**	Oxs : **Oxshott**	W Mole : **West Molesey**
Cobh : **Cobham**	Hanw : **Hanworth**	Rich : **Richmond**	Whit : **Whitton**
E Mos : **East Molesey**	Hers : **Hersham**	Sun : **Sunbury**	Wor Pk : **Worcester Park**
Eps : **Epsom**	Hin W : **Hinchley Wood**	Surb : **Surbiton**	
Eps D : **Epsom Downs**	Houn : **Hounslow**	Sutt : **Sutton**	
Esh : **Esher**	Isle : **Isleworth**	Tad : **Tadworth**	

A

	Abinger Rd. W4 . . . . .1B 6	Addington Ct. SW14 . . . . .7A 6	Agar Cl. KT6: Surb 6G 23
	Aboyne Dr. SW20 . . . . .6D 18	Addison Bri. Pl. W14 . . . . .1J 7	Agar Ho. KT1: King T 6C 36
	Acacia Av. TW8: Bford 4C 4	Addison Gdns. KT5: Surb 1G 23	Agates La. KT21: Asht 7E 32
Abbey Ct. TW12: Hamp 4F 15	Acacia Dr. SM3: Sutt 5J 25	Addison Gro. W4 . . . . .1B 6	Ailsa Av. TW1: Twick 2B 10
Abbey Gdns. W6: Lon 3H 7	SM7: Bans 3G 35	Addison Rd. TW11: Tedd 3C 16	Ailsa Rd. TW1: Twick 2C 10
Abbey Wlk. KT8: W Mole 7G 15	Acacia Gro. KT3: N Mald 7A 18	W14 . . . . .1J 7	Aintree Est. *SW6* 4H 7
Abbots Av. KT19: Eps 7H 29	Acacia Rd. TW12: Hamp 3F 15	Addison Ter. *W4* 1K 5	(off Aintree St.)
Abbotsbury Rd. SM4: Mord 2K 25	Accommodation Rd.	(off Chiswick Rd.)	Aintree St. SW6 . . . . .4H 7
Abbot's Ho. W14 . . . . .1J 7	KT17: Ewe 2D 30	Adecroft Way KT8: W Mole 7H 15	Airedale Av. W4 . . . . .1C 6
(off St Mary Abbots Ter.)	**AC Court** KT7: T Ditt 3B 22	Adela Av. KT3: N Mald 2E 24	Airedale Av. Sth. W4 . . . . .2C 6
Abbotsleigh Cl. SM2: Sutt 4K 31	Ace Pde. KT9: Chess 7F 23	*Adela Ho.* W6 . . . . .2F 7	Air Links Ind. Est. TW13: Hanw . .7D 8
Abbots Mead TW10: Ham 1E 16	Ackmar Rd. SW6 . . . . .5K 7	(off Queen Caroline St.)	Air Pk. Way TW13: Felt 6A 8
Abbotsmede Cl. TW1: Twick 6A 10	Acorn Cl. TW12: Hamp 3G 15	Adelaide Rd. KT6: Surb 2F 23	Aisgill Av. W14 . . . . .2J 7
Abbotstone Rd. SW15 . . . . .7F 7	Acorns Way KT10: Esh 2H 27	KT12: Walt T 7A 20	(not continuous)
Abbott Av. SW20 . . . . .5G 19	Acqua Ho. TW9: Kew 4J 5	SW18 . . . . .2K 13	Aiten Pl. W6 . . . . .1D 6
Abbott Cl. TW12: Hamp 3D 14	Acre Rd. KT2: King T 1D **36** (5F **17**)	TW9: Rich 1G 11	Akehurst St. SW15 . . . . .3D 12
Abbotts Rd. SM3: Cheam 1H 31	Acropolis Ho. KT1: King T 5E 36	TW11: Tedd 3A 16	Akerman Rd. KT6: Surb 3D 22
Abbott's Tilt KT12: Hers 7D 20	Acton La. W4 . . . . .1K 5	Adelaide Ter. TW8: Bford 2E 4	Alan Rd. SW19 . . . . .2H 19
Abercorn M. TW10: Rich 1G 11	(not continuous)	Adelphi Ct. W4 . . . . .3A 6	Alba M. SW18 . . . . .6K 13
Abingdon W14 . . . . .1J 7	Acton Sports Club 1H 5	Adelphi Rd. KT17: Eps 2A 34	Albany Cl. KT10: Esh 5F 27
(off Kensington Village)	Acuba Rd. SW18 . . . . .6K 13	Adeney Cl. W6 . . . . .3G 7	SW14 . . . . .1J 11
Abingdon Gdns. W8 . . . . .1K 7	Adams Cl. KT5: Surb 3G 23	Adie Rd. W6 . . . . .1F 7	Albany Cres. KT10: Clay 3K 27
Abingdon Rd. W8 . . . . .1K 7	Adams End TW8: Bford 4D 4	Admark Ho. KT18: Eps 4J 33	Albany M. KT2: King T 3E 16
Abingdon Vs. W8 . . . . .1K 7	Adams Wlk.	Admiral Ho. TW1: Tedd 1B 16	Albany Pde. TW8: Bford 3F 5
Abinger Av. SM2: Cheam 5F 31	KT1: King T 3C **36** (6F **17**)	Admiral Rd. TW11: Tedd 3A 16	Albany Pk. Rd. KT2: King T 3E 16
Abinger Gdns. TW7: Isle 1K 9	Adam Wlk. SW6 . . . . .4F 7	Admiralty Way TW11: Tedd 3A 16	Albany Pas. TW10: Rich 2F 11

A-Z Richmond & Kingston 37

Albany Pl.—Astonville St.

Albany Pl. TW8: Bford 3E **4**
Albany Reach KT7: T Ditt 2A **22**
Albany Rd. KT3: N Mald 1A **24**
KT12: Hers 1C **26**
SW19 2K **19**
TW8: Bford 3E **4**
TW10: Rich 2G **11**
Albany Ter. *TW10: Rich 2G **11***
(off Albany Pas.)
Albemarle SW19 6G **13**
Albemarle Av. TW2: Whit 5E **8**
Albemarle Gdns.
KT3: N Mald 1A **24**
Alberta Av. SM1: Sutt 1H **31**
Albert Dr. SW19 6H **13**
Albert Gro. SW20 5G **19**
Albertine Cl. KT17: Eps D 5E **34**
Albert Rd.
KT1: King T 3E **36** (6G **17**)
KT3: N Mald 1C **24**
KT17: Eps 2C **34**
KT21: Asht 7G **33**
TW1: Twick 5A **10**
TW3: Houn 1F **9**
TW10: Rich 2F **11**
TW11: Tedd 3A **16**
TW12: Hamp H 2H **15**
Albert Ter. *W6 2D **6***
(off Beavor La.)
Albion Ct. *W6 1E **6***
(off Albion Pl.)
Albion Gdns. W6 1E **6**
Albion M. W6 1E **6**
Albion Pl. W6 1E **6**
Albion Rd. KT2: King T 5K **17**
TW2: Twick 5K **9**
TW3: Houn 1F **9**
Albon Ho. *SW18 3K **13***
(off Neville Gill Cl.)
Albury Av. SM2: Cheam 5F **31**
TW7: Isle 4A **4**
Albury Cl. KT19: Eps 5J **29**
TW12: Hamp 3G **15**
Albury Rd. KT9: Chess 2F **29**
Alcorn Cl. SM3: Sutt 6K **25**
Aldensley Rd. W6 1E **6**
Alderbury Rd. SW13 3D **6**
Alder Lodge SW6 5F **7**
Alderman Judge Mall
KT1: King T 4C **36** (6F **17**)
Alder Rd. SW14 7A **6**
Alders, The TW13: Hanw 1D **14**
Aldersbrook Dr. KT2: King T 3G **17**
Alders Gro. KT8: E Mos 2J **21**
Alderton Ct. *KT8: W Mole 1E **20***
(off Walton Rd.)
Alderville Rd. SW6 6J **7**
Aldrich Gdns. SM3: Cheam 7J **25**
Aldridge Ri. KT3: N Mald 4B **24**
Alexa Ct. SM2: Sutt 3K **31**
W8 1K **7**
Alexander Cl. TW2: Twick 6K **9**
Alexander Godley Cl.
KT21: Asht 7G **33**
Alexander Ho. *KT2: King T 2C **36***
(off Seven Kings Way)
Alexandra Av. SM1: Sutt 7K **25**
W4 4A **6**
Alexandra Cl. KT12: Walt T 6A **20**
Alexandra Dr. KT5: Surb 4H **23**
Alexandra Gdns. W4 4B **6**
Alexandra Ho. *W6 2F **7***
(off Queen Caroline St.)
Alexandra Mans.
*KT17: Eps 2C **34***
(off Alexandra Rd.)
Alexandra M. SW19 3J **19**
Alexandra Rd. KT2: King T 4H **17**
KT7: T Ditt 2A **22**
KT17: Eps 2C **34**
SW14 7A **6**
SW19 3J **19**
TW1: Twick 3D **10**
TW8: Bford 3E **4**
TW9: Kew 6G **5**
Alexandra Sq. SM4: Mord 2K **25**
Alexandra Way KT19: Eps 7H **29**
Alfred Cl. W4 1A **6**
Alfred Rd.
KT1: King T 6D **36** (7F **17**)
TW13: Felt 6B **8**
Alfreton Cl. SW19 7G **13**
Alfriston KT5: Surb 3G **23**
Alfriston Cl. KT5: Surb 2G **23**
Algar Cl. TW7: Isle 7B **4**
Algar Rd. TW7: Isle 7B **4**
Alice Gilliatt Ct. *W14 3J **7***
(off Star Rd.)
Alice M. TW11: Tedd 2A **16**
Alice Way TW3: Houn 1G **9**
Alkerden Rd. W4 2B **6**
Allan Cl. KT3: N Mald 2A **24**
Allbrook Cl. TW11: Tedd 2K **15**
Allen Cl. TW16: Sun 5A **14**
Allenford Ho. *SW15 3C **12***
(off Tunworth Cres.)
Allen Rd. TW16: Sun 5A **14**
Allen St. W8 1K **7**
Allenswood SW19 5H **13**
Allestree Rd. SW6 4H **7**
Allgood Cl. SM4: Mord 3G **25**
Allington Cl. SW19 2G **19**
All Saints Pas. SW18 2K **13**
Alma Cres. SM1: Sutt 2H **31**
Alma Ho. TW8: Bford 3F **5**
Alma Rd. KT10: Esh 5K **21**
Alma Ter. W8 1K **7**
Almer Rd. SW20 4D **18**
Almond Gro. TW8: Bford 4C **4**
Almond Rd. KT19: Eps 7A **30**
Almshouse La. KT9: Chess 5D **28**
Alpha Pl. SM4: Mord 5G **25**
Alpha Rd. KT5: Surb 3G **23**
TW11: Tedd 2J **15**
Alpine Av. KT5: Surb 6K **23**
Alpine Rd. KT12: Walt T 4A **20**
Alric Av. KT3: N Mald 7B **18**
Alsom Av. KT4: Wor Pk 7D **24**
Alston Cl. KT6: Surb 4C **22**
Alt Gro. SW19 4J **19**
Alton Cl. TW7: Isle 6A **4**
Alton Gdns. TW2: Whit 4J **9**
Alton Rd. SW15 5D **12**
TW9: Rich 1F **11**
Alverstone Av. SW19 6K **13**
Alverstone Rd. KT3: N Mald 1C **24**
Alway Av. KT19: Ewe 2A **30**
Alwyn Av. W4 2A **6**
Alwyne Rd. SW19 3J **19**
Amalgamated Dr. TW8: Bford 3B **4**
Amberley Gdns. KT19: Ewe 7C **24**
Amberley Way SM4: Mord 4J **25**
TW4: Houn 2B **8**
Amberside Cl. TW7: Isle 3J **9**
Amberwood Ri. KT3: N Mald 3B **24**
Amblecote KT11: Cobh 7D **26**
Ambleside SW19 5H **13**
Ambleside Av. KT12: Walt T 5B **20**
Amelia Ho. *W6 2F **7***
(off Queen Caroline St.)
Amenity Way SM4: Mord 4F **25**
American International University of London, The *4F **11***
(in Richmond University)
Amerland Rd. SW18 2J **13**
Amesbury Cl. KT4: Wor Pk 5F **25**
Amesbury Rd. TW13: Felt 6C **8**
Amhurst Gdns. TW7: Isle 6B **4**
Amis Av. KT19: Ewe 3J **29**
Amity Gro. SW20 5E **18**
Amor Rd. W6 1F **7**
Amyand Cotts. TW1: Twick 3C **10**
Amyand La. TW1: Twick 4C **10**
Amyand Pk. Gdns.
TW1: Twick 4C **10**
Amyand Pk. Rd. TW1: Twick 4B **10**
Ancaster Cres. KT3: N Mald 3D **24**
Anchorage Cl. SW19 2K **19**
Ancill Cl. W6 3H **7**
Anderson Cl. KT19: Eps 1J **33**
SM3: Sutt 5K **25**
Anderson Pl. TW3: Houn 1G **9**
Andover Cl. KT19: Eps 7A **30**
Andover Rd. TW2: Twick 5J **9**
Andrewes Ho. SM1: Sutt 7K **25**
Andrew Reed Ho. *SW18 4H **13***
(off Linstead Way)
Andrews Cl. KT4: Wor Pk 6G **25**
KT17: Eps 3C **34**
Angelfield TW3: Houn 1G **9**
Angel M. SW15 4D **12**
Angel Rd. KT7: T Ditt 4B **22**
Angel Wlk. W6 1F **7**
Anglers, The KT1: King T 5B **36**
Anglers Cl. TW10: Ham 1D **16**
Anglers Reach KT6: Surb 2E **22**
Anglesea Ho. KT1: King T 7B **36**
Anglesea Rd.
KT1: King T 7B **36** (1E **22**)
Angus Cl. KT9: Chess 2H **29**
Anlaby Rd. TW11: Tedd 2K **15**
Annandale Rd. W4 2B **6**
Anne Boleyn's Wlk.
KT2: King T 2F **17**
SM3: Cheam 4G **31**
Anne Case M. KT3: N Mald 7A **18**
Anne Way KT8: W Mole 1G **21**
Anselm Rd. SW6 3K **7**
Anstice Cl. W4 4B **6**
Anton Cres. SM1: Sutt 7K **25**
Antrobus Cl. SM1: Sutt 2J **31**
Antrobus Rd. W4 1K **5**
Anvil Rd. TW16: Sun 7A **14**
Aperdele Rd. KT22: Lea 7B **32**
APEX CORNER 7E **8**
Apex Retail Pk. TW13: Hanw 7E **8**
Appleby Cl. TW2: Twick 6J **9**
Appleby Ho. KT19: Eps 7A **30**
Apple Gth. TW8: Bford 1E **4**
Applegarth KT10: Clay 2A **28**
Applegarth Rd. W14 1G **7**
Apple Gro. KT9: Chess 1F **29**
Apple Mkt. KT1: King T 4B **36**
Appleton Gdns.
KT3: N Mald 3D **24**
Approach Rd. KT8: W Mole 2F **21**
SW20 6F **19**
April Cl. KT21: Asht 7G **33**
TW13: Felt 7A **8**
Apsley Ho. TW4: Houn 1E **8**
Apsley Rd. KT3: N Mald 7K **17**
Aquarius TW1: Twick 5C **10**
Arabella Dr. SW15 1B **12**
Aragon Av. KT7: T Ditt 2A **22**
KT17: Ewe 6E **30**
Aragon Ct. KT8: E Mos 1H **21**
Aragon Rd. KT2: King T 2F **17**
SM4: Mord 3G **25**
Arbrook Chase KT10: Esh 3H **27**
Arbrook Hall KT10: Clay 3A **28**
Arbrook La. KT10: Esh 3H **27**
Arcade Pde. KT9: Chess 2E **28**
Archdale Pl. KT3: N Mald 7J **17**
Archel Rd. W14 3J **7**
Archer Cl. KT2: King T 4F **17**
Archer M. TW12: Hamp H 3H **15**
Arch Rd. KT12: Hers 7C **20**
Archway Cl. SW19 7K **13**
Archway M. *SW15 1H **13***
(off Putney Bri. Rd.)
Archway St. SW13 7B **6**
Ardleigh Gdns. SM3: Sutt 4K **25**
Ardmay Gdns. KT6: Surb 2F **23**
Ardrossan Gdns.
KT4: Wor Pk 7D **24**
Ardshiel Cl. SW15 7G **7**
Argent Ct. KT6: Chess 7H **23**
Argon M. SW6 4K **7**
Argyle Av. TW3: Houn 3F **9**
(not continuous)
Argyle Pl. W6 1E **6**
Argyle Rd. TW3: Houn 2G **9**
Argyll Mans. *W14 1H **7***
(off Hammersmith Rd.)
Ark, The *W6 2G **7***
(off Talgarth Rd.)
Arklow M. KT6: Surb 6F **23**
Arlesey Cl. SW15 2H **13**
Arlington Cl. SM1: Sutt 6K **25**
TW1: Twick 3D **10**
Arlington Gdns. W4 2K **5**
Arlington Ho. TW9: Kew 4J **5**
Arlington M. TW1: Twick 3C **10**
Arlington Pk. Mans.
*W4 2K **5***
(off Sutton La. Nth.)
Arlington Pas. TW11: Tedd 1A **16**
Arlington Rd. KT6: Surb 3E **22**
TW1: Twick 3D **10**
TW10: Ham 6E **10**
TW11: Tedd 1A **16**
Armadale Rd. SW6 4K **7**
TW14: Felt 2A **8**
Armfield Cl. KT8: W Mole 2E **20**
Armoury Way SW18 2K **13**
Armstrong Rd. TW13: Hanw 2D **14**
Arnal Cres. SW18 4H **13**
Arndale Wlk. SW18 2K **13**
Arnewood Cl. SW15 5D **12**
Arnison Rd. KT8: E Mos 1J **21**
Arnold Cres. TW7: Isle 2J **9**
Arnold Dr. KT9: Chess 3E **28**
Arnold Mans. *W14 3J **7***
(off Queen's Club Gdns.)
Arnott Cl. W4 1A **6**
Arosa Rd. TW1: Twick 3E **10**
(not continuous)
Arragon Rd. SW18 5K **13**
TW1: Twick 4B **10**
Arran Way KT10: Esh 6G **21**
Arrow Ct. *SW5 1K **7***
(off W. Cromwell Rd.)
Arterberry Rd. SW20 4F **19**
Arthur Henderson Ho.
*SW6 6J **7***
(off Fulham Rd.)
Arthur Rd. KT2: King T 4H **17**
KT3: N Mald 2E **24**
SW19 2J **19**
Arundale KT1: King T 7B **36**
Arundel Av. KT17: Ewe 6E **30**
SM4: Mord 1J **25**
Arundel Cl. TW12: Hamp H 2G **15**
Arundel Ct. *SW13 3E **6***
(off Arundel Ter.)
Arundel Mans. *SW6 5J **7***
(off Kelvedon Rd.)
Arundel Rd. KT1: King T 6J **17**
SM2: Cheam 4J **31**
TW4: Houn 1B **8**
Arundel Ter. SW13 3E **6**
Arun Ho. KT2: King T 1B **36** (5E **16**)
Asbridge Ct. *W6 1E **6***
(off Dalling Rd.)
Ashbourne Gro. W4 2B **6**
Ashbourne Ter. SW19 4J **19**
Ashburnham Pk. KT10: Esh 7H **21**
Ashburnham Rd.
TW10: Ham 7C **10**
Ashburton Ent. Cen.
SW15 3F **13**
Ashby Av. KT9: Chess 3H **29**
Ash Cl. KT3: N Mald 6A **18**
Ashcombe Av. KT6: Surb 4E **22**
Ashcombe Rd. SW19 2K **19**
Ashcombe Sq. KT3: N Mald 7K **17**
Ashcombe St. SW6 6K **7**
Ash Ct. KT19: Ewe 1K **29**
SW19 4H **19**
Ashcroft Rd. KT9: Chess 7G **23**
Ashcroft Sq. W6 1F **7**
Ashdale Cl. TW2: Whit 4H **9**
Ashdale Way TW2: Whit 4G **9**
Ashdown Pl. KT7: T Ditt 4B **22**
KT17: Ewe 4C **30**
Ashdown Rd.
KT1: King T 4C **36** (6F **17**)
KT17: Eps 2C **34**
Ashe Ho. TW1: Twick 3E **10**
Ashen Gro. SW19 7K **13**
Ashfield Av. TW13: Felt 5A **8**
Ashfield Cl. TW10: Ham 5F **11**
Ashfield Ho. *W14 2J **7***
(off W. Cromwell Rd.)
Ashington Rd. SW6 6J **7**
Ashleigh Ct. *W5 1E **4***
(off Murray Rd.)
Ashleigh Rd. SW14 7B **6**
Ashley Av. KT18: Eps 2A **34**
SM4: Mord 2K **25**
Ashley Cen. KT18: Eps 2A **34**
Ashley Ct. KT18: Eps 2A **34**
Ashley Dr. KT12: Walt T 7A **20**
SM7: Bans 3K **35**
TW2: Whit 4G **9**
Ashley Gdns. TW10: Ham 6E **10**
ASHLEY PARK 7A **20**
Ashley Pk. Rd. KT12: Walt T 7A **20**
Ashley Rd. KT7: T Ditt 3A **22**
KT18: Eps, Eps D 2A **34**
TW9: Rich 7F **5**
TW12: Hamp 5F **15**
Ashley Sq. *KT18: Eps 2A **34***
(off Ashley Cen.)
Ashlone Rd. SW15 7F **7**
Ashlyns Way KT9: Chess 3E **28**
Ashmere Cl. SM3: Cheam 2G **31**
Ash M. KT18: Eps 2B **34**
Ashmore Ho. *W14 1H **7***
(off Russell Rd.)
Ashmount Ter. W5 1E **4**
Ashridge Way SM4: Mord 7J **19**
TW16: Sun 3A **14**
Ash Rd. SM3: Sutt 4H **25**
ASHTEAD 7G **33**
Ashtead Gap KT22: Lea 5C **32**
ASHTEAD PARK 7H **33**
Ashtead Station (Rail) 6F **33**
Ashtead Woods Rd.
KT21: Asht 6D **32**
Ashton Cl. KT12: Hers 3A **26**
SM1: Sutt 1K **31**
Ashton Gdns. TW4: Houn 1E **8**
Ash Tree Cl. KT6: Surb 6F **23**
Ashurst KT18: Eps 3A **34**
Ashway Cen., The
KT2: King T 2D **36** (5F **17**)
Askill Dr. SW15 2H **13**
Aspen Gdns. W6 2E **6**
Aspenlea Rd. W6 3G **7**
Aspen Way SM7: Bans 3G **35**
TW13: Felt 7A **8**
Assher Rd. KT12: Hers 7D **20**
Astede Pl. KT21: Asht 7G **33**
Astley Ho. *SW13 3E **6***
(off Wyatt Dr.)
Aston Cl. KT21: Asht 7D **32**
Aston Rd. KT10: Clay 2K **27**
SW20 6F **19**
Astonville St. SW18 5K **13**

38 A-Z Richmond & Kingston

Aston Way—Belgravia M.

Aston Way KT18: Eps 4C 34
Astor Cl. KT2: King T 3J 17
Astrid Ho. TW13: Felt 6B 8
Atalanta St. SW6 . . . . .4G 7
Atbara Rd. TW11: Tedd 3C 16
Atcham Rd. TW3: Houn 1H 9
Athelstan Ho. *KT1: King T* *1G 23*
(off Athelstan Rd.)
Athelstan Rd. KT1: King T 1G 23
Athena Cl.
KT1: King T 5E 36 (7G 17)
Atherley Way TW4: Houn 4E 8
Atherton Dr. SW19 . . . . .1G 19
Atherton Rd. SW13 . . . . .4D 6
Athlone KT10: Clay 3K 27
Atney Rd. SW15 . . . . .1H 13
Attfield Ct. KT1: King T 4E 36
Atwell Pl. KT7: T Ditt 5A 22
Atwood Av. TW9: Kew 6H 5
Atwood Ho. *W14* *1J 7*
(off Beckford Cl.)
Atwood Rd. W6 . . . . .1E 6
Atwoods All. TW9: Kew 5H 5
Aubyn Sq. SW15 . . . . .2D 12
Auckland Rd. KT1: King T 1G 23
Auden Pl. SM3: Cheam 7F 25
Audley Ct. TW2: Twick 7J 9
Audley Firs KT12: Hers 7B 20
Audley Pl. SM2: Sutt 4K 31
Audley Rd. TW10: Rich 2G 11
Audric Cl. KT2: King T 5H 17
Augusta Cl. KT8: W Mole 1E 20
Augusta Rd. TW2: Twick 6H 9
Augustine Rd. W14 . . . . .1G 7
Augustus Cl. TW8: Bford 4D 4
Augustus Ct. TW13: Hanw 1E 14
Augustus Rd. SW19 . . . . .5G 13
Aura Ho. TW9: Kew 5J 5
Auriol Cl. KT4: Wor Pk 7B 24
Auriol Pk. Rd. KT4: Wor Pk 7B 24
Auriol Rd. W14 . . . . .1H 7
Austin Cl. TW1: Twick 2D 10
Austyn Gdns. KT5: Surb 5J 23
Austyns Pl. KT17: Ewe 5D 30
Autumn Dr. SM2: Sutt 5K 31
Avalon Cl. SW20 . . . . .6H 19
Avante KT1: King T 5B 36 (7E 16)
Avebury Pk. KT6: Surb 4E 22
Avebury Rd. SW19 . . . . .5J 19
Avening Rd. SW18 . . . . .4K 13
Avening Ter. SW18 . . . . .4K 13
Avenue, The KT4: Wor Pk 6C 24
KT5: Surb 3G 23
KT10: Clay 3K 27
KT17: Ewe 4E 30
KT22: Oxs 7A 28
SM2: Cheam 6J 31
SM3: Cheam 4F 31
TW1: Twick 2C 10
TW3: Houn 2G 9
TW9: Kew 6G 5
TW12: Hamp 3E 14
TW16: Sun 5A 14
W4 . . . . .1B 6
Avenue Elmers KT6: Surb 2F 23
Avenue Gdns. SW14 . . . . .7B 6
TW11: Tedd 4A 16
Avenue Pde. TW16: Sun 7A 14
Avenue Rd.
KT1: King T 5D 36 (7F 17)
KT3: N Mald 1B 24
KT18: Eps 3A 34
SM2: Sutt 6K 31
SM7: Bans 4K 35
SW20 . . . . .6E 18
TW7: Isle 5A 4
TW8: Bford 2D 4
TW11: Tedd 4B 16
TW12: Hamp 5G 15
Avenue Sth. KT5: Surb 4H 23
Avenue Ter. KT3: N Mald 7K 17
Averill St. W6 . . . . .3G 7
Avern Gdns. KT8: W Mole 1G 21
Avern Rd. KT8: W Mole 1G 21
Avon Cl. KT4: Wor Pk 6D 24
Avon Ct. SW15 . . . . .2H 13
Avondale Av. KT4: Wor Pk 5C 24
KT10: Hin W 7B 22
Avondale Cl. KT12: Hers 2B 26
Avondale Gdns. TW4: Houn 2E 8
Avondale Rd. SW14 . . . . .7B 6
SW19 . . . . .2K 19
Avon Ho. KT2: King T 1B 36 (5E 16)
W14 . . . .*1J 7*
(off Kensington Village)
Avonmore Gdns. W14 . . . . .1J 7
Avonmore Pl. W14 . . . . .1H 7
Avonmore Rd. W14 . . . . .1H 7
Axwood KT18: Eps 4K 33
Aylett Rd. TW7: Isle 6A 4
Ayliffe Cl. KT1: King T 6H 17
Aylward Rd. SW20 . . . . .6J 19
Aynhoe Mans. *W14* *1G 7*
(off Aynhoe Rd.)
Aynhoe Rd. W14 . . . . .1G 7
Aynscombe Path SW14 . . . . .6K 5

B

Babbacombe Cl. KT9: Chess 2E 28
Baber Bri. Cvn. Site
TW14: Felt 2B 8
Baber Dr. TW14: Felt 3B 8
Back Grn. KT12: Hers 3B 26
Back La. TW8: Bford 3E 4
TW10: Ham 7D 10
Back Rd. TW11: Tedd 4K 15
Baddeley Ho. *KT8: W Mole* *2F 21*
(off Down St.)
Baden Powell Cl.
KT6: Surb 6G 23
Badger Cl. TW13: Felt 7A 8
Badgers Copse KT4: Wor Pk 6C 24
Badger's Ct. KT17: Eps 2B 34
Badgers Wlk. KT3: N Mald 6B 18
Bagley's La. SW6 . . . . .5K 7
Bagot Cl. KT21: Asht 5G 33
Bahram Rd. KT19: Eps 6A 30
Bailey Cres. KT9: Chess 4D 28
Bailey M. *W4* *3J 5*
(off Hervert Gdns.)
Bainbridge Cl. TW10: Ham 2F 17
Bakers End SW20 . . . . .6H 19
Bakery M. KT6: Surb 5H 23
Bakewell Way KT3: N Mald 6B 18
Balaam Ho. SM1: Sutt 1K 31
Balaclava Rd. KT6: Surb 4D 22
Balfern Gro. W4 . . . . .2B 6
Balfour Pl. SW15 . . . . .1E 12
Balgowan Cl. KT3: N Mald 2B 24
Ballard Cl. KT2: King T 4A 18
Ballards Grn. KT20: Tad 7H 35
Balmain Lodge *KT5: Surb* *1F 23*
(off Cranes Pk. Av.)
Balmoral Cl. SW15 . . . . .3G 13
Balmoral Ct. KT4: Wor Pk 6E 24
SM2: Sutt 4K 31
Balmoral Cres. KT8: W Mole 7F 15
Balmoral Ho. *W14* *1H 7*
(off Windsor Way)
Balmoral Rd.
KT1: King T 7E 36 (1G 23)
KT4: Wor Pk 7E 24
Balmoral Way SM2: Sutt 6K 31
Balmuir Gdns. SW15 . . . . .1F 13
Balquhain Cl. KT21: Asht 6E 32
Baltic Cen., The TW8: Bford 2E 4
Balvernie Gro. SW18 . . . . .4J 13
Balvernie M. SW18 . . . . .4K 13
Banbury Ct. SM2: Sutt 4K 31
Bangalore St. SW15 . . . . .7F 7
Banim St. W6 . . . . .1E 6
Bank La. KT2: King T 4F 17
SW15 . . . . .2B 12
Bankside Cl. TW7: Isle 1A 10
Bankside Dr. KT7: T Ditt 5C 22
Bannow Cl. KT19: Ewe 7B 24
Banstead Rd. KT17: Ewe 6E 30
SM7: Bans 6E 30
Banstead Station (Rail) 3J 35
Barb M. W6 . . . . .1F 7
Barclay Cl. SW6 . . . . .4K 7
Barclay Rd. SW6 . . . . .4K 7
Bardolph Rd. TW9: Rich 7G 5
Bargate Cl. KT3: N Mald 4D 24
Barge Wlk.
KT1: Hamp W 5A 36 (7E 16)
KT8: E Mos 7J 15
Barham Rd. SW20 . . . . .4D 18
Barker Cl. KT3: N Mald 1J 23
TW9: Rich 6J 5
Barkston Gdns. SW5 . . . . .1K 7
Barley Mow Pas. W4 . . . . .2A 6
Barlow Rd. TW12: Hamp 4F 15
Barnard Cl. TW16: Sun 4A 14
Barnard Gdns. KT3: N Mald 1D 24
Barn Cl. KT18: Eps 4K 33
Barneby Cl. TW2: Twick 5K 9
Barn Elms Athletic Track 6E 6
Barn Elms Pk. SW15 . . . . .7F 7
BARNES 6C 6
Barnes All. TW12: Hamp 6H 15
Barnes Av. SW13 . . . . .4D 6
Barnes Bridge Station (Rail) 6C 6
Barnes End KT3: N Mald 2D 24
Barnes High St. SW13 . . . . .6C 6
Barnes Station (Rail) 7D 6
Barnett Wood La. KT21: Asht 7D 32
KT22: Lea 7D 32
Barnfield KT3: N Mald 3B 24
Barnfield Av. KT2: King T 1E 16
Barnfield Gdns. KT2: King T 1F 17
Barnlea Cl. TW13: Hanw 6D 8
Barnsbury Cl. KT3: N Mald 1K 23
Barnsbury Cres. KT5: Surb 5K 23
Barnsbury La. KT5: Surb 6J 23
Barnscroft SW20 . . . . .7E 18
BARNES HOSPITAL 7B 6
Barons, The TW1: Twick 3C 10
BARONS COURT 2H 7
Baron's Ct. Rd. W14 . . . . .2H 7
Barons Court Station (Tube) 2H 7
Barons Court Theatre *2H 7*
(off Comeragh Rd.)
Baronsfield Rd. TW1: Twick 3C 10
Barons Ga. W4 . . . . .1K 5
Baron's Hurst KT18: Eps 5K 33
Barons Keep W14 . . . . .2H 7
Baronsmead Rd. SW13 . . . . .5D 6
Barrack Rd. TW4: Houn 1C 8
Barrington Rd. SM3: Sutt 6K 25
Barrosa Dr. TW12: Hamp 5F 15
Barrowgate Rd. W4 . . . . .2K 5
Barrow Hill KT4: Wor Pk 6B 24
Barrow Hill Cl. KT4: Wor Pk 6B 24
Barrow Wlk. TW8: Bford 3D 4
Barton Ct. *W14* *2H 7*
(off Baron's Ct. Rd.)
Barton Grn. KT3: N Mald 6A 18
Barton Green Theatre 6A 18
Barton Rd. W14 . . . . .2H 7
Barwell Bus. Pk. KT9: Chess 4E 28
Barwell Ct. KT9: Chess 4C 28
Basden Gro. TW13: Hanw 6F 9
Basden Ho. TW13: Hanw 6F 9
Basildene Rd. TW4: Houn 1C 8
Basing Cl. KT7: T Ditt 4A 22
Basingfield Rd. KT7: T Ditt 4A 22
Basing Rd. SM7: Bans 3J 35
Basing Way KT7: T Ditt 4A 22
Basuto Rd. SW6 . . . . .5K 7
Batavia Cl. TW16: Sun 5A 14
Batavia Rd. TW16: Sun 5A 14
Bathgate Rd. SW19 . . . . .7G 13
Bath Pas.
KT1: King T 4B 36 (6E 16)
Bath Pl. *W6* *2F 7*
(off Peabody Est.)
Bath Rd. TW3: Houn 1F 9
W4 . . . . .1B 6
Baths App. SW6 . . . . .4J 7
Bathurst Av. SW19 . . . . .5K 19
Baulk, The SW18 . . . . .4K 13
Baygrove M.
KT1: Hamp W 1A 36 (5D 16)
Bayleaf Cl. TW12: Hamp H 2J 15
Baylis M. TW1: Twick 4B 10
Bayonne Rd. W6 . . . . .3H 7
Bazalgette Cl. KT3: N Mald 2A 24
Bazalgette Gdns.
KT3: N Mald 2A 24
Beach Gro. TW13: Hanw 6F 9
Beach Ho. *SW5* *2K 7*
(off Philbeach Gdns.)
TW13: Hanw 6F 9
Beacon Cl. SM7: Bans 5G 35
Beaconsfield Cl. W4 . . . . .2K 5
Beaconsfield Gdns.
KT10: Clay 4K 27
Beaconsfield Pl. KT17: Eps 1B 34
Beaconsfield Rd.
KT3: N Mald 6A 18
KT5: Surb 4G 23
KT10: Clay 4K 27
TW1: Twick 3C 10
W4 . . . . .1A 6
Beaconsfield Wlk. SW6 . . . . .5J 7
Beacon Way SM7: Bans 5G 35
Beadon Rd. W6 . . . . .1F 7
Beaford Gro. SW20 . . . . .7H 19
Beagle Cl. TW13: Felt 1A 14
Beard Rd. KT2: King T 2G 17
Beard's Hill TW12: Hamp 5F 15
Beard's Hill Cl. TW12: Hamp 5F 15
Bearfield Rd. KT2: King T 4F 17
Bear Rd. TW13: Hanw 1C 14
Beatrice Ho. *W6* *2F 7*
(off Queen Caroline St.)
Beatrice Rd. TW10: Rich 2G 11
Beauchamp Rd.
KT8: W Mole, E Moss 2G 21
SM1: Sutt 1K 31
TW1: Twick 4B 10
Beauchamp Ter. SW15 . . . . .7E 6
Beauclerc Ct. TW16: Sun 6B 14
Beauclerk Cl. TW13: Felt 5A 8
Beaufort Cl. SW15 . . . . .4E 12
Beaufort Ct. SW6 . . . . .3K 7
TW10: Ham 1D 16
Beaufort M. SW6 . . . . .3J 7
Beaufort Rd.
KT1: King T 7D 36 (1F 23)
TW1: Twick 4D 10
TW10: Ham 1D 16
Beaufort Way KT17: Ewe 4D 30
Beaulieu Cl. TW1: Twick 3E 10
TW4: Houn 2E 8
Beaulieu Pl. W4 . . . . .1K 5
Beaumont *W14* *1J 7*
(off Kensington Village)
Beaumont Av. TW9: Rich 7G 5
W14 .2J 7
Beaumont Cl. KT2: King T 4H 17
Beaumont Ct. W4 . . . . .2K 5
Beaumont Cres. W14 . . . . .2J 7
Beaumont Pl. TW7: Isle 2A 10
Beaumont Rd. SW19 . . . . .4H 13
W4 . . . . .1K 5
Beaver Cl. SM4: Mord 4F 25
TW12: Hamp 5G 15
Beavers Cres. TW4: Houn 1B 8
Beavers La. TW4: Houn 1B 8
Beavers La. Campsite
TW4: Houn 1C 8
Beavor Gro. *W6* *2D 6*
(off Beavor La.)
Beavor La. W6 . . . . .2D 6
Bechtel Ho. *W6* *1G 7*
(off Hammersmith Rd.)
Becketts Cl. TW14: Felt 3A 8
Becketts Pl.
KT1: Hamp W 2A 36 (5E 16)
Beckford Cl. W14 . . . . .1J 7
Bective Pl. SW15 . . . . .1J 13
Bective Rd. SW15 . . . . .1J 13
Bedfont La. TW13: Felt 5A 8
TW14: Felt 5A 8
Bedford Cl. W4 . . . . .3B 6
Bedford Cnr. *W4* *1B 6*
(off South Pde.)
BEDFORD PARK 1A 6
Bedford Pk. Cnr. W4 . . . . .1B 6
Bedford Pk. Mans. W4 . . . . .1A 6
Bedford Pas. *SW6* *4H 7*
(off Dawes Rd.)
Bedford Rd. KT4: Wor Pk 6F 25
TW2: Twick 7J 9
W4 . . . . .1A 6
Bedgebury Gdns. SW19 . . . . .6H 13
Bedster Gdns. KT8: W Mole 6G 15
Beech Av. TW8: Bford 4C 4
Beech Cl. KT11: Cobh 7F 27
KT12: Hers 1B 26
SW15 . . . . .4D 12
SW19 . . . . .3F 19
TW16: Sun 6C 14
Beech Cl. Ct. KT11: Cobh 7E 26
Beech Ct. KT6: Surb 4E 22
Beechcroft Av. KT3: N Mald 5K 17
Beechcroft Rd. KT9: Chess 7G 23
SW14 . . . . .7K 5
Beechen Cliff Way TW7: Isle 6A 4
Beeches, The SM7: Bans 5K 35
Beeches Rd. SM3: Sutt 5H 25
Beech Gro. KT3: N Mald 7A 18
KT18: Tatt C 6E 34
Beechmore Gdns.
SM3: Cheam 6G 25
Beecholme SM7: Bans 3H 35
Beech Rd. KT17: Eps 4C 34
Beechrow TW10: Ham 1F 17
Beech Wlk. KT17: Ewe 7D 30
Beech Way KT17: Eps 4C 34
TW2: Twick 7F 9
Beechwood Av. TW9: Kew 5H 5
TW16: Sun 3A 14
Beechwood Cl. KT6: Surb 4D 22
Beechwood Ct. *KT12: Walt T* *7A 20*
(off Station Av.)
TW16: Sun 3A 14
W4 . . . . .3A 6
Beechwood Dr. KT11: Cobh 7F 27
Beechwood Gro. KT6: Surb 4D 22
Beecot La. KT12: Walt T 6B 20
Beeston Way TW14: Felt 3B 8
BEGGAR'S HILL 3C 30
Beggar's Hill KT17: Ewe 4C 30
Beggars Roost La. SM1: Sutt 3K 31
Begonia Pl. TW12: Hamp 3F 15
Beldham Gdns. KT8: W Mole 6G 15
Belfield Rd. KT19: Ewe 5A 30
Belgrade Rd. TW12: Hamp 5G 15
Belgrave Cl. KT12: Hers 1A 26
Belgrave Ct. W4 . . . . .2K 5
Belgrave Cres. TW16: Sun 5A 14
Belgrave Rd. SW13 . . . . .4C 6
TW4: Houn 1E 8
TW16: Sun 5A 14
Belgravia M. KT1: King T 1E 22

Brentford Fountain Leisure Cen. 2H 5
Brentford Ho. TW1: Twick 4C 10
Brentford Musical Mus. 3F 5
Brentford Station (Rail) 3D 4
Brent Lea TW8: Bford 4D 4
Brent Rd. TW8: Bford 3D 4
Brent Side TW8: Bford 3D 4
Brentside Executive Cen.
TW8: Bford 3C 4
Brentwaters Bus. Pk.
TW8: Bford 4D 4
Brent Way TW8: Bford 4E 4
Brentwick Gdns. TW8: Bford 1F 5
Brettgrave KT19: Eps 6K 29
Brett Ho. Cl. SW15 4G 13
Brewers La. TW9: Rich 2E 10
Brewery La. TW1: Twick 4A 10
Brewery M. Cen. TW7: Isle 7B 4
Brewhouse La. SW15 7H 7
Briane Rd. KT19: Eps 6K 29
Briar Cl. TW7: Isle 2A 10
TW12: Hamp 2E 14
Briar Ct. SM3: Cheam 7F 25
SW15 1E 12
Briar Rd. TW2: Twick 5K 9
Briar Wlk. SW15 1E 12
Briarwood Ct. *KT4: Wor Pk 5D 24*
(off Avenue, The)
Briarwood Rd. KT17: Ewe 3D 30
Briavels Ct. KT18: Eps 4B 34
Brick Farm Cl. TW9: Kew 5J 5
Brickfield Cl. TW8: Bford 4D 4
Bridge Av. W6 1F 7
Bridge Av. Mans. *W6 2F 7*
(off Bridge Av.)
Bridge Cl. TW11: Tedd 1A 16
Bridgefield Cl. SM7: Bans 4F 35
Bridgefield Rd. SM1: Sutt 3K 31
Bridge Gdns. KT8: E Mos 1J 21
Bridgeman Rd. TW11: Tedd 3B 16
Bridgepark SW18 2K 13
Bridge Rd. KT8: E Mos 1J 21
KT9: Chess 2F 29
KT17: Eps 1C 34
TW1: Twick 3C 10
TW7: Isle 1J 9
Bridges Pl. SW6 5J 7
Bridges Rd. SW19 3K 19
Bridges Rd. M. SW19 3K 19
Bridge St. TW9: Rich 2E 10
W4 1A 6
Bridge Vw. W6 2F 7
Bridge Way TW2: Whit 4H 9
Bridge Wharf Rd. TW7: Isle 7C 4
Bridgewood Rd.
KT4: Wor Pk 1D 30
Bridle Cl.
KT1: King T 7B 36 (1E 22)
KT19: Ewe 2A 30
TW16: Sun 7A 14
Bridle End KT17: Eps 2C 34
Bridle La. TW1: Twick 3C 10
Bridle Path, The KT17: Ewe 6F 31
Bridle Rd. KT10: Clay 3C 28
KT17: Eps 2C 34
Bridleway Cl. KT17: Ewe 6F 31
Bright Ho. *KT1: King T 5B 36*
(off Kingston Hall Rd.)
Brighton Rd. KT6: Surb 3D 22
SM2: Bans, Sutt 7K 31
SM7: Bans 7H 35
Brindles, The SM7: Bans 6J 35
Brinkley KT1: King T 6H 17
Brinkley Rd. KT4: Wor Pk 6E 24
Brinsworth Cl. TW2: Twick 5J 9
Brinsworth Ho. TW2: Twick 6J 9
Brisbane Av. SW19 5K 19
Brisson Cl. KT10: Esh 2E 26
Bristol Gdns. SW15 4F 13
Bristow Rd. TW3: Houn 1H 9
Britannia Ct. *KT2: King T 1B 36*
(off Skerne Wlk.)
Britannia La. TW2: Whit 4H 9
Britannia Rd. KT5: Surb 4G 23
SW6 4K 7
(not continuous)
British Gro. W4 2C 6
British Gro. Pas. W4 2C 6
British Gro. Sth. *W4 2C 6*
(off British Gro. Pas.)
Brittain Rd. KT12: Hers 2C 26
Broad Cl. KT12: Hers 7C 20
Broadfields KT8: E Mos 3K 21
Broadhurst KT21: Asht 5F 33
Broadhurst Cl. TW10: Rich 2G 11
Broadlands TW13: Hanw 7F 9
Broadlands Ct. *TW9: Kew 4H 5*
(off Kew Gdns. Rd.)
Broadlands Way KT3: N Mald 3C 24
Broad La. TW12: Hamp 4E 14
Broad Mead KT21: Asht 6G 33
Broadmead W14 1H 7
Broadmead Av. KT4: Wor Pk 4D 24
Broadmead Cl. TW12: Hamp 3F 15
Broadoaks KT6: Surb 6J 23
Broad St. TW11: Tedd 3A 16
Broad Wlk. KT18: Tatt C 7G 35
TW9: Kew 4G 5
Broad Wlk., The KT8: E Mos 1A 22
Broadway, The KT7: T Ditt 5K 21
SM3: Cheam 3H 31
SW13 6B 6
SW19 3J 19
Broadway Arc. *W6 1F 7*
(off Hammersmith B'way.)
Broadway Av. TW1: Twick 3C 10
Broadway Cen., The W6 1F 7
Broadway Chambers *W6 1F 7*
(off Hammersmith B'way.)
Broadway Ct. SW19 3K 19
Broadway Pl. SW19 3J 19
Broadway Squash & Fitness Cen. *1G 7*
(off Chalk Hill Rd.)
Broadwood Ter. W8 1J 7
Brockbridge Ho. SW15 3C 12
Brockenhurst KT8: W Mole 2E 20
Brockenhurst Av.
KT4: Wor Pk 5B 24
Brockham Cl. SW19 2J 19
Brocks Dr. SM3: Cheam 7H 25
Brockshot Cl. TW8: Bford 2E 4
Brompton Cl. TW4: Houn 2E 8
Brompton Pk. Cres. SW6 3K 7
Bronsart Rd. SW6 4H 7
Bronson Rd. SW20 6G 19
Bronte Ct. *W14 1G 7*
(off Girdler's Rd.)
Brook Cl. KT19: Ewe 5B 30
SW20 7E 18
Brookers Cl. KT21: Asht 6D 32
Brookfield Gdns. KT10: Clay 3A 28
Brook Gdns. KT2: King T 5K 17
SW13 7C 6
BROOK GREEN 1G 7
Brook Grn. W6 1G 7
Brook Grn. Flats *W14 1G 7*
(off Dunsany Rd.)
Brook Ho. *W6 1F 7*
(off Shepherd's Bush Rd.)
Brooklands Av. SW19 6K 13
Brooklands Ct. KT1: King T 7B 36
Brooklands Pl.
TW12: Hamp H 2G 15
Brooklands Rd. KT7: T Ditt 5A 22
Brook La. Bus. Cen.
TW8: Bford 2E 4
Brook La. Nth. TW8: Bford 2E 4
(not continuous)
Brook Mead KT19: Ewe 3B 30
Brook Rd. KT6: Surb 6F 23
TW1: Twick 3B 10
Brook Rd. Sth. TW8: Bford 3E 4
Brookside Cl. TW13: Felt 7A 8
Brookside Cres.
KT4: Wor Pk 5D 24
Brooks La. W4 3H 5
Brooks Rd. W4 2H 5
Brook St. KT1: King T 4C 36 (6F 17)
Brookville Rd. SW6 4J 7
Brook Way KT22: Lea 7B 32
Brookwood Av. SW13 6C 6
Brookwood Rd. SW18 5J 13
Broom Cl. KT10: Esh 2G 27
TW11: Tedd 4E 16
Broome Ct. KT20: Tad 7H 35
Broome Rd. TW12: Hamp 4E 14
Broomfield TW16: Sun 5A 14
Broomfield Ride KT22: Oxs 7J 27
Broomfield Rd. KT5: Surb 5G 23
TW9: Kew 5G 5
TW11: Tedd 3D 16
Broomfields KT10: Esh 2H 27
Broomhill Rd. SW18 2K 13
Broomhouse La. SW6 6K 7
(not continuous)
Broomhouse Rd. SW6 6K 7
Broomloan La. SM1: Sutt 6K 25
Broom Lock TW11: Tedd 3D 16
Broom Pk. TW11: Tedd 4E 16
Broom Rd. TW11: Tedd 2C 16
Broom Water TW11: Tedd 3D 16
Broom Water W. TW11: Tedd 2D 16
Brough Cl. KT2: King T 2E 16
Broughton Av. TW10: Ham 7C 10
Browells La. TW13: Felt 6A 8
(not continuous)
Brown Bear Ct. TW13: Hanw 1C 14
Browning Av. KT4: Wor Pk 5E 24
Browning Cl. TW12: Hamp 1E 14
Brown's Rd. KT5: Surb 4G 23
Broxholme Ho. *SW6 5K 7*
(off Harwood Rd.)
Brumfield Rd. KT19: Ewe 2K 29
Brunel University
Osterley Campus 4A 4
Twickenham Campus 1C 10
Brunel Wlk. TW2: Whit 4F 9
Brunswick Cl. KT7: T Ditt 5A 22
KT12: Walt T 6B 20
TW2: Twick 7J 9
Brunswick Rd. KT2: King T 5H 17
Bryanston Av. TW2: Whit 5G 9
Buckhold Rd. SW18 3K 13
Buckingham Av.
KT8: W Mole 6G 15
TW14: Felt 3A 8
Buckingham Cl. TW12: Hamp 2E 14
Buckingham Ct. SM2: Sutt 5K 31
Buckingham Gdns.
KT8: W Mole 6G 15
Buckingham Rd.
KT1: King T 7E 36 (1G 23)
TW10: Ham 6E 10
TW12: Hamp 1E 14
Buckland Rd. KT9: Chess 2G 29
SM2: Cheam 6F 31
Bucklands Rd. TW11: Tedd 3D 16
Buckland's Wharf
KT1: King T 3A 36 (6E 16)
Buckland Way KT4: Wor Pk 5F 25
Buckleigh Av. SW20 7H 19
Bucklers All. SW6 3J 7
(not continuous)
Buckles Way SM7: Bans 5H 35
Bucknills Cl. KT18: Eps 3K 33
Budd's All. TW1: Twick 2D 10
Buer Rd. SW6 6H 7
Bullard Rd. TW11: Tedd 3K 15
Bull's All. SW14 6A 6
Bunbury Way KT17: Eps D 5E 34
Burberry Cl. KT3: N Mald 6B 18
Burden Cl. TW8: Bford 2D 4
Burdenshott Av. TW10: Rich 1J 11
Burdett Av. SW20 5D 18
Burdett Rd. TW9: Rich 6G 5
Burdon La. SM2: Cheam 4H 31
Burdon Pk. SM2: Cheam 5J 31
Burford Ho. KT17: Ewe 7F 31
TW8: Bford 2E 4
Burford La. KT17: Ewe 7F 31
Burford Rd. KT4: Wor Pk 4C 24
SM1: Sutt 6K 25
TW8: Bford 2F 5
Burges Gro. SW13 4E 6
Burgess Cl. TW13: Hanw 1D 14
Burgess Rd. SM1: Sutt 1K 31
Burgh Cft. KT17: Eps 4C 34
Burghfield KT17: Eps 4C 34
BURGH HEATH 7H 35
Burgh Heath Rd.
KT17: Eps, Eps D 3C 34
Burghley Av. KT3: N Mald 5A 18
Burghley Hall Cl. SW19 5H 13
Burghley Ho. SW19 7H 13
Burghley Rd. SW19 1G 19
Burgh Mt. SM7: Bans 4J 35
Burgh Wood SM7: Bans 4H 35
Burgoine Quay KT1: Hamp W 5E 16
BURHILL 5A 26
Burhill Rd. KT12: Hers 5A 26
Burke Cl. SW15 1B 12
Burlea Cl. KT12: Hers 2A 26
Burleigh Pl. SW15 2G 13
Burleigh Rd. SM3: Sutt 5H 25
Burlington Av. TW9: Kew 5H 5
Burlington Gdns. SW6 6H 7
W4 2K 5
Burlington La. W4 4K 5
Burlington M. SW15 2J 13
Burlington Pl. SW6 6H 7
Burlington Rd. KT3: N Mald 1C 24
SW6 6H 7
W4 2K 5
Burnaby Cres. W4 3K 5
Burnaby Gdns. W4 3J 5
Burne Jones Ho. W14 1H 7
Burnell Av. TW10: Ham 2D 16
Burnet Gro. KT19: Eps 2K 33
Burney Av. KT5: Surb 2G 23
Burnfoot Av. SW6 5H 7
Burnham Dr. KT4: Wor Pk 6G 25
Burnham St. KT2: King T 5H 17
Burnham Way W13 1C 4
Burns Dr. SM7: Bans 3H 35
Burnside KT21: Asht 7G 33
Burnside Cl. TW1: Twick 3B 10
Burnthwaite Rd. SW6 4J 7
Burritt Rd. KT1: King T 6H 17
Burr Rd. SW18 5K 13
Burstock Rd. SW15 1H 13
Burston Rd. SW15 2G 13
Burstow Rd. SW20 5H 19
Burtenshaw Rd. KT7: T Ditt 4B 22
Burton Cl. KT9: Chess 4E 28
Burton Ct. KT7: T Ditt 3B 22
Burton Rd.
KT2: King T 1D 36 (4F 17)
Burton's Rd. TW12: Hamp H 1G 15
Burwell *KT1: King T 6H 17*
(off Excelsior Rd.)
Burwood Cl. KT6: Surb 5H 23
KT12: Hers 3B 26
BURWOOD PARK 7A 26
Burwood Pk. Rd. KT12: Hers 1A 26
Burwood Rd. KT12: Hers 3A 26
Busch Cl. TW7: Isle 5C 4
Bush Cotts. SW18 2K 13
Bushey Ct. SW20 7E 18
Bushey La. SM1: Sutt 7K 25
BUSHEY MEAD 6G 19
Bushey Rd. SM1: Sutt 7K 25
SW20 7E 18
Bushey Shaw KT21: Asht 6C 32
Bush Rd. TW9: Kew 3G 5
Bushwood Rd. TW9: Kew 3H 5
Bushy Ct. *KT1: Hamp W 5D 16*
(off Up. Teddington Rd.)
Bushy Pk. Gdns. TW11: Tedd 2J 15
Bushy Pk. Rd. TW11: Tedd 4C 16
(not continuous)
Bushy Rd. TW11: Tedd 3A 16
Bute Av. TW10: Ham 6F 11
Bute Gdns. TW10: Ham 5F 11
W6 1G 7
Butlers Cl. TW3: Houn 1E 8
Butterfield Cl. TW1: Twick 3A 10
Buttermere Cl. SM4: Mord 3G 25
Buttermere Dr. SW15 2H 13
Butterwick W6 1G 7
Butts, The TW8: Bford 3D 4
TW16: Sun 7B 14
Butts Cres. TW13: Hanw 7F 9
Buxton Cres. SM3: Cheam 7H 25
Buxton Dr. KT3: N Mald 6A 18
Buxton Rd. SW14 7B 6
Byatt Wlk. TW12: Hamp 3D 14
Bychurch End TW11: Tedd 2A 16
Byeway, The SW14 7K 5
Byeways TW2: Twick 7G 9
Byeways, The KT5: Surb 2H 23
Byfeld Gdns. SW13 5D 6
Byfield Rd. TW7: Isle 7B 4
Byron Av. KT3: N Mald 2D 24
Byron Cl. KT12: Walt T 5D 20
TW12: Hamp 1E 14
Byron Ct. *W7 1B 4*
(off Boston Rd.)
Byward Av. TW14: Felt 3B 8
Byway, The KT19: Ewe 1C 30
Byways, The KT21: Asht 7E 32

C

Caci Ho. *W14 1J 7*
(off Kensington Village)
Cadbury Cl. TW7: Isle 5B 4
Cadman Ct. *W4 2J 5*
(off Chaseley Dr.)
Cadmer Cl. KT3: N Mald 1B 24
Cadnam Point SW15 5E 12
Cadogan Cl. TW11: Tedd 2K 15
Cadogan Rd. KT6: Surb 2E 22
Caen Wood Rd. KT21: Asht 7D 32
Caerleon Cl. KT10: Clay 4C 28
Cairn Ct. KT17: Ewe 6C 30
Cairngorm Cl. TW11: Tedd 2B 16
Caithness Dr. KT18: Eps 3A 34
Caithness Rd. W14 1G 7
Calcott Ct. *W14 1H 7*
(off Blythe Rd.)
Caldbeck Av. KT4: Wor Pk 6D 24
Caldecote *KT1: King T 6H 17*
(off Excelsior Cl.)
Caldwell Ho. *SW13 4F 7*
(off Trinity Chu. Rd.)
California Cl. SM2: Sutt 6K 31
California Rd. KT3: N Mald 1J 23
Calonne Rd. SW19 1G 19
Calverley Rd. KT17: Ewe 3D 30
Camac Rd. TW2: Twick 5J 9
Cambalt Rd. SW15 2G 13
Camberley Av. SW20 6E 18
Camberley Cl. SM3: Cheam 7G 25
Camborne Rd. SM2: Sutt 4K 31
SM4: Mord 2G 25
SW18 4K 13
Cambourne Wlk. TW10: Rich 3E 10

Cambria Cl.—Chase Gdns.

Cambria Cl. TW3: Houn 1F 9
Cambria Ct. TW14: Felt 4A 8
Cambrian Rd. TW10: Rich 3G 11
Cambridge Av. KT3: N Mald 7B 18
(not continuous)
Cambridge Cl. SW20 5E 18
TW4: Houn 1D 8
Cambridge Cotts. TW9: Kew 3H 5
Cambridge Ct. *W6 1F 7*
(off Shepherd's Bush Rd.)
Cambridge Cres.
TW11: Tedd 2B 16
Cambridge Gdns.
KT1: King T 6H 17
Cambridge Gro. W6 1E 6
Cambridge Gro. Rd.
KT1: King T 7H 17
(not continuous)
Cambridge Ho. *W6 1E 6*
(off Cambridge Gro.)
Cambridge Pk. TW1: Twick 3D 10
Cambridge Pk. Ct.
TW1: Twick 4E 10
Cambridge Rd. KT1: King T 6G 17
KT3: N Mald 1A 24
KT8: W Mole 1E 20
KT12: Walt T 3A 20
SW13 6C 6
SW20 5D 18
TW1: Twick 3E 10
TW4: Houn 1D 8
TW9: Kew 4H 5
TW11: Tedd 1A 16
TW12: Hamp 4E 14
Cambridge Rd. Nth. W4 2J 5
Cambridge Rd. Sth. W4 2J 5
Camden Av. TW13: Felt 5B 8
Camden Gdns. SM1: Sutt 2K 31
Camden Rd. SM1: Sutt 2K 31
Camel Gro. KT2: King T 2E 16
Camellia Pl. TW2: Whit 4G 9
Camelot Cl. SW19 1J 19
Camm Gdns. KT1: King T 6G 17
KT7: T Ditt 4A 22
Campana Rd. SW6 5K 7
Campbell Cl. TW2: Twick 5J 9
Campbell Rd. KT8: E Mos 7K 15
TW2: Twick 6J 9
Campen Cl. SW19 6H 13
Campion Rd. SW15 1F 13
TW7: Isle 5A 4
Camp Rd. SW19 2E 18
(not continuous)
Camp Vw. SW19 2E 18
Camrose Av. TW13: Felt 1B 14
Camrose Cl. SM4: Mord 1K 25
Canbury Av.
KT2: King T 1E 36 (5G 17)
Canbury Bus. Cen.
KT2: King T 2D 36 (5F 17)
Canbury Bus. Pk.
KT2: King T 2D 36
Canbury Ct. KT2: King T 4E 16
Canbury Pk. Rd.
KT2: King T 2D 36 (5F 17)
Canbury Pas.
KT2: King T 2B 36 (5E 16)
Candler M. TW1: Twick 4B 10
Canford Gdns. KT3: N Mald 3B 24
Canford Pl. TW11: Tedd 3D 16
Can Hatch KT20: Tad 7H 35
Cannizaro Rd. SW19 3F 19
Cannon Cl. SW20 7F 19
TW12: Hamp 3G 15
Cannon Hill La. SW20 2G 25
Cannons Health Club
Fulham 5G 7
Cannon Way KT8: W Mole 1F 21
Canons La. KT20: Tad 7H 35
Canterbury Hall KT4: Wor Pk 4E 24
Canterbury Ho. *KT19: Eps 7H 29*
(off Queen Alexandra's Way)
Canterbury Rd. TW13: Hanw 6D 8
Capital Interchange Way
TW8: Bford 2H 5
Cardiff Rd. W7 1B 4
Cardigan Rd. SW13 6D 6
TW10: Rich 3F 11
Cardinal Av. KT2: King T 2F 17
SM4: Mord 3H 25
Cardinal Cl. KT4: Wor Pk 7D 24
SM4: Mord 3H 25
Cardinal Cres. KT3: N Mald 6K 17
Cardinal Dr. KT12: Walt T 5C 20
Cardinal Pl. SW15 1G 13
Cardinal Rd. TW13: Felt 5A 8
Cardinals Wlk. TW12: Hamp 4H 15
Cardington Sq. TW4: Houn 1C 8
Cardross St. W6 1E 6
Carisbrooke Ct. SM2: Cheam 4J 31
Carisbrooke Ho. *KT2: King T 2C 36*
(off Seven Kings Way)
Carleton Cl. KT10: Esh 5J 21
Carlingford Rd. SM4: Mord 3G 25
Carlisle Cl. KT2: King T 5H 17
Carlisle M. KT2: King T 5H 17
Carlisle Rd. SM1: Sutt 3J 31
TW12: Hamp 4G 15
Carlson Ct. SW15 1J 13
Carlton Av. TW14: Felt 3B 8
Carlton Cl. KT9: Chess 3E 28
Carlton Cres. SM3: Cheam 7H 25
Carlton Dr. SW15 2G 13
Carlton Ho. TW3: Houn 3F 9
Carlton Pk. Av. SW20 6G 19
Carlton Rd. KT3: N Mald 6B 18
KT12: Walt T 4A 20
SW14 7K 5
Carlton Vs. SW15 2H 13
Carlyle Cl. KT8: W Mole 6G 15
Carlyle Ho. *KT8: W Mole 2F 21*
(off Down St.)
Carlyle Pl. SW15 1G 13
Carlyle Rd. W5 1D 4
Carmalt Gdns. KT12: Hers 2B 26
SW15 1F 13
Carmel Lodge *SW6 3K 7*
(off Lillie Rd.)
Carmichael Ct. *SW13 6C 6*
(off Grove Rd.)
Carnegie Cl. KT6: Surb 6G 23
Carnegie Pl. SW19 7G 13
Carnforth Cl. KT19: Ewe 3J 29
Carnwath Rd. SW6 7K 7
Caroline Ho. *W6 2F 7*
(off Queen Caroline St.)
Caroline Rd. SW19 4J 19
Caroline Wlk. *W6 3H 7*
(off Lillie Rd.)
Carpenter Cl. KT17: Ewe 5C 30
Carpenters Ct. TW2: Twick 6K 9
Carrara Wharf SW6 7H 7
Carrick Cl. TW7: Isle 7B 4
Carrick Ga. KT10: Esh 7H 21
Carrington Av. TW3: Houn 2G 9
Carrington Cl. KT2: King T 2K 17
Carrington Pl. KT10: Esh 1G 27
Carrington Rd. TW10: Rich 1H 11
Carrow Rd. KT12: Walt T 7C 20
Carslake Rd. SW15 3F 13
Carters Cl. KT4: Wor Pk 6G 25
Carters Rd. KT17: Eps 4C 34
Carter's Yd. SW18 2K 13
Carthew Rd. W6 1E 6
Cartwright Way SW13 4E 6
Carville Cres. TW8: Bford 1F 5
Cascades Ct. SW19 4J 19
CASSEL HOSPITAL, THE 1E 16
Cassidy Rd. SW6 4K 7
(not continuous)
Cassilis Rd. TW1: Twick 2C 10
Castello Av. SW15 2F 13
CASTELNAU 3E 6
Castelnau SW13 5D 6
Castelnau Gdns. SW13 3E 6
Castelnau Mans. *SW13 3E 6*
(off Castelnau, not continuous)
Castelnau Row SW13 3E 6
Castle Av. KT17: Ewe 5D 30
Castle Cl. SW19 7G 13
Castlecombe Dr. SW19 4G 13
Castlegate TW9: Rich 7G 5
Castle Ho. SM2: Sutt 3K 31
Castlemaine Av. KT17: Ewe 5E 30
Castle M. TW12: Hamp 5G 15
(not continuous)
Castle Pde. KT17: Ewe 4D 30
Castle Pl. W4 1B 6
Castle Rd. KT18: Eps 4J 33
TW7: Isle 6A 4
Castle Row W4 2A 6
Castle St.
KT1: King T 3C 36 (6F 17)
Castleton Cl. SM7: Bans 4K 35
Castleton Dr. SM7: Bans 4K 35
Castletown Rd. W14 2H 7
Castle Vw. KT18: Eps 3J 33
Castle Wlk. TW16: Sun 7B 14
Castle Way KT17: Ewe 6D 30
SW19 7G 13
TW13: Hanw 1B 14
Castle Yd. TW10: Rich 2E 10
CASUALTY PLUS 2D 4
Catherine Ct. SW19 2J 19
Catherine Dr. TW9: Rich 1F 11
Catherine Gdns. TW3: Houn 1J 9
Catherine Rd. KT6: Surb 2E 22
Catherine Wheel Rd.
TW8: Bford 4E 4
Cato's Hill KT10: Esh 7G 21
Causeway, The KT9: Chess 1F 29
KT10: Clay 4A 28
SW18 1K 13
(not continuous)
SW19 2F 19
TW4: Houn 1A 8
TW11: Tedd 3A 16
TW14: Felt, Houn 1A 8
Cavalier Ct. KT5: Surb 3G 23
Cavalry Cres. TW4: Houn 1C 8
Cavalry Gdns. SW15 2J 13
Cavell Way KT19: Eps 7H 29
Cavendish Av. KT3: N Mald 2D 24
Cavendish Dr. KT10: Clay 2K 27
Cavendish Rd. KT3: N Mald 1C 24
W4 5K 5
Cavendish Ter. TW13: Felt 6A 8
Caverleigh Way KT4: Wor Pk 5D 24
Cave Rd. TW10: Ham 1D 16
Caversham Av. SM3: Cheam 6H 25
Caversham Ho. KT1: King T 4C 36
Caversham Rd.
KT1: King T 3E 36 (6G 17)
Cawdor Cres. W7 1B 4
Caxton M. TW8: Bford 3E 4
Cecil Cl. KT9: Chess 1E 28
Cecil Rd. SM1: Sutt 3J 31
SW19 4K 19
Cedar Av. TW2: Whit 3G 9
Cedar Cl. KT8: E Mos 1K 21
KT10: Esh 3E 26
KT17: Eps 3C 34
SW15 1A 18
Cedar Ct. SW19 7G 13
TW8: Bford 3D 4
Cedarcroft Rd. KT9: Chess 1G 29
Cedar Hgts. TW10: Ham 5F 11
Cedar Hill KT18: Eps 5K 33
Cedar Ho. TW9: Kew 5J 5
Cedarland Ter. SW20 4E 18
Cedarne Rd. SW6 4K 7
Cedar Rd. KT8: E Mos 1K 21
TW11: Tedd 2B 16
Cedars, The TW11: Tedd 3A 16
Cedars Rd. KT1: Hamp W 5D 16
SM4: Mord 1K 25
SW13 6D 6
W4 2K 5
Cedar Ter. TW9: Rich 1F 11
Cedar Vw. KT1: King T 6B 36
Cedar Wlk. KT10: Clay 3A 28
Celandine Rd. KT12: Hers 1D 26
Centaur Ct. TW8: Bford 2F 5
Centaurs Bus. Pk. TW7: Isle 3B 4
Central Av. KT8: W Mole 1E 20
TW3: Houn 1H 9
Central Mall *SW18 3K 13*
(off South Mall)
Central Pde. KT6: Surb 3F 23
KT8: W Mole 1E 20
TW14: Felt 4B 8
Central Pk. Est. TW4: Houn 2C 8
Central Rd. KT4: Wor Pk 5D 24
SM4: Mord 3K 25
Central School Path
SW14 7K 5
Central Wlk. *KT19: Eps 2A 34*
(off Station App.)
Central Way TW14: Felt 2A 8
Centre, The TW3: Houn 1G 9
TW13: Felt 6A 8
Centre Ct. Shop. Cen.
SW19 3J 19
Century Ho. SW15 1G 13
Ceylon Rd. W14 1G 7
Chadacre Rd. KT17: Ewe 3E 30
Chadwick Av. SW19 3K 19
Chadwick Cl. SW15 4C 12
TW11: Tedd 3B 16
Chadwick M. W4 3J 5
Chadwick Pl. KT6: Surb 4D 22
Chadworth Way KT10: Clay 2J 27
Chaffers Mead KT21: Asht 5G 33
Chaffinch Cl. KT6: Surb 7H 23
Chailey Pl. KT12: Hers 1D 26
Chalcot Cl. SM2: Sutt 4K 31
Chalcott Gdns. KT6: Surb 5D 22
Chaldon Rd. SW6 4H 7
Chalfont Way W13 1C 4
Chalford Cl. KT8: W Mole 1F 21
Chalgrove Av. SM4: Mord 2K 25
CHALKER'S CORNER 7J 5
Chalk Hill Rd. W6 1G 7
Chalk La. KT18: Eps, Eps D 4A 34
(not continuous)
KT21: Asht 7H 33
Chalk Paddock KT18: Eps 4A 34
Chalk Pit Rd. KT18: Eps D 7K 33
SM7: Bans 6K 35
Chalky La. KT9: Chess 6E 28
Challis Rd. TW8: Bford 2E 4
Challoner Cres. W14 2J 7
Challoners Cl. KT8: E Mos 1J 21
Challoner St. W14 2J 7
Chalmers Way TW14: Felt 2A 8
Chamberlain Wlk.
TW13: Hanw 1D 14
(off Swift Rd.)
Chamberlain Way KT6: Surb 4F 23
Chamberlens Garages
W6 1E 6
(off Dalling Rd.)
Chambon Pl. W6 1D 6
Champneys Cl. SM2: Cheam 4J 31
Chancellor's Rd. W6 2F 7
Chancellor's St. W6 2F 7
Chancellors Wharf W6 2F 7
Chanctonbury Gdns.
SM2: Sutt 4K 31
Chandler Cl. TW12: Hamp 5F 15
Chandler Ct. TW14: Felt 3A 8
Chandos Av. W5 1D 4
Channon Ct. *KT6: Surb 2F 23*
(off Maple Rd)
Chanton Dr. SM2: Cheam 6F 31
Chantry Hurst KT18: Eps 4A 34
Chantry Rd. KT9: Chess 2G 29
Chapel Gro. KT18: Tatt C 7F 35
Chapelier Ho. SW18 1K 13
Chapel Mill Rd. KT1: King T 7G 17
Chapel Rd. TW1: Twick 4C 10
TW3: Houn 1G 9
Chapel Way KT18: Tatt C 7F 35
Chapel Yd. *SW18 2K 13*
(off Wandsworth High St.)
Chapman Sq. SW19 6G 13
Chapter Way TW12: Hamp 1F 15
Chara Pl. W4 3A 6
Charcot Ho. SW15 3C 12
Chardin Rd. W4 1B 6
CHARING CROSS HOSPITAL 3G 7
Charing Cross Sports Club 3G 7
Charles Babbage Cl.
KT9: Chess 4D 28
Charles Harrod Ct.
SW13 3F 7
(off Somerville Av.)
Charles Ho. *W14 1J 7*
(off Kensington High St.)
Charles Lesser Ho.
KT9: Chess 2E 28
Charles Rd. SW19 5K 19
Charles St. SW13 6B 6
Charleston Cl. TW13: Felt 7A 8
Charlesworth Pl. SW13 7B 6
Charleville Mans. *W14 2H 7*
(off Charleville Rd.)
Charleville M. TW7: Isle 1C 10
Charleville Rd. W14 2H 7
Charlotte Ct. KT10: Esh 2H 27
W6 1D 6
(off Invermead Cl.)
Charlotte Ho. *W6 2F 7*
(off Queen Caroline St.)
Charlotte M. *KT10: Esh 1G 27*
(off Heather Pl.)
W14 1H 7
Charlotte Rd. SW13 5C 6
Charlotte Sq. TW10: Rich 3G 11
Charlton Av. KT12: Hers 1A 26
Charlton Ho. TW8: Bford 3F 5
Charlwood Ho. TW9: Kew 4J 5
Charlwood Rd. SW15 1G 13
Charlwood Ter. SW15 1G 13
Charminster Av. SW19 6K 19
Charminster Ct. KT6: Surb 4E 22
Charminster Rd.
KT4: Wor Pk 5G 25
Charmouth Ct. TW10: Rich 2G 11
Charnwood Av. SW19 6K 19
Charnwood Cl. KT3: N Mald 1B 24
Charrington Bowl 6J 23
Charter Ct. KT3: N Mald 7B 18
Charter Cres. TW4: Houn 1D 8
Charter Quay KT1: King T 4B 36
Charter Rd. KT1: King T 7J 17
Charter Sq. KT1: King T 6J 17
Chartfield Av. SW15 2E 12
Chartfield Sq. SW15 2G 13
Chartwell Gdns.
SM3: Cheam 7H 25
Chartwell Pl. KT18: Eps 3B 34
SM3: Cheam 7J 25
Chase, The KT21: Asht 7D 32
SW20 5H 19
TW16: Sun 5A 14
Chase Ct. SW20 6H 19
TW7: Isle 6B 4
Chase End KT19: Eps 1A 34
Chase Gdns. TW2: Whit 4J 9

Chaseley Dr.—Claygate Lodge Cl.

Chaseley Dr. W4 . . . . . 2J 5
Chasemore Ho. SW6 . . . . . 4H 7
(off Williams Cl.)
Chase Rd. KT19: Eps 1A 34
Chaseside Av. SW20 . . . . . 5H 19
Chatham Cl. SM3: Sutt 4J 25
Chatham Rd. KT1: King T 6H 17
Chatsfield KT17: Ewe 6D 30
Chatsworth Av. SW20 . . . . . 5H 19
Chatsworth Cl. W4 . . . . . 3K 5
Chatsworth Ct. W8 . . . . . 1K 7
(off Pembroke Rd.)
Chatsworth Cres. TW3: Houn 1J 9
Chatsworth Gdns.
KT3: N Mald 2C 24
Chatsworth Lodge W4 . . . . . 2A 6
(off Bourne Pl.)
Chatsworth Pl. TW11: Tedd 1B 16
Chatsworth Rd. SM3: Cheam 2G 31
W4 . . . . . 3K 5
Chatterton Ct. TW9: Kew 6G 5
Chaucer Av. TW9: Rich 7H 5
Chaucer Cl. SM7: Bans 3H 35
Chaucer Gdns. SM1: Sutt 7K 25
(not continuous)
Chaucer Ho. SM1: Sutt 7K 25
(off Chaucer Gdns.)
Chaucer Mans. W14 . . . . . 3H 7
(off Queen's Club Gdns.)
Chaucer Rd. SM1: Sutt 7K 25
Chave Cft. KT18: Tatt C 7F 35
Chavecroft Ter. KT18: Tatt C 7F 35
CHEAM 3H 31
Cheam Comn. Rd.
KT4: Wor Pk 6E 24
Cheam Leisure Cen. 1G 31
Cheam Mans. SM3: Cheam 4H 31
Cheam Pk. Way
SM3: Cheam 3H 31
Cheam Rd. KT17: Ewe 6D 30
SM1: Sutt 3J 31
SM2: Cheam 6D 30
Cheam Station (Rail) 4H 31
CHEAM VILLAGE 3H 31
Cheeseman Cl.
TW12: Hamp 3D 14
Cheesemans Ter. W14 . . . . . 2J 7
(not continuous)
Chelmsford Cl. SM2: Sutt 5K 31
W6 . . . . . 3G 7
Chelsea Cl. KT4: Wor Pk 4D 24
TW12: Hamp H 2H 15
Chelsea FC 4K 7
Chelsea Gdns. SM3: Cheam 7H 25
Cheltenham Av. TW1: Twick 4B 10
Cheltenham Cl. KT3: N Mald 7K 17
Chelverton Rd. SW15 . . . . . 1G 13
Chelwood Cl. KT17: Eps 1C 34
Chelwood Gdns. TW9: Kew 6H 5
Chelwood Gdns. Pas.
TW9: Kew 6H 5
Chenies Ho. W4 . . . . . 4C 6
(off Corney Reach Way)
Chepstow Cl. SW15 . . . . . 2H 13
Cherimoya Gdns.
KT8: W Mole 7G 15
Cheriton Ct. KT12: Walt T 5B 20
Cherry Cl. SM4: Mord 1H 25
SM7: Bans 3G 35
W5 . . . . . 1E 4
Cherry Cres. TW8: Bford 4C 4
Cherry Gth. TW8: Bford 2E 4
Cherry Orchard KT21: Asht 7J 33
Cherry Orchard Gdns.
KT8: W Mole 7E 14
Cherry Orchard Rd.
KT8: W Mole 7F 15
Cherry Way KT19: Ewe 3A 30
Cherry Wood Cl. KT2: King T 4H 17
Cherrywood Ct. TW11: Tedd 2B 16
Cherrywood Dr. SW15 . . . . . 2G 13
Cherrywood La. SM4: Mord 1H 25
Chertsey Ct. SW14 . . . . . 7J 5
Chertsey Dr. SM3: Cheam 6H 25
Chertsey La. KT19: Eps 1H 33
Chertsey Rd. TW1: Twick 3A 10
TW2: Twick 6G 9
Chervil Cl. TW13: Felt 7A 8
Cherwell Ct. KT19: Ewe 1K 29
Chesfield Rd. KT2: King T 4F 17
Chesham Cl. SM2: Cheam 6H 31
Chesham Rd. KT1: King T 6H 17
Cheshire Gdns. KT9: Chess 3E 28
Chesilton Rd. SW6 . . . . . 5J 7
CHESSINGTON 2G 29
Chessington Cl. KT19: Ewe 3K 29
Chessington Hall Gdns.
KT9: Chess 4E 28
Chessington Hill Pk.
KT9: Chess 2H 29
Chessington Ho. KT17: Ewe 5C 30
(off Spring St.)
Chessington North Station (Rail)
. . . . . 2F 29
Chessington Pde. KT9: Chess 3E 28
Chessington Pk. KT9: Chess 1H 29
Chessington Rd. KT17: Ewe 5A 30
KT19: Ewe 3H 29
Chessington South Station (Rail)
. . . . . 4E 28
Chessington Sports Cen. 4E 28
Chessington World of Adventures
. . . . . 6D 28
Chesson Rd. W14 . . . . . 3J 7
Chester Av. TW2: Whit 5E 8
TW10: Rich 3G 11
Chester Cl. SM1: Sutt 6K 25
SW13 . . . . . 7E 6
TW10: Rich 3G 11
Chesterfield Ct. KT5: Surb 2F 23
(off Cranes Pk.)
Chesterfield Dr. KT10: Hin W 6B 22
Chesterfield Rd. KT19: Ewe 4A 30
W4 . . . . . 3K 5
Chesterman Ct. W4 . . . . . 4B 6
(off Corney Reach Way)
Chester Rd. SW19 . . . . . 3F 19
Chesters, The KT3: N Mald 5B 18
Chesterton Cl. SW18 . . . . . 2K 13
Chesterton Sq. W8 . . . . . 1K 7
Chesterton Ter. KT1: King T 6H 17
Chestnut All. SW6 . . . . . 3J 7
Chestnut Av. KT8: E Mos 7A 16
KT10: Esh 4J 21
KT19: Ewe 1B 30
SW14 . . . . . 7A 6
TW8: Bford 1E 4
TW11: Tedd 6A 16
TW12: Hamp 4F 15
Chestnut Ct. SW6 . . . . . 3J 7
TW13: Hanw 2C 14
Chestnut Gro. KT3: N Mald 7A 18
TW7: Isle 1B 10
Chestnut Ho. W4 . . . . . 1B 6
(off Orchard, The)
Chestnut Pl. KT17: Ewe 7D 30
Chestnut Rd. KT2: King T 4F 17
SW20 . . . . . 6G 19
TW2: Twick 6K 9
Chestnuts, The KT12: Walt T 6A 20
Chestnut Way TW13: Felt 7A 8
Chetwode Dr. KT18: Tatt C 7G 35
Chetwode Rd. KT20: Tad 7G 35
Cheviot Cl. SM7: Bans 4K 35
Cheyham Gdns. SM2: Cheam 6G 31
Cheyham Way SM2: Cheam 6H 31
Cheyne Av. TW2: Whit 5E 8
Cheyne Hill
KT5: Surb 7E 36 (1G 23)
Chichester Cl. TW12: Hamp 3E 14
Chichester Ct. KT17: Ewe 5C 30
Chichester Ho. KT19: Eps 1H 33
Chichester Way TW14: Felt 4B 8
Chiddingstone Cl. SM2: Sutt 6K 31
Chiddingstone St. SW6 . . . . . 6K 7
Chilcombe Ho. SW15 . . . . . 4D 12
(off Fontley Way)
Childerley KT1: King T 7H 17
(off Burritt Rd.)
Childerley St. SW6 . . . . . 5H 7
Child's M. SW5 . . . . . 1K 7
(off Child's Pl.)
Child's Pl. SW5 . . . . . 1K 7
Child's St. SW5 . . . . . 1K 7
Child's Wlk. SW5 . . . . . 1K 7
(off Child's St.)
Chillingworth Gdns.
TW1: Twick 7A 10
Chilmark Gdns. KT3: N Mald 3D 24
Chiltern Av. TW2: Whit 5F 9
Chiltern Cl. KT4: Wor Pk 5F 25
Chiltern Dr. KT5: Surb 3H 23
Chilton Av. W5 . . . . . 1E 4
Chilton Rd. TW9: Rich 7H 5
Chilvers Cl. TW2: Twick 6K 9
Chilworth Ct. SW19 . . . . . 5G 13
Chippenham KT1: King T 6G 17
(off Excelsior Cl.)
Chipstead Rd. SM7: Bans 6J 35
(not continuous)
Chipstead St. SW6 . . . . . 5K 7
Chisholm Ct. W6 . . . . . 2D 6
Chisholm Rd. TW10: Rich 3G 11
Chislehurst Rd. TW10: Rich 2F 11
CHISWICK 2A 6
Chiswick Bri. W4 . . . . . 6K 5
Chiswick Comn. Rd. W4 . . . . . 1A 6
Chiswick Community Sports Hall
. . . . . 4A 6
Chiswick Ct. W4 . . . . . 1J 5
Chiswick High Rd. TW8: Bford 2H 5
(not continuous)
W4 . . . . . 2J 5
Chiswick House 3B 6
Chiswick La. W4 . . . . . 2B 6
Chiswick La. Sth. W4 . . . . . 3C 6
Chiswick Mall W4 . . . . . 3C 6
W6 . . . . . 3C 6
Chiswick Pk. W4 . . . . . 1J 5
Chiswick Park Station (Tube) 1K 5
Chiswick Plaza W4 . . . . . 3K 5
Chiswick Quay W4 . . . . . 5K 5
Chiswick Rd. W4 . . . . . 1K 5
CHISWICK RDBT. 2H 5
Chiswick Sq. W4 . . . . . 3B 6
Chiswick Staithe W4 . . . . . 5K 5
Chiswick Station (Rail) 4K 5
Chiswick Ter. W4 . . . . . 1K 5
(off Chiswick Rd.)
Chiswick Village W4 . . . . . 3H 5
Chiswick Wharf W4 . . . . . 3C 6
Chivenor Gro. KT2: King T 2E 16
Chobham Gdns. SW19 . . . . . 6G 13
Cholmley Rd. KT7: T Ditt 3C 22
Cholmley Ter. KT7: T Ditt 4C 22
(off Portsmouth Rd.)
Cholmley Vs. KT7: T Ditt 3C 22
(off Portsmouth Rd.)
Cholmondeley Wlk.
TW9: Rich 2D 10
(not continuous)
Christabel Cl. TW7: Isle 7A 4
Christchurch Av. TW11: Tedd 2B 16
Christchurch Flats TW9: Rich 7F 5
Christchurch Gdns.
KT19: Eps 7J 29
Christ Chu. Mt. KT19: Eps 1J 33
(not continuous)
Christchurch Pl. KT19: Eps 7J 29
Christ Chu. Rd. KT19: Eps 1F 33
SW14 . . . . . 2J 11
Christchurch Rd. KT5: Surb 3G 23
Chudleigh Rd. TW2: Twick 3K 9
(not continuous)
Chumleigh Wlk. KT5: Surb 1G 23
Church Av. SW14 . . . . . 7A 6
Church Cl. KT17: Eps 2B 34
Church Ct. TW9: Rich 2E 10
Church Est. Almshouses
TW9: Rich 1G 11
(off Sheen Rd.)
Church Farm La.
SM3: Cheam 3H 31
Churchfield Mans. SW6 . . . . . 6J 7
(off New Kings Rd.)
Churchfield Rd. KT12: Walt T 4A 20
Churchfields KT8: W Mole 7F 15
Churchfields Av. TW13: Hanw 7E 8
Church Ga. SW6 . . . . . 7H 7
Church Grn. KT12: Hers 3B 26
Church Gro.
KT1: Hamp W 3A 36 (5D 16)
Church Hill SW19 . . . . . 2J 19
Church Hill Rd. KT6: Surb 2F 23
SM3: Cheam 7G 25
Churchill Rd. KT19: Eps 7H 29
Church La. KT7: T Ditt 3A 22
KT9: Chess 3G 29
KT18: Tad 6G 35
SW19 . . . . . 5J 19
TW1: Twick 5B 10
TW10: Ham 5F 11
TW11: Tedd 2A 16
Church Mdw. KT6: Surb 6D 22
Church Pas. KT6: Surb 2F 23
TW1: Twick 5C 10
Church Path SW14 . . . . . 7A 6
(not continuous)
SW19 . . . . . 6J 19
(not continuous)
W3 . . . . . 1K 5
(not continuous)
Church Ri. KT9: Chess 3G 29
Church Rd.
KT1: King T 3E 36 (6G 17)
KT4: Wor Pk 5B 24
KT6: Surb 5D 22
KT8: E Mos 1J 21
KT10: Clay 3A 28
KT17: Eps 1B 34
KT19: Ewe 4A 30
KT21: Asht 7E 32
SM3: Cheam 3H 31
SW13 . . . . . 6C 6
SW19 . . . . . 2H 19
TW9: Rich 1F 11
TW10: Ham 1E 16
TW11: Tedd 1K 15
TW13: Hanw 2C 14
Church Side KT18: Eps 2J 33
Church St.
KT1: King T 3B 36 (6E 16)
KT10: Esh 1G 27
KT17: Eps 2B 34
KT17: Ewe 5D 30
TW1: Twick 5B 10
TW7: Isle 7C 4
TW12: Hamp 5H 15
TW16: Sun 7A 14
W4 . . . . . 3C 6
Church Stretton Rd.
TW3: Houn 2H 9
Church Ter. TW10: Rich 2E 10
Church Vw. TW10: Rich 2F 11
Churchview Rd. TW2: Twick 5J 9
Church Villa TW16: Sun 7A 14
Church Wlk. KT7: T Ditt 3A 22
SW13 . . . . . 5D 6
SW15 . . . . . 2E 12
SW20 . . . . . 7F 19
TW8: Bford 3D 4
(not continuous)
TW9: Rich 2E 10
Churchward Ho. W14 . . . . . 2J 7
(off Ivatt Pl.)
Churston Dr. SM4: Mord 2G 25
Chuters Gro. KT17: Eps 1C 34
Cineworld Cinema
Feltham 6A 8
Wandsworth 2K 13
Circle Gdns. SW19 . . . . . 6K 19
City Wharf Ho. KT7: T Ditt 3C 22
Clancarty Rd. SW6 . . . . . 6K 7
Clandon Cl. KT17: Ewe 3C 30
Clandon Ter. SW20 . . . . . 6G 19
Clare Cres. KT22: Lea 7B 32
Clare Hill KT10: Esh 3G 27
Clare Lawn Av. SW14 . . . . . 2K 11
Clare M. SW6 . . . . . 4K 7
Claremont Av. KT3: N Mald 2D 24
KT10: Esh 3E 26
KT12: Hers 1C 26
TW16: Sun 5A 14
Claremont Cl. KT12: Hers 2B 26
Claremont Dr. KT10: Esh 5F 27
Claremont End KT10: Esh 3G 27
Claremont Gdns. KT6: Surb 2F 23
Claremont Gro. W4 . . . . . 4B 6
Claremont Ho. SM2: Sutt 4K 31
Claremont Landscape Garden
. . . . . 4E 26
Claremont La. KT10: Esh 2G 27
CLAREMONT PARK 4F 27
Claremont Pk. Rd.
KT10: Esh 3G 27
Claremont Rd. KT6: Surb 2F 23
KT10: Clay 4K 27
TW1: Twick 4C 10
TW11: Tedd 2A 16
Claremont Ter. KT7: T Ditt 4C 22
Claremount Cl. KT18: Tatt C 6F 35
Claremount Gdns.
KT18: Tatt C 6F 35
Clarence Av. KT3: N Mald 6K 17
Clarence Cl. KT12: Hers 1A 26
Clarence Ct. W6 . . . . . 1E 6
(off Cambridge Gro.)
Clarence Ho. KT12: Hers 2A 26
(off Queens Rd.)
Clarence La. SW15 . . . . . 3B 12
Clarence Rd. KT12: Hers 1A 26
SM1: Sutt 2K 31
SW19 . . . . . 3K 19
TW9: Kew 5G 5
TW11: Tedd 3A 16
W4 . . . . . 2H 5
Clarence St.
KT1: King T 3B 36 (6E 16)
(not continuous)
TW9: Rich 1F 11
Clarence Ter. TW3: Houn 1G 9
Clarendon Ct. TW9: Kew 5G 5
Clarendon Cres. TW2: Twick 7J 9
Clarendon Dr. SW15 . . . . . 1F 13
Clare Pl. SW15 . . . . . 4C 12
Clare Rd. TW4: Houn 1E 8
Clare Wood KT22: Lea 7C 32
Claridge Ct. SW6 . . . . . 6J 7
Clarkes Av. KT4: Wor Pk 5G 25
Claudia Pl. SW19 . . . . . 5H 13
Clavering Av. SW13 . . . . . 3E 6
Clavering Cl. TW1: Twick 1B 16
Claverton KT21: Asht 6F 33
Claxton Gro. W6 . . . . . 2G 7
Claybrook Rd. W6 . . . . . 3G 7
CLAYGATE 3A 28
Claygate La. KT7: T Ditt 5B 22
KT10: Clay, Hin W 6B 22
Claygate Lodge Cl.
KT10: Clay 4K 27

Claygate Station (Rail)—Cranbrook Dr.

Claygate Station (Rail) 3K 27
Clayhill KT5: Surb 2H 23
Claymore Cl. SM4: Mord 4K 25
Clayponds Av. TW8 . . . . .1F 5
Clayponds Gdns. W5 . . . . .1E 4
(not continuous)
CLAYPONDS HOSPITAL 1F 5
Clayponds La. TW8: Bford 2F 5
(not continuous)
Clayton Cres. TW8: Bford 2E 4
Clayton Ho. *SW13* *4F 7*
(off Trinity Chu. Rd.)
Clayton Rd. KT9: Chess 1D 28
KT17: Eps 1B 34
TW7: Isle 1K 9
Clearwater Pl. KT6: Surb 3D 22
Cleaveland Rd. KT6: Surb 2E 22
Cleaves Almshouses
KT2: King T 3D 36
Cleeve Way SW15 . . . . .4C 12
Clem Attlee Ct. SW6 . . . . .3J 7
Clem Attlee Pde. *SW6* *3J 7*
(off Nth. End Rd.)
Clement Cl. W4 . . . . .1A 6
Clement Rd. SW19 . . . . .2H 19
Clements Ct. TW4: Houn 1C 8
Clements Mead KT22: Lea 7B 32
Clements Pl. TW8: Bford 2E 4
Clements Rd. KT12: Walt T 6A 20
Clensham Ct. SM1: Sutt 6K 25
Clensham La. SM1: Sutt 6K 25
Clevedon Rd. KT1: King T 6H 17
TW1: Twick 3E 10
(not continuous)
Cleveland Av. SW20 . . . . .6J 19
TW12: Hamp 4E 14
W4 .1C 6
Cleveland Cl. KT12: Walt T 7A 20
Cleveland Gdns.
KT4: Wor Pk 6B 24
SW13 . . . . .6C 6
Cleveland Ri. SM4: Mord 4G 25
Cleveland Rd. KT3: N Mald 1B 24
KT4: Wor Pk 6B 24
SW13 . . . . .6C 6
TW7: Isle 1B 10
W4 .1K 5
Cleves Av. KT17: Ewe 5E 30
Cleves Ct. KT17: Eps 1C 34
Cleves Rd. TW10: Ham 7D 10
Cleves Way TW12: Hamp 4E 14
Clifden Rd. TW1: Twick 5A 10
TW8: Bford 3E 4
Clifford Av. SW14 . . . . .7J 5
(not continuous)
Clifford Haigh Ho. SW6 . . . . .4G 7
Clifford Ho. *W14* *1J 7*
(off Edith Vs.)
Clifford Rd. TW10: Ham 6E 10
Clifton Av. TW13: Felt 7B 8
Clifton Ct. KT5: Surb 4G 23
Clifton Gdns. W4 . . . . .1A 6
(not continuous)
Clifton Pde. TW13: Felt 7B 8
Clifton Pk. Av. SW20 . . . . .6F 19
Clifton Pl. SM7: Bans 4K 35
Clifton Rd. KT2: King T 4G 17
SW19 . . . . .3G 19
TW11: Tedd 1K 15
Clifton Wlk. *W6* *1E 6*
(off King St.)
Clinton Av. KT8: E Mos 1H 21
Clinton Ho. *KT6: Surb* *4E 22*
(off Lovelace Gdns)
Clippesby Cl. KT9: Chess 3G 29
Clitherow Ct. TW8: Bford 2D 4
Clitherow Pas. TW8: Bford 2D 4
Clitherow Rd. TW8: Bford 2C 4
Cliveden Rd. SW19 . . . . .5J 19
Clive Rd. KT10: Esh 1G 27
TW1: Twick 1A 16
Clockhouse, The SW19 . . . . .7F 13
Clockhouse Cl. SW19 . . . . .6F 13
Clockhouse Pl. SW15 . . . . .3H 13
Clock Twr. Ind. Est. TW7: Isle 7A 4
Clock Twr. Rd. TW7: Isle 7A 4
Cloister Cl. TW11: Tedd 2C 16
Cloisters, The *TW7: Isle* *7B 4*
(off Pulteney Cl.)
Cloisters Mall
KT1: King T 3B 36 (6F 17)
Cloncurry St. SW6 . . . . .6G 7
Clonmel Rd. SW6 . . . . .4J 7
TW11: Tedd 1J 15
Clonmore St. SW18 . . . . .5J 13
Close, The KT3: N Mald 6K 17
KT6: Surb 3F 23
KT10: Esh 3G 27
SM3: Sutt 4J 25
TW9: Rich 7J 5
Clovelly Ct. *KT17: Eps* *2C 34*
(off Alexandra Rd.)
Cluny M. SW5 . . . . .1K 7
Clyde Flats *SW6* *4J 7*
(off Rhylston Rd.)
Clyde Ho.
KT2: King T 1B 36 (5E 16)
Clyde Rd. SM1: Sutt 2K 31
Clydesdale Cl. TW7: Isle 7A 4
Clydesdale Gdns.
TW10: Rich 1J 11
Clymping Dene TW14: Felt 4A 8
Coach Ho. La. SW19 . . . . .1G 19
Coalecroft Rd. SW15 . . . . .1F 13
Coates Wlk. TW8: Bford 3F 5
Cobbett Rd. TW2: Whit 5F 9
Cobblers Wlk.
TW12: Hamp, Tedd 5H 15
(not continuous)
Cobb's Hall *W6* *3G 7*
(off Fulham Pal. Rd.)
Cobb's Rd. TW4: Houn 1E 8
Cobham Av. KT3: N Mald 2D 24
Cobham Rd. KT1: King T 6H 17
Cochrane Rd. SW19 . . . . .4H 19
COCKCROW HILL 5E 22
Cocks Cres. KT3: N Mald 1C 24
Coda Cen., The SW6 . . . . .4H 7
Colborne Way KT4: Wor Pk 7F 25
Colcokes Rd. SM7: Bans 5K 35
Coldstream Gdns.
SW18 . . . . .3J 13
Colebrook Cl. SW15 . . . . .4G 13
Cole Ct. TW1: Twick 4B 10
Colehill Gdns. SW6 . . . . .6H 7
Colehill La. SW6 . . . . .5H 7
Coleman Ct. SW18 . . . . .4K 13
COLE PARK 3B 10
Cole Pk. Gdns. TW1: Twick 2B 10
Cole Pk. Rd. TW1: Twick 2B 10
Cole Pk. Vw. TW1: Twick 3B 10
Coleridge Ct. *W14* *1G 7*
(off Blythe Rd.)
Cole Rd. TW1: Twick 3B 10
Coleshill Rd. TW11: Tedd 3K 15
Colet Ct. *W6* *1G 7*
(off Hammersmith Rd.)
Colet Gdns. W14 . . . . .1G 7
Colinette Rd. SW15 . . . . .1F 13
Coliston Pas. SW18 . . . . .4K 13
Coliston Rd. SW18 . . . . .4K 13
College Av. KT17: Eps 3C 34
College Cl. TW2: Twick 5J 9
College Ct. *W6* *2F 7*
(off Queen Caroline St.)
College Dr. KT7: T Ditt 4K 21
College Gdns. KT3: N Mald 2C 24
College Rd. KT17: Eps 3C 34
TW7: Isle 5A 4
College Rdbt.
KT1: King T 5C 36 (7F 17)
College Wlk.
KT1: King T 5D 36 (7F 17)
Collier Cl. KT19: Ewe 3H 29
Collingwood Av. KT5: Surb 5K 23
Collingwood Cl. TW2: Whit 4F 9
Collingwood Pl.
KT12: Walt T 7A 20
Collingwood Rd. SM1: Sutt 7K 25
Collins Path TW12: Hamp 3E 14
Collis All. TW2: Twick 5K 9
Colman Cl. KT18: Tatt C 6F 35
Colne Ct. KT19: Ewe 1K 29
Colne Dr. KT12: Walt T 7C 20
Colne Rd. TW1: Twick 5A 10
TW2: Twick 5K 9
Colonial Av. TW2: Whit 3H 9
Colonial Dr. W4 . . . . .1K 5
Colston Rd. SW14 . . . . .1K 11
Columbia Av. KT4: Wor Pk 4C 24
Columbia Sq. SW14 . . . . .1K 11
Colville Rd. W3 . . . . .1J 5
Colwith Rd. W6 . . . . .3F 7
Combemartin Rd.
SW18 . . . . .4H 13
Comberton *KT1: King T* *6H 17*
(off Eureka Rd.)
Comeragh M. W14 . . . . .2H 7
Comeragh Rd. W14 . . . . .2H 7
Commerce Rd. TW8: Bford 3D 4
Common, The KT21: Asht 5E 32
Commondale SW15 . . . . .7F 7
Commonfield Rd. SM7: Bans 3K 35
Common La. KT10: Clay 4B 28
Common Rd. KT10: Clay 3B 28
SW13 . . . . .7E 6
W4 .1B 6
Common Side KT18: Eps 4H 33
Commonside Cl. SM2: Sutt 7K 31
Community Way KT10: Esh 1H 27
Compass Hill TW10: Rich 3E 10
Compton Cl. KT10: Esh 3J 27
Compton Cres. KT9: Chess 2F 29
W4 .3K 5
Compton Rd. SW19 . . . . .3J 19
Conaways Cl. KT17: Ewe 6D 30
Concord Ct. KT1: King T 5E 36
Concord Ho. KT3: N Mald 7B 18
Conifer Gdns. SM1: Sutt 6K 25
Conifer Pk. KT17: Eps 7B 30
Conifers Cl. TW11: Tedd 4C 16
Coniger Rd. SW6 . . . . .6K 7
Coniston Cl. SW13 . . . . .4C 6
SW20 . . . . .3G 25
W4 .4K 5
Coniston Rd. TW2: Whit 3G 9
Coniston Way KT9: Chess 7F 23
Connaught Av. SW14 . . . . .7K 5
TW4: Houn 1D 8
Connaught M. SW6 . . . . .5H 7
Connaught Rd. KT3: N Mald 1B 24
TW10: Rich 2G 11
TW11: Tedd 2J 15
Conrad Dr. KT4: Wor Pk 5F 25
Consfield Av. KT3: N Mald 1D 24
Consort M. TW7: Isle 2J 9
Constable Ct. *W4* *2J 5*
(off Chaseley Dr.)
Constable Gdns. TW7: Isle 2J 9
Constance Rd. TW2: Whit 4G 9
Convent Gdns. W5 . . . . .1D 4
Conway Rd. SW20 . . . . .5F 19
TW4: Houn 4E 8
TW13: Hanw 2C 14
Conway Wlk. TW12: Hamp 3E 14
Conyers Cl. KT12: Hers 2C 26
Cookes La. SM3: Cheam 3H 31
COOMBE 4A 18
Coombe Bank KT2: King T 5B 18
Coombe Cl. TW3: Houn 1F 9
Coombe Cres. TW12: Hamp 4E 14
Coombe End KT2: King T 4A 18
Coombefield Cl. KT3: N Mald 2B 24
Coombe Gdns. KT3: N Mald 1C 24
SW20 . . . . .6D 18
Coombe Hill Glade
KT2: King T 4B 18
Coombe Hill Rd. KT2: King T 4B 18
Coombe Ho. Chase
KT3: N Mald 5A 18
COOMBE LANE 5C 18
Coombe La. SW20 . . . . .5C 18
Coombe La. Flyover
SW20 . . . . .5C 18
Coombe La. W. KT2: King T 5J 17
Coombe Neville KT2: King T 4A 18
Coombe Pk. KT2: King T 2K 17
Coombe Pl. KT2: King T 2K 17
Coombe Ridings KT2: King T 2K 17
Coombe Ri. KT2: King T 5K 17
Coombe Rd. KT2: King T 5H 17
KT3: N Mald 6B 18
TW12: Hamp 3E 14
W4 .2B 6
Coombe Wlk. SM1: Sutt 7K 25
Coombe Wood Rd.
KT2: King T 2K 17
Coomer M. SW6 . . . . .3J 7
Coomer Pl. SW6 . . . . .3J 7
Coomer Rd. SW6 . . . . .3J 7
Coopers Ct. *TW7: Isle* *6A 4*
(off Woodlands Rd.)
Copenhagen Way
KT12: Walt T 7A 20
Cope Pl. W8 . . . . .1K 7
Coppard Gdns. KT9: Chess 3D 28
Copper Mill Dr. TW7: Isle 6A 4
Coppice Cl. SW20 . . . . .7F 19
Coppice Dr. SW15 . . . . .3E 12
Coppsfield KT8: W Mole 7F 15
Copse Edge Av. KT17: Eps 2C 34
Copse Glade KT6: Surb 4E 22
COPSE HILL 4E 18
Copse Hill SW20 . . . . .5D 18
Copsem Dr. KT10: Esh 3G 27
Copsem La. KT10: Esh, Oxs 3H 27
KT22: Oxs 3H 27
Copsem Way KT10: Esh 4H 27
Copsem Wood KT22: Oxs 7H 27
Coptain Ho. SW18 . . . . .1K 13
Copthall Gdns. TW1: Twick 5A 10
Coram Ho. *W4* *2B 6*
(off Wood St.)
Corban Rd. TW3: Houn 1F 9
Corbet Rd. KT17: Ewe 6B 30
Corbiere Ct. SW19 . . . . .3G 19
Corelli Ct. *SW5* *1K 7*
(off W. Cromwell Rd.)
Corfe Cl. KT21: Asht 7D 32
Corkran Rd. KT6: Surb 4E 22
Cormorant Pl. SM1: Sutt 2J 31
Cornelia Ho. *TW1: Twick* *3E 10*
(off Denton Rd.)
Cornercroft *SM3: Cheam* *2G 31*
(off Wickham Av.)
Corney Reach Way W4 . . . . .4B 6
Corney Rd. W4 . . . . .3B 6
Cornish Ho. TW8: Bford 2G 5
Cornwall Av. KT10: Clay 4A 28
Cornwall Gro. W4 . . . . .2B 6
Cornwall Rd. SM2: Sutt 4J 31
TW1: Twick 4B 10
Coronation Wlk. TW2: Whit 5F 9
Corporate Dr. TW13: Felt 7A 8
Corporation Av. TW4: Houn 1D 8
Corscombe Cl. KT2: King T 2K 17
Cortayne Ct. TW2: Twick 6K 9
Cortayne Rd. SW6 . . . . .6J 7
Cortis Rd. SW15 . . . . .3E 12
Cortis Ter. SW15 . . . . .3E 12
Cotherstone KT19: Ewe 6A 30
Cotman Cl. SW15 . . . . .3G 13
Cotsford Av. KT3: N Mald 2K 23
Cotswold Cl. KT2: King T 3K 17
KT10: Hin W 6A 22
Cotswold Rd. TW12: Hamp 2F 15
Cotswold Way KT4: Wor Pk 6F 25
Cottage Gro. KT6: Surb 3E 22
Cottage Rd. KT19: Ewe 4A 30
Cottenham Dr. SW20 . . . . .4E 18
Cottenham Pde. SW20 . . . . .6E 18
COTTENHAM PARK 5E 18
Cottenham Pk. Rd.
SW20 . . . . .5D 18
(not continuous)
Cottenham Pl. SW20 . . . . .4E 18
Cotterill Rd. KT6: Surb 6F 23
Cottimore Av. KT12: Walt T 5A 20
Cottimore Cres.
KT12: Walt T 4A 20
Cottimore La. KT12: Walt T 4A 20
(not continuous)
Cottimore Ter. KT12: Walt T 4A 20
Cottington Rd. TW13: Hanw 1C 14
Couchmore Av. KT10: Hin W 6K 21
Country Way TW13: Hanw 3A 14
County Pde. TW8: Bford 4E 4
Court Cl. TW2: Twick 7G 9
Court Cl. Av. TW2: Twick 7G 9
Court Cres. KT9: Chess 2E 28
Courtenay Av. SM2: Sutt 5K 31
Courtenay Rd. KT4: Wor Pk 7F 25
Court Farm Av. KT19: Ewe 2A 30
Court Farm Gdns. KT19: Eps 7K 29
Courthope Rd. SW19 . . . . .2H 19
Courthope Vs. SW19 . . . . .4H 19
Court Ho. Mans. KT19: Eps 1A 34
Courtlands TW10: Rich 2H 11
Courtlands Av. KT10: Esh 3E 26
TW9: Kew 6J 5
TW12: Hamp 3E 14
Courtlands Cres. SM7: Bans 4K 35
Courtlands Dr. KT19: Ewe 3B 30
Courtlands Rd. KT5: Surb 4H 23
Court La. KT19: Eps 2K 33
Courtney Pl. KT11: Cobh 7E 26
Court Rd. SM7: Bans 5K 35
Court Royal SW15 . . . . .2H 13
Court Way TW2: Twick 4A 10
Coutts Av. KT9: Chess 2F 29
Coval Gdns. SW14 . . . . .1J 11
Coval La. SW14 . . . . .1J 11
Coval Pas. SW14 . . . . .1K 11
Coval Rd. SW14 . . . . .1J 11
Coverts Rd. KT10: Clay 4A 28
Cowleaze Rd.
KT2: King T 2D 36 (5F 17)
Cowley Cres. KT12: Hers 1B 26
Cowley Rd. SW14 . . . . .7B 6
Cowper Rd. KT2: King T 2G 17
Coxdean KT18: Tatt C 7F 35
Cox Ho. *W6* *3H 7*
(off Field Rd.)
Cox La. KT9: Chess 1G 29
KT19: Ewe 2J 29
(not continuous)
Coxwold Path KT9: Chess 4F 29
Crabtree La. SW6 . . . . .4F 7
(not continuous)
Craddocks Av. KT21: Asht 6F 33
Craddocks Cl. KT21: Asht 5H 33
Craddocks Pde. KT21: Asht 6F 33
(not continuous)
Craig Rd. TW10: Ham 1D 16
Crammond Cl. W6 . . . . .3H 7
Cranborne Av. KT6: Surb 7H 23
Cranbourne Cl. KT12: Hers 3B 26
Cranbrook Ct. TW8: Bford 3D 4
Cranbrook Dr. KT10: Esh 5H 21
TW2: Whit 5G 9

Cranbrook Rd. SW19 4H 19
TW4: Houn 1E 8
W4 2B 6
Crane Av. TW7: Isle 2B 10
Cranebank M. TW1: Twick 1B 10
Cranebrook TW2: Twick 6H 9
Crane Ct. KT19: Ewe 1K 29
Craneford Cl. TW2: Twick 4A 10
Craneford Way TW2: Twick 4K 9
Crane Ho. TW13: Hanw 7F 9
Crane Mead Ct. TW1: Twick 4A 10
Crane Pk. Island Nature Reserve 6E 8
Crane Pk. Rd. TW2: Whit 6G 9
Crane Rd. TW2: Twick 5K 9
Cranes Dr. KT5: Surb 1F 23
Cranes Pk.
KT5: Surb 7D 36 (1F 23)
Cranes Pk. Av.
KT5: Surb 7E 36 (1F 23)
Cranes Pk. Cres. KT5: Surb 1G 23
Crane Way TW2: Whit 4H 9
Cranford Cl. SW20 4E 18
Cranford Ri. KT10: Esh 2H 27
Cranleigh Ct. TW9: Rich 7H 5
Cranleigh Gdns. KT2: King T 3G 17
Cranleigh Rd. KT10: Esh 5H 21
SW19 7K 19
Cranmer Av. W13 1C 4
Cranmer Cl. SM4: Mord 3G 25
Cranmer Rd. KT2: King T 2F 17
TW12: Hamp H 2G 15
Craven Cottage 6G 7
Craven Gdns. SW19 2K 19
Craven Rd. KT2: King T 5G 17
Cray Av. KT21: Asht 5F 33
Crayke Hill KT9: Chess 4F 29
Crediton Way KT10: Clay 2B 28
Creek Cotts. *KT8: E Mos* *1K 21*
(off Creek Rd.)
Creek Rd. KT8: E Mos 1K 21
Crefeld Cl. W6 3H 7
Creighton Rd. W5 1E 4
Cremorne Gdns. KT19: Ewe 6A 30
Crescent, The KT3: N Mald 7K 17
KT6: Surb 2F 23
KT8: W Mole 1F 21
KT18: Eps 3H 33
(not continuous)
SM2: Sutt 7K 31
SW13 6C 6
SW19 7K 13
Crescent Ct. KT6: Surb 2E 22
Crescent Gdns. SW19 7K 13
Crescent Rd. KT2: King T 4H 17
SW20 5G 19
Crescent Stables SW15 2H 13
Cresford Rd. SW6 5K 7
Cressage Ho. *TW8: Bford* *3F 5*
(off Ealing Rd.)
Cressinghams, The
KT18: Eps 2A 34
Cresswell Rd. TW1: Twick 3E 10
TW13: Hanw 7D 8
Crest, The KT5: Surb 2H 23
Creston Way KT4: Wor Pk 5G 25
Crestway SW15 3D 12
Crestwood Way TW4: Houn 2D 8
Cricketers Cl. KT9: Chess 1E 28
Crieff Ct. TW11: Tedd 4D 16
Crispen Rd. TW13: Hanw 1D 14
Crispin Cl. KT21: Asht 7G 33
Crisp Rd. W6 2F 7
Cristowe Rd. SW6 6J 7
Criterion Bldgs. *KT7: T Ditt* *4C 22*
(off Portsmouth Rd.)
Croft, The KT17: Eps 3C 34
Croft End Cl. KT9: Chess 7G 23
Crofters Cl. TW7: Isle 2J 9
Crofton KT21: Asht 7F 33
Crofton Av. KT12: Walt T 7B 20
W4 4A 6
Crofton Ter. TW9: Rich 1G 11
Croftway TW10: Ham 7C 10
Cromerhyde SM4: Mord 2K 25
Cromer Vs. Rd. SW18 3J 13
Cromford Rd. SW18 2K 13
Cromford Way KT3: N Mald 5A 18
Cromwell Av. KT3: N Mald 2C 24
W6 2E 6
Cromwell Cl. KT12: Walt T 5A 20
Cromwell Cres. SW5 1K 7
CROMWELL HOSPITAL, THE 1K 7
Cromwell Pl. SW14 7K 5
Cromwell Rd.
KT2: King T 2D 36 (5F 17)
KT4: Wor Pk 7A 24
KT12: Walt T 5A 20
SW5 1K 7
SW19 2K 19
Cromwell Rd. TW3: Houn 1F 9
TW11: Tedd 3B 16
TW13: Felt 5A 8
Cromwell St. TW3: Houn 1F 9
Crondace Rd. SW6 5K 7
Crondall Ho. SW15 4D 12
Crooked Billet SW19 3F 19
Crookham Rd. SW6 5J 7
Crosby Cl. TW13: Hanw 7D 8
Cross Deep TW1: Twick 6A 10
Cross Deep Gdns.
TW1: Twick 6A 10
Cross Lances Rd. TW3: Houn 1G 9
Crosslands Rd. KT19: Ewe 3A 30
Cross Rd. KT2: King T 4G 17
SM2: Sutt 6K 31
SW19 4K 19
TW13: Hanw 1D 14
Cross St. SW13 6B 6
TW12: Hamp H 2H 15
Crossway KT12: Walt T 6A 20
SW20 1F 25
Crossways, The KT5: Surb 5J 23
Crown Arc.
KT1: King T 4B 36 (6E 16)
Crown Cl. KT12: Walt T 4B 20
Crown La. SM4: Mord 1K 25
Crown M. W6 1D 6
Crown Pde. SM4: Mord 7K 19
Crown Pas. *KT1: King T* *4B 36*
(off Church St.)
Crown Rd. KT3: N Mald 5K 17
SM1: Sutt 1K 31
SM4: Mord 1K 25
TW1: Twick 3C 10
Crown Ter. TW9: Rich 1G 11
Crowntree Cl. TW7: Isle 3A 4
Crowther Av. TW8: Bford 1F 5
Crowther Cl. *SW6* *3J 7*
(off Bucklers All.)
Crowthorne Cl. SW18 4J 13
Croxall Ho. KT12: Walt T 3B 20
Croylands Dr. KT6: Surb 4F 23
Crutchfield La. KT12: Walt T 6A 20
Cudas Cl. KT19: Ewe 7C 24
Cuddington Av. KT4: Wor Pk 7C 24
Cuddington Ct. SM2: Cheam 5G 31
Cuddington Glade KT19: Eps 1H 33
Cuddington Pk. Cl.
SM7: Bans 2J 35
Cuddington Way
SM2: Cheam 1G 35
Cudham Cl. SM2: Sutt 6K 31
Cullerne Cl. KT17: Ewe 6C 30
Culsac Rd. KT6: Surb 6F 23
Culverhay KT21: Asht 5F 33
Cumberland Cl. KT19: Ewe 6B 30
SW20 4G 19
TW1: Twick 3C 10
Cumberland Cres. W14 1H 7
(not continuous)
Cumberland Dr. KT9: Chess 7F 23
KT10: Hin W 6B 22
Cumberland Ho. KT2: King T 4J 17
Cumberland Pl. TW16: Sun 1A 20
Cumberland Rd. SW13 5C 6
TW9: Kew 4H 5
Cumbrae Gdns. KT6: Surb 6E 22
Cumnor Gdns. KT17: Ewe 3D 30
Cunliffe Pde. KT19: Ewe 7C 24
Cunliffe Rd. KT19: Ewe 7C 24
Cunnington St. W4 1K 5
Curlew Ct. KT6: Surb 7H 23
Currie Hill Cl. SW19 1J 19
Curtis Rd. KT19: Ewe 1K 29
TW4: Houn 4E 8
Curvan Cl. KT17: Ewe 6C 30
Cusack Cl. TW1: Twick 1A 16
Cutthroat All. TW10: Ham 6D 10
Cyclamen Cl. TW12: Hamp 3F 15
Cyclamen Way KT19: Ewe 2K 29
Cygnet Av. TW14: Felt 4B 8
Cygnets, The TW13: Hanw 1D 14
Cypress Av. TW2: Whit 4H 9
Cypress Ct. SM1: Sutt 2K 31
Cypress Way SM7: Bans 3G 35

D

D'Abernon Chase KT22: Oxs 3B 32
D'Abernon Cl. KT10: Esh 7F 21
Daffodil Pl. TW12: Hamp 3F 15
Dagmar Rd. KT2: King T 5G 17
Dain Ct. *W8* *1K 7*
(off Lexham Gdns.)
Dairy Wlk. SW19 1H 19
Daisy La. SW6 7K 7
Dale Ct. *KT2: King T* *4G 17*
(off York Rd.)
Dale Rd. SM1: Sutt 1J 31
Daleside Rd. KT19: Ewe 3A 30
Dale St. W4 2B 6
Dalewood Gdns.
KT4: Wor Pk 6E 24
Dallas Rd. SM3: Cheam 3H 31
Dalling Rd. W6 1E 6
Dallington Cl. KT12: Hers 3B 26
Dalmeny Cres. TW3: Houn 1J 9
Dalmeny Rd. KT4: Wor Pk 7E 24
Dalmore Av. KT10: Clay 3A 28
Dancer Rd. SW6 5J 7
TW9: Rich 7H 5
Danebury Av. SW15 3B 12
(not continuous)
Danehurst TW8: Bford 4D 4
Danehurst Ct. KT17: Eps 2C 34
Danehurst St. SW6 5H 7
Danemere St. SW15 7F 7
Danesbury Rd. TW13: Felt 5A 8
Danesfield Cl. KT12: Walt T 7A 20
Danesmead KT11: Cobh 7F 27
Danetree Cl. KT19: Ewe 4K 29
Danetree Rd. KT19: Ewe 4K 29
Daniel Cl. TW4: Houn 4E 8
Daniel Way SM7: Bans 3K 35
Dan Mason Dr. W4 6K 5
Da Palma Ct. *SW6* *3K 7*
(off Anselm Rd.)
Daphne Ct. KT4: Wor Pk 6B 24
Darby Cres. TW16: Sun 6B 14
Darby Gdns. TW16: Sun 6B 14
D'Arcy Pl. KT21: Asht 6G 33
Darcy Rd. KT21: Asht 6G 33
SM3: Cheam 7G 25
TW7: Isle 5B 4
Darell Rd. TW9: Rich 7H 5
Darfur St. SW15 7G 7
Darlan Rd. SW6 4J 7
Darlaston Rd. SW19 4G 19
Darley Dr. KT3: N Mald 6A 18
Darling Ho. TW1: Twick 3E 10
Dartmouth Ho. *KT2: King T* *2C 36*
(off Seven Kings Way)
Dartmouth Pl. W4 3B 6
Darwin Rd. W5 2D 4
Davenport Cl. TW11: Tedd 3B 16
David Lloyd Leisure
Cheam 4G 31
Epsom 6H 29
Merton 7G 19
David Twigg Cl.
KT2: King T 1D 36 (5F 17)
Davis Rd. KT9: Chess 1H 29
Davmor Ct. TW8: Bford 2D 4
Dawes Av. TW7: Isle 2B 10
Dawes Ct. KT10: Esh 1G 27
Dawes Rd. SW6 4H 7
Dawson Rd. KT1: King T 7G 17
Dax Ct. TW16: Sun 7B 14
Daylesford Av. SW15 1D 12
Deacon Rd.
KT2: King T 2E 36 (5G 17)
Deacons Ct. TW1: Twick 6A 10
Deacons Wlk.
TW12: Hamp 1F 15
Deal M. W5 1E 4
Dealtry Rd. SW15 1F 13
Deanhill Ct. SW14 1J 11
Deanhill Rd. SW14 1J 11
Dean Rd. TW3: Houn 2G 9
TW12: Hamp 2F 15
Deans Cl. W4 3J 5
Deans La. *W4* *3J 5*
(off Deans Cl.)
Deans Rd. SM1: Sutt 7K 25
Debden Cl. KT2: King T 2E 16
De Brome Rd. TW13: Felt 5B 8
De Burgh Pk. SM7: Bans 4K 35
Deepdale SW19 1G 19
Deepwell Cl. TW7: Isle 5B 4
Deerhurst Cl. TW13: Felt 1A 14
Deerhurst Cres.
TW12: Hamp H 2H 15
Dee Rd. TW9: Rich 1G 11
Deer Pk. Cl. KT2: King T 4J 17
Dee Way KT19: Ewe 6B 30
Defoe Av. TW9: Kew 4H 5
Delacy Ct. SM2: Sutt 7K 31
Delaford St. SW6 4H 7
Delamere Rd. SW20 5G 19
Delaporte Cl. KT17: Eps 1B 34
Delcombe Av. KT4: Wor Pk 5F 25
Delft Ho. KT2: King T 1E 36
Dell, The TW8: Bford 3D 4
TW14: Felt 4A 8
Dellbow Rd. TW14: Felt 2A 8
Dell La. KT17: Ewe 2D 30
Dell Rd. KT17: Ewe 3D 30
Dells Cl. TW11: Tedd 3A 16
Dell Wlk. KT3: N Mald 6B 18
Delorme St. W6 3G 7
Delta Cl. KT4: Wor Pk 7C 24
Delta Pk. SW18 1K 13
Delta Rd. KT4: Wor Pk 7B 24
Delvino Rd. SW6 5K 7
De Mel Cl. KT19: Eps 1J 33
Dempster Cl. KT6: Surb 5D 22
Denbigh Cl. SM1: Sutt 2J 31
Denbigh Gdns. TW10: Rich 2G 11
Dene, The KT8: W Mole 2E 20
SM2: Cheam 7J 31
Dene Cl. KT4: Wor Pk 6C 24
Dene Gdns. KT7: T Ditt 6B 22
Denehurst Gdns. TW2: Twick 4J 9
TW10: Rich 1H 11
Dene Rd. KT21: Asht 7G 33
Denewood KT17: Eps 2B 34
Denham Rd. KT17: Eps 1C 34
TW14: Felt 4B 8
Denleigh Gdns. KT7: T Ditt 3K 21
Denman Dr. KT10: Clay 2B 28
Denmark Av. SW19 4H 19
Denmark Ct. SM4: Mord 3K 25
Denmark Rd.
KT1: King T 5C 36 (7F 17)
SW19 3G 19
TW2: Twick 7J 9
Denmead Ho. *SW15* *3C 12*
(off Highcliffe Dr.)
Dennan Rd. KT6: Surb 5G 23
Denning Cl. TW12: Hamp 2E 14
Denningtons, The
KT4: Wor Pk 6B 24
Dennis Ho. SM1: Sutt 7K 25
Dennis Pk. Cres. SW20 5H 19
Dennis Rd. KT8: E Mos 1H 21
Denton Gro. KT12: Walt T 6D 20
Denton Rd. TW1: Twick 3E 10
Deodar Rd. SW15 1H 13
Depot Rd. KT17: Eps 2B 34
Derby Arms Rd. KT18: Eps D 6C 34
Derby Cl. KT18: Tatt C 7E 34
Derby Day Experience, The 6C 34
Derby Rd. KT5: Surb 5H 23
SM1: Sutt 3J 31
SW14 1J 11
SW19 4K 19
TW3: Houn 1G 9
Derby Sq., The *KT19: Eps* *2A 34*
(off High St.)
Derby Stables Rd.
KT18: Eps D 6C 34
Derek Av. KT19: Ewe 3H 29
Derek Cl. KT19: Ewe 2J 29
Derwent Av. SW15 1B 18
Derwent Cl. KT10: Clay 3K 27
Derwent Lodge KT4: Wor Pk 6E 24
Derwent Rd. SW20 3G 25
TW2: Whit 3G 9
Desborough Ho. *W14* *3J 7*
(off Nth. End Rd.)
Devas Rd. SW20 5F 19
Devereux La. SW13 4E 6
Devey Cl. KT2: King T 4C 18
Devitt Cl. KT21: Asht 5H 33
Devoke Way KT12: Walt T 6C 20
Devon Av. TW2: Twick 5H 9
Devon Ct. TW12: Hamp 4F 15
Devoncroft Gdns.
TW1: Twick 4B 10
Devonhurst Pl. W4 2A 6
Devon Rd. KT12: Hers 1B 26
SM2: Cheam 5H 31
Devonshire Dr. KT6: Surb 5E 22
Devonshire Gdns. W4 4K 5
Devonshire M. W4 2B 6
Devonshire Pas. W4 2B 6
Devonshire Rd. TW13: Hanw 7D 8
W4 2B 6
Devonshire St. W4 2B 6
Devon Way KT9: Chess 2D 28
KT19: Ewe 2J 29
Dewsbury Ct. W4 1K 5
Dewsbury Gdns.
KT4: Wor Pk 7D 24
Diana Gdns. KT6: Surb 6G 23
Diana Ho. SW13 5C 6
Dibdin Cl. SM1: Sutt 7K 25
Dibdin Rd. SM1: Sutt 7K 25
Diceland Rd. SM7: Bans 5J 35
Dickens Cl. TW10: Ham 6F 11
Dickenson Rd. TW13: Hanw 2B 14
Dickerage La. KT3: N Mald 7K 17
Dickerage Rd. KT1: King T 5K 17
KT3: N Mald 5K 17
Dieppe Cl. W14 2J 7
Digby Mans. *W6* *2E 6*
(off Hammersmith Bri. Rd.)
Digdens Ri. KT18: Eps 4K 33

Dilton Gdns. SW15	5D 12
Dimes Pl. W6	1E 6
Dinton Rd. KT2: King T	4G 17
Dirdene Cl. KT17: Eps	1C 34
Dirdene Gdns. KT17: Eps	1C 34
Dirdene Gro. KT17: Eps	1B 34
Disbrowe Rd. W6	3H 7
Disraeli Cl. W4	1A 6
Disraeli Gdns. SW15	1J 13
Disraeli Rd. SW15	1H 13
Distillery La. W6	2F 7
Distillery Rd. W6	2F 7
Distillery Wlk. TW8: Bford	3F 5
Ditton Cl. KT7: T Ditt	4B 22
Ditton Grange Cl. KT6: Surb	5E 22
Ditton Grange Dr. KT6: Surb	5E 22
Ditton Hill KT6: Surb	5D 22
Ditton Hill Rd. KT6: Surb	5D 22
Ditton Lawn KT7: T Ditt	5B 22
Ditton Reach KT7: T Ditt	3C 22
Ditton Rd. KT6: Surb	6E 22
Divis Way SW15	3E 12
(off Dover Pk. Dr.)	
Dock Rd. TW8: Bford	4E 4
Dockwell's Ind. Est.	
TW14: Felt	2A 8
Dolby Rd. SW6	6J 7
Dollary Pde. KT1: King T	7J 17
(off Kingston Rd.)	
Dolman Rd. W4	1A 6
Dolphin Cl. KT6: Surb	2E 22
Dolphin Sq. W4	4B 6
Dolphin St.	
KT1: King T	3C 36 (6F 17)
Donald Woods Gdns.	
KT5: Surb	6J 23
Doneraile St. SW6	6G 7
Donnelly Ct. SW6	4H 7
(off Dawes Rd.)	
Donnington Rd. KT4: Wor Pk	6D 24
Donovan Cl. KT19: Eps	6A 30
Doone Cl. TW11: Tedd	3B 16
Dora Rd. SW19	2K 19
Dorchester Gro. W4	2B 6
Dorchester Ho. TW9: Kew	4J 5
Dorchester M. KT3: N Mald	1A 24
Dorchester Rd. KT4: Wor Pk	5F 25
TW1: Twick	3D 10
Dorey Ho. TW8: Bford	4D 4
(off High St.)	
Doria Rd. SW6	6J 7
Dorien Rd. SW20	6G 19
Dorking Cl. KT4: Wor Pk	6G 25
Dorking Rd. KT18: Eps	5H 33
Dorling Dr. KT17: Eps	1C 34
Dormay St. SW18	2K 13
Dorncliffe Rd. SW6	6H 7
Dorney Way TW4: Houn	2D 8
Dorset Cl. KT17: Eps	1C 34
Dorset Rd. SM2: Sutt	6K 31
SW19	5K 19
Dorset Sq. KT19: Ewe	6A 30
Dorset Way TW2: Twick	5J 9
Dorville Cres. W6	1E 6
Douai Gro. TW12: Hamp	5H 15
Douglas Av. KT3: N Mald	1E 24
Douglas Cl. KT1: King T	7D 36
Douglas Ho. KT6: Surb	5G 23
Douglas Johnstone Ho.	
SW6	3J 7
(off Clem Attlee Ct.)	
Douglas Mans. TW3: Houn	1G 9
Douglas M. SM7: Bans	5J 35
Douglas Rd. KT1: King T	6J 17
KT6: Surb	6G 23
KT10: Esh	6G 21
TW3: Houn	1G 9
Douglas Sq. SM4: Mord	3K 25
Dounesforth Gdns.	
SW18	5K 13
Dovecote Gdns. SW14	7A 6
Dover Ho. Rd. SW15	1D 12
Dover Pk. Dr. SW15	3E 12
Dover Ter. TW9: Rich	6G 5
(off Sandycombe Rd.)	
Dowdeswell Cl. SW15	1B 12
Dowler Ct. KT2: King T	1D 36
Downbury M. SW18	2K 13
Downes Cl. TW1: Twick	3C 10
Downe Ter. TW10: Rich	3F 11
Downfield KT4: Wor Pk	5C 24
Down Hall Rd.	
KT2: King T	2B 36 (5E 16)
Downham Ct. KT12: Walt T	7B 20
(off Long Lodge Dr.)	
Downland Cl. KT18: Tatt C	7E 34
Downland Gdns. KT18: Tatt C	7E 34
Downland Way KT18: Tatt C	7E 34
Down Pl. W6	1E 6
Down Rd. TW11: Tedd	3C 16

Downs, The SW20	4G 19
Downs Av. KT18: Eps	3B 34
Downs Hill Rd. KT18: Eps	3B 34
Downs Ho. Rd. KT18: Eps D	7B 34
Downside TW18: Eps	3B 34
TW1: Twick	7A 10
Downside Wlk. TW8: Bford	3E 4
(off Windmill Rd.)	
Downs Lodge Ct. KT17: Eps	3B 34
Downs Rd. KT18: Eps	3B 34
SM2: Sutt	6K 31
Downs Side SM2: Cheam	7J 31
Down St. KT8: W Mole	2F 21
Downs Vw. TW7: Isle	5A 4
Downs Way KT18: Eps	5C 34
Downs Wood KT18: Tatt C	6E 34
Doyle Ho. SW13	4F 7
(off Trinity Chu. Rd.)	
Draco Ga. SW15	7F 7
Dragons Health Club	
Epsom	1A 30
Drake Cl. KT5: Surb	1F 23
(off Cranes Pk. Av.)	
Drake Rd. KT9: Chess	2H 29
Drake's Cl. KT10: Esh	1F 27
Drax Av. SW20	4D 18
Draxmont SW19	3H 19
Draycot Rd. KT6: Surb	5H 23
Draycott M. SW6	6J 7
(off Laurel Bank Gdns.)	
Draymans Way TW7: Isle	7A 4
Drayton Cl. TW4: Houn	2E 8
Drey Ct. KT4: Wor Pk	5C 24
DRIFT BRIDGE	3F 35
Driftway, The SM7: Bans	4F 35
Drive, The KT2: King T	4K 17
KT6: Surb	4F 23
KT10: Esh	5H 21
KT19: Ewe	3C 30
SM2: Cheam	1J 35
SM7: Bans	6H 35
SW6	6H 7
SW20	4F 19
TW14: Felt	4B 8
Drive Mans. SW6	6H 7
(off Fulham Rd.)	
Dromore Rd. SW15	3H 13
Drovers Ct. KT1: King T	3D 36
Drumaline Ridge	
KT4: Wor Pk	6B 24
Drummond Gdns. KT19: Eps	7K 29
Drummond Pl. TW1: Twick	4C 10
Drummonds Pl. TW9: Rich	1F 11
Dryad St. SW15	7G 7
Dryburgh Rd. SW15	7E 6
Dryden Mans. W14	3H 7
(off Queen's Club Gdns.)	
Ducks Wlk. TW1: Twick	2D 10
Dudley Dr. SM4: Mord	5H 25
Dudley Gro. KT18: Eps	3K 33
Dudley Rd.	
KT1: King T	5E 36 (7G 17)
KT12: Walt T	4A 20
SW19	3K 19
TW9: Rich	6G 5
Duke of Cambridge Cl.	
TW2: Whit	3J 9
Duke Rd. W4	2A 6
Dukes Av. KT2: King T	1E 16
KT3: N Mald	7B 18
TW4: Houn	1D 8
TW10: Ham	1D 16
W4	2A 6
Dukes Cl. TW12: Hamp	2E 14
Dukes Ct. KT19: Ewe	5B 30
SW14	6A 6
Dukes Ga. W4	1K 5
Dukes Grn. Av. TW14: Felt	2A 8
Dukes Head Pas.	
TW12: Hamp	4H 15
Dukes Rd. KT12: Hers	2C 26
Duke St. TW9: Rich	1E 10
Dumbleton Cl. KT1: King T	5J 17
Dunbar Ct. KT12: Walt T	5B 20
Dunbar Rd. KT3: N Mald	1K 23
Dunbridge Ho. SW15	3C 12
(off Highcliffe Dr.)	
Duncan Rd. KT20: Tad	7H 35
TW9: Rich	1F 11
Dundas Gdns. KT8: W Mole	7G 15
Dundela Gdns. KT4: Wor Pk	1E 30
Dundonald Rd. SW19	4H 19
(not continuous)	
Dundonald Road Stop (CT)	4J 19
Dungarvan Av. SW15	1D 12
Dunhill Point SW15	5D 12
Dunleary Cl. TW4: Houn	4E 8
Dunmore Rd. SW20	5F 19
Dunmow Cl. TW13: Hanw	7D 8
Dunnymans Rd. SM7: Bans	4J 35

Dunsany Rd. W14	1G 7
Dunsford Way SW15	3E 12
Dunsmore Rd. KT12: Walt T	3A 20
Dunstable Rd. KT8: W Mole	1E 20
TW9: Rich	1F 11
Dunstall Rd. SW20	3E 18
Dunstall Way KT8: W Mole	7G 15
Dunster Av. SM4: Mord	5G 25
Dunton Cl. KT6: Surb	5F 23
Dunvegan Cl. KT8: W Mole	1G 21
Dupont Rd. SW20	6G 19
Durban Rd. KT9: Chess	1F 29
Durford Cres. SW15	5E 12
Durham Cl. SW20	6E 18
Durham Ct. TW11: Tedd	4J 15
Durham Rd. SW20	5E 18
TW14: Felt	4B 8
W5	1E 4
Durham Wharf TW8: Bford	4D 4
Durlston Rd. KT2: King T	3F 17
Durnsford Av. SW19	6K 13
Durnsford Rd. SW19	6K 13
Durrell Rd. SW6	5J 7
Durrels Ho. W14	1J 7
(off Warwick Gdns.)	
Durrington Av. SW20	4F 19
Durrington Pk. Rd.	
SW20	5F 19
Dutch Gdns. KT2: King T	3J 17
Dutch Yd. SW18	2K 13
Duxberry Av. TW13: Felt	7B 8
Dyer Ho. TW12: Hamp	5G 15
Dyers La. SW15	1E 12
Dymes Path SW19	6G 13
Dynevor Rd. TW10: Rich	2F 11
Dysart Av. KT2: King T	2D 16

E

Ealing Pk. Gdns. W5	1D 4
Ealing Pk. Mans. W5	1E 4
(off Sth. Ealing Rd.)	
Ealing Rd. TW8: Bford	1E 4
Ealing Rd. Trad. Est.	
TW8: Bford	2E 4
Eardley Cres. SW5	2K 7
Earldom Rd. SW15	1F 13
Earle Gdns. KT2: King T	4F 17
Earl Rd. SW14	1K 11
EARL'S COURT	2K 7
Earls Court Exhibition Building	
	2K 7
Earl's Ct. Gdns. SW5	1K 7
Earls Ct. Rd. SW5	1K 7
W8	1K 7
Earl's Ct. Sq. SW5	2K 7
Earl's Court Station (Tube)	1K 7
Earlsfield Ho. KT2: King T	2B 36
(off Skerne Rd.)	
Earls Ter. W8	1J 7
Earls Wlk. W8	1K 7
Earsby St. W14	1H 7
(not continuous)	
Eashing Point SW15	5E 12
(off Wanborough Dr.)	
Eastbank Rd.	
TW12: Hamp H	2H 15
Eastbourne Gdns. SW14	7K 5
Eastbourne Rd. TW8: Bford	2D 4
TW13: Felt	6C 8
W4	3K 5
Eastbury Gro. W4	2B 6
Eastbury Rd.	
KT2: King T	1C 36 (4F 17)
Eastcote Av. KT8: W Mole	2E 20
Eastcote Ho. KT17: Eps	1B 34
Eastcroft Rd. KT19: Ewe	4B 30
Eastdean Av. KT18: Eps	2J 33
EAST EWELL	6F 31
Eastfields Av. SW18	1K 13
Eastgate SM7: Bans	3J 35
East La. KT1: King T	5B 36 (7E 16)
Eastleigh Wlk. SW15	4D 12
EAST MOLESEY	4E 20
Eastmont Rd. KT10: Hin W	6K 21
East Putney Station (Tube)	2H 13
East Rd. KT2: King T	1D 36 (5F 17)
EAST SHEEN	1K 11
E. Sheen Av. SW14	2A 12
East St. KT17: Eps	2B 34
TW8: Bford	4D 4
Eastway KT19: Eps	7A 30
SM4: Mord	2G 25
East W. Link Rd.	
KT2: King T	1B 36 (5E 16)
Eastwick Rd. KT12: Hers	3A 26
Eaton Dr. KT2: King T	4H 17
Eaton Rd. TW3: Houn	1J 9

Ebbas Way KT18: Eps	4J 33
Ebbisham Cen., The	
KT19: Eps	2A 34
Ebbisham Rd. KT4: Wor Pk	6F 25
KT18: Eps	3J 33
Ebor Cotts. SW15	7B 12
Eddiscombe Rd. SW6	6J 7
Ede Cl. TW3: Houn	1E 8
Ede Ct. KT17: Eps	1C 34
Edenfield Gdns.	
KT4: Wor Pk	7C 24
Edenhurst Av. SW6	7J 7
Edensor Gdns. W4	4B 6
Edensor Rd. W4	4B 6
Eden St. KT1: King T	4B 36 (6E 16)
Eden Wlk.	
KT1: King T	4C 36 (6F 17)
Edgar Cl. KT3: N Mald	6B 18
Edgarley Ter. SW6	5H 7
Edgar Rd. TW4: Houn	4E 8
Edgecombe Ho. SW19	5H 13
Edgecoombe Cl. KT2: King T	4A 18
Edge Hill SW19	4G 19
Edge Hill Ct. SW19	4G 19
Edgehill Ct. KT12: Walt T	5B 20
Edinburgh Ct. KT1: King T	5C 36
SW20	2G 25
Edith Gdns. KT5: Surb	4J 23
Edith Ho. W6	2F 7
(off Queen Caroline St.)	
Edith Rd. W14	1H 7
Edith Summerskill Ho.	
SW6	4J 7
(off Clem Attlee Est.)	
Edith Vs. W14	1J 7
Edmund Gro. TW13: Hanw	6E 8
Edna Rd. SW20	6G 19
Edward Cl. TW12: Hamp H	2H 15
Edwardes Pl. W8	1J 7
Edwardes Sq. W8	1J 7
Edward Rd. TW12: Hamp H	2H 15
Edwards Cl. KT4: Wor Pk	6G 25
Edwin Rd. TW1: Twick	5A 10
TW2: Twick	5K 9
Edwin Stray Ho. TW13: Hanw	6F 9
Edwyn Ho. SW18	3K 13
(off Neville Gill Cl.)	
Eel Pie Island TW1: Twick	5B 10
Effie Pl. SW6	4K 7
Effie Rd. SW6	4K 7
Effingham Lodge KT1: King T	1E 22
Effingham Rd. KT6: Surb	4C 22
Effra Rd. SW19	3K 19
Egbury Ho. SW15	3C 12
(off Tangley Gro.)	
Egerton Rd. KT3: N Mald	1C 24
TW2: Twick	4K 9
Egham Cl. SM3: Cheam	6H 25
SW19	6H 13
Egham Cres. SM3: Cheam	7H 25
Egliston M. SW15	7F 7
Egliston Rd. SW15	7F 7
Egmont Av. KT6: Surb	5G 23
Egmont Ct. KT12: Walt T	4A 20
Egmont Rd. KT3: N Mald	1C 24
KT6: Surb	5G 23
KT12: Walt T	4A 20
Elborough St. SW18	5K 13
Eleanor Av. KT19: Ewe	6A 30
Eleanor Gro. SW13	7B 6
Eleanor Ho. W6	2F 7
(off Queen Caroline St.)	
Electric Pde. KT6: Surb	3E 22
Elfin Gro. TW11: Tedd	2A 16
Elgar Av. KT5: Surb	5H 23
Elgar Ct. W14	1H 7
(off Blythe Rd.)	
Eliot Cl. SW18	3K 13
Eliot Gdns. SW15	1D 12
Elizabeth Cl. SM1: Sutt	7J 25
Elizabeth Cotts. TW9: Kew	5G 5
Elizabeth Ct.	
KT2: King T	1C 36 (5F 17)
TW11: Tedd	2K 15
TW16: Sun	7B 14
(off Elizabeth Gdns.)	
Elizabeth Gdns. TW7: Isle	1B 10
TW16: Sun	7B 14
Elizabeth Ho. SM3: Cheam	3H 31
(off Park La.)	
W6	2F 7
(off Queen Caroline St.)	
Elizabeth Way TW13: Hanw	1B 14
Ellaline Rd. W6	3G 7
Elland Rd. KT12: Walt T	6C 20
Ellenborough Pl. SW15	1D 12
Ellen Wilkinson Ho. SW6	3J 7
(off Clem Attlee Ct.)	
Elleray Rd. TW11: Tedd	3A 16
Ellerby St. SW6	5G 7

Ellerdine Rd.—Fauconberg Ct.

Ellerdine Rd. TW3: Houn 1H 9
Ellerker Gdns. TW10: Rich 3F 11
Ellerman Av. TW2: Whit 5E 8
Ellerton Rd. KT6: Surb 6G 23
SW13 . . . . .5D 6
SW20 . . . . .4D 18
Ellesmere Ct. W4 . . . . .2A 6
Ellesmere Rd. TW1: Twick 3D 10
W4 . . . . .3K 5
Ellingham Rd. KT9: Chess 3E 28
Ellington Way KT18: Tatt C 6E 34
Elliott Rd. W4 . . . . .1B 6
Ellisfield Dr. SW15 . . . . .4D 12
Ellison Rd. SW13 . . . . .6C 6
Ellswood Ct. KT6: Surb 4E 22
Elm Bank Gdns. SW13 . . . . .6B 6
Elmbridge Av. KT5: Surb 2J 23
Elmbridge Leisure Cen. 2A 20
Elmbrook Cl. TW16: Sun 5A 14
Elmbrook Rd. SM1: Sutt 1J 31
Elm Cl. KT5: Surb 4K 23
SW20 . . . . .1F 25
TW2: Twick 6G 9
Elm Ct. KT8: W Mole 1G 21
Elm Cres.
KT2: King T 2D 36 (5F 17)
Elmcroft Cl. KT9: Chess 7F 23
Elmcroft Dr. KT9: Chess 7F 23
Elmdene KT5: Surb 5K 23
Elm Dr. TW16: Sun 6B 14
Elmer Gdns. TW7: Isle 1J 9
Elmers Dr. TW11: Tedd 3C 16
Elmfield Av. TW11: Tedd 2A 16
Elm Gdns. KT10: Clay 3A 28
KT18: Tatt C 7F 35
Elmgate Av. TW13: Felt 7A 8
Elm Gro. KT2: King T 2D 36 (5F 17)
KT12: Walt T 5A 20
KT18: Eps 3K 33
SW19 . . . . .4H 19
Elm Gro. Rd. SW13 . . . . .5D 6
Elm Ho. *KT2: King T* *4G 17*
(off Elm Rd.)
Elm Lodge SW6 . . . . .5F 7
Elm Rd. KT2: King T 2E 36 (5G 17)
KT3: N Mald 6A 18
KT9: Chess 1F 29
KT10: Clay 3A 28
KT17: Ewe 3C 30
SW14 .7K 5
Elm Rd. W. SM3: Sutt 4J 25
Elms, The KT10: Clay 4A 28
SW13 .7C 6
Elmshaw Rd. SW15 . . . . .2D 12
Elmshorn KT17: Eps D 5F 35
Elmsleigh Ho. *TW2: Twick* *6J 9*
(off Staines Rd.)
Elmsleigh Rd. TW2: Twick 6J 9
Elmslie Cl. KT18: Eps 3K 33
Elmstead Cl. KT19: Ewe 2B 30
Elmstead Gdns.
KT4: Wor Pk 7D 24
Elmstone Rd. SW6 . . . . .5K 7
Elm Tree Av. KT10: Esh 4J 21
Elmtree Rd. TW11: Tedd 1K 15
Elm Wlk. SW20 . . . . .1F 25
Elm Way KT4: Wor Pk 7F 25
KT19: Ewe 2A 30
Elmwood Av. TW13: Felt 6A 8
Elmwood Cl. KT17: Ewe 4D 30
KT21: Asht 6E 32
Elmwood Ct. KT21: Asht 6E 32
Elmwood Dr. KT17: Ewe 3D 30
Elmwood Rd. W4 . . . . .3K 5
Elsenham St. SW18 . . . . .5J 13
Elsinore Ho. *W6* *2G 7*
(off Fulham Pal. Rd.)
Elsinore Way TW9: Rich 7J 5
Elsrick Av. SM4: Mord 2K 25
Elstead Ct. SM3: Sutt 5H 25
Elsworthy KT7: T Ditt 3K 21
Elthiron Rd. SW6 . . . . .5K 7
Elthorne Ct. TW13: Felt 5B 8
Elthorne Sports Cen. 1A 4
Elton Cl. KT1: Hamp W 4D 16
Elton Rd. KT2: King T 5G 17
Elvedon Rd. KT11: Cobh 7A 26
Ely Cl. KT3: N Mald 6C 18
Elysium Pl. *SW6* *6J 7*
(off Elysium St.)
Elysium St. SW6 . . . . .6J 7
Emanuel Dr. TW12: Hamp 2E 14
Embankment SW15 . . . . .6G 7
(not continuous)
Embankment, The
TW1: Twick 5B 10
Ember Cen. KT12: Walt T 6D 20
Embercourt Rd. KT7: T Ditt 3K 21
Ember Farm Av. KT8: E Mos 3J 21
Ember Farm Way KT8: E Mos 3J 21
Ember Gdns. KT7: T Ditt 4K 21
Ember La. KT8: E Mos 4J 21
KT10: Esh 4J 21
Embleton Wlk. TW12: Hamp 2E 14
Emily Davison Dr.
KT18: Tatt C 7E 34
Emlyn Gdns. W12 . . . . .1C 6
Emmeline Ct. KT12: Walt T 4B 20
Emms Pas.
KT1: King T 4B 36 (6E 16)
Empress App. SW6 . . . . .2K 7
Empress Pl. SW6 . . . . .2K 7
Empress State Bldg.
SW6 . . . . .2K 7
Enclave, The SW13 . . . . .6C 6
Endsleigh Gdns. KT6: Surb 3D 22
KT12: Hers 2B 26
Endway KT5: Surb 4J 23
Energize Fitness Club *2H 7*
(in Hammersmith & West London College)
Enfield Rd. TW8: Bford 2E 4
Enfield Wlk. TW8: Bford 2E 4
Engadine St. SW18 . . . . .5J 13
England Way KT3: N Mald 1J 23
Enmore Gdns. SW14 . . . . .2A 12
Enmore Rd. SW15 . . . . .1F 13
Ennerdale Cl. SM1: Sutt 1J 31
Ennerdale Rd. TW9: Rich 6G 5
Ennismore Av. W4 . . . . .1C 6
Ennismore Gdns. KT7: T Ditt 3K 21
Ennor Ct. SM3: Cheam 7F 25
Enterprise Ho. KT12: Walt T 4A 20
Enterprise Way SW18 . . . . .1K 13
TW11: Tedd 3A 16
Epirus M. SW6 . . . . .4K 7
Epirus Rd. SW6 . . . . .4J 7
Epple Rd. SW6 . . . . .5J 7
EPSOM .2A 34
Epsom Bus. Pk. KT17: Eps 7B 30
EPSOM DAY SURGERY UNIT 2C 34
EPSOM DOWNS 7B 34
Epsom Downs Racecourse 7C 34
Epsom Downs Station (Rail) 4E 34
Epsom Gap KT22: Lea 4C 32
EPSOM GENERAL HOSPITAL 4K 33
Epsom La. Nth.
KT18: Tad, Tatt C 7E 34
Epsom Playhouse *2A 34*
(off Ashley Av.)
Epsom Rd. KT17: Ewe 7C 30
KT21: Asht 7G 33
SM3: Sutt 4J 25
SM4: Mord 4J 25
Epsom Station (Rail) 2A 34
Epworth Rd. TW7: Isle 4C 4
Ericcson Cl. SW18 . . . . .2K 13
Erncroft Way TW1: Twick 3A 10
Ernest Cotts. KT17: Ewe 4C 30
Ernest Gdns. W4 . . . . .3J 5
Ernest Rd. KT1: King T 6J 17
Ernest Sq. KT1: King T 6J 17
Ernle Rd. SW20 . . . . .4E 18
Ernshaw Pl. SW15 . . . . .2H 13
Erpingham Rd. SW15 . . . . .7F 7
Erridge Rd. SW19 . . . . .6K 19
Errol Gdns. KT3: N Mald 1D 24
ESHER .1G 27
Esher Av. KT12: Walt T 4A 20
SM3: Cheam 7G 25
Esher By-Pass KT9: Chess 3D 28
KT10: Clay 6F 27
KT10: Esh 6F 27
KT11: Cobh 7A 26
KT22: Oxs 6F 27
Esher Cl. KT10: Esh 2G 27
ESHER COMMON 6H 27
Esher Gdns. SW19 . . . . .6G 13
Esher Grn. KT10: Esh 7G 21
Esher Grn. Dr. KT10: Esh 7G 21
Esher Pk. Av. KT10: Esh 1G 27
Esher Pl. Av. KT10: Esh 7F 21
Esher Rd. KT8: E Mos 3J 21
KT12: Hers 2C 26
Esher Station (Rail) 6J 21
Esmond Gdns. W4 . . . . .1A 6
Esmond Rd. W4 . . . . .1A 6
Esmond St. SW15 . . . . .1H 13
Esporta Health & Fitness
Grove Park 5B 6
Gunnersbury 1J 5
Kingston upon Thames *1C 36*
(off East W. Link Rd.)
Wimbledon 3J 19
Essex Av. TW7: Isle 1K 9
Essex Cl. SM4: Mord 4G 25
Essex Ct. SW13 . . . . .6C 6
Essex Pl. W4 . . . . .1K 5
(not continuous)
Essex Pl. Sq. W4 . . . . .1A 6
Essex Rd. W4 . . . . .1A 6
(not continuous)
Estcourt Rd. SW6 . . . . .4J 7
Estella Av. KT3: N Mald 1E 24
Estridge Cl. TW3: Houn 1F 9
Eternit Wlk. SW6 . . . . .5F 7
Ethel Bailey Cl. KT19: Eps 1H 33
Ethelbert Rd. SW20 . . . . .5G 19
Eton Av. KT3: N Mald 2A 24
Eton St. TW9: Rich 2F 11
Etwell Pl. KT5: Surb 3G 23
Eureka Rd. KT1: King T 6H 17
Eustace Rd. SW6 . . . . .4K 7
Evans Gro. TW13: Hanw 6F 9
Evans Ho. TW13: Hanw 6F 9
Evelyn Cl. TW2: Whit 4G 9
Evelyn Gdns. TW9: Rich 1F 11
Evelyn Mans. *W14* *3H 7*
(off Queen's Club Gdns.)
Evelyn Rd. TW9: Rich 7F 5
TW10: Ham 7D 10
W4 . . . . .1A 6
Evelyn Ter. TW9: Rich 7F 5
Evelyn Way KT19: Eps 7H 29
Evenwood Cl. SW15 . . . . .2H 13
Everatt Cl. SW18 . . . . .3J 13
Everdon Rd. SW13 . . . . .3D 6
Everington St. W6 . . . . .3G 7
(not continuous)
Eve Rd. TW7: Isle 1B 10
Eversfield Rd. TW9: Kew 6G 5
Evershed Wlk. W4 . . . . .1K 5
Eversley Pk. SW19 . . . . .3E 18
Eversley Rd. KT5: Surb 1G 23
Evesham Cl. SM2: Sutt 4K 31
Evesham Ct. TW10: Rich 3G 11
Evesham Grn. SM4: Mord 3K 25
Evesham Ter. KT6: Surb 3E 22
Ewald Rd. SW6 . . . . .6J 7
EWELL 5C 30
Ewell By-Pass KT17: Ewe 4D 30
Ewell Ct. Av. KT19: Ewe 2B 30
Ewell Downs Rd. KT17: Ewe 7D 30
Ewell East Station (Rail) 6E 30
Ewell Gro. Ct. *KT17: Ewe* *5C 30*
(off West St.)
Ewell Ho. *KT17: Ewe* *6C 30*
(off Ewell Ho. Gro.)
Ewell Ho. Gro. KT17: Ewe 6C 30
Ewell Ho. Pde *KT17: Ewe* *6C 30*
(off Epsom Rd.)
Ewell Pk. Gdns. KT17: Ewe 4D 30
Ewell Pk. Way KT17: Ewe 3D 30
Ewell Rd. KT6: Surb 3F 23
(Surbiton Hill Rd.)
KT6: Surb 4C 22
(Thornhill Rd.)
SM3: Cheam 3G 31
Ewell West Station (Rail) 5B 30
Ewhurst Cl. SM2: Cheam 5F 31
Excelsior Cl. KT1: King T 6H 17
Exeter Ct. *KT6: Surb* *2F 23*
(off Maple Rd.)
Exeter Ho. SW15 . . . . .3F 13
TW13: Hanw *6E 8*
(off Watermill Way)
Exeter M. SW6 . . . . .4K 7
Exeter Rd. TW13: Hanw 7E 8
Eyot Gdns. W6 . . . . .2C 6
Eyot Grn. W4 . . . . .2C 6

F

Fabian Rd. SW6 . . . . .4J 7
Faggs Rd. TW14: Felt 2A 8
Fairacre KT3: N Mald 7B 18
Fairacres KT11: Cobh 7C 26
SW15 . . . . .1C 12
Fairbriar Ct. *KT18: Eps* *2B 34*
(off Hereford Cl.)
Fairburn Ct. SW15 . . . . .2H 13
Fairburn Ho. *W14* *2J 7*
(off Ivatt Pl.)
Faircroft Ct. TW11: Tedd 3B 16
Fairdale Gdns. SW15 . . . . .1E 12
Fairfax Av. KT17: Ewe 5E 30
Fairfax Cl. KT12: Walt T 5A 20
Fairfax Ho. KT1: King T 5E 36
Fairfax M. SW15 . . . . .1F 13
Fairfax Pl. W14 . . . . .1H 7
Fairfax Rd. TW11: Tedd 3B 16
W4 . . . . .1B 6
Fairfield KT1: King T 4E 36 (6G 17)
Fairfield Av. TW2: Whit 5G 9
Fairfield Cl. KT19: Ewe 2B 30
Fairfield E.
KT1: King T 3D 36 (6F 17)
Fairfield Nth.
KT1: King T 3D 36 (6F 17)
Fairfield Pl.
KT1: King T 5D 36 (7F 17)
Fairfield Rd.
KT1: King T 4D 36 (6F 17)
(not continuous)
Fairfield Sth.
KT1: King T 4D 36 (6F 17)
Fairfields Rd. TW3: Houn 1H 9
Fairfield Trade Pk.
KT1: King T 7G 17
Fairfield Way KT19: Ewe 2B 30
Fairfield W.
KT1: King T 4D 36 (6F 17)
Fairford Gdns. KT4: Wor Pk 6C 24
Fairhall Ct. KT5: Surb 4G 23
Fairholme Cres. KT21: Asht 6D 32
Fairholme Rd. SM1: Sutt 3J 31
W14 . . . . .2H 7
Fairlands Av. SM1: Sutt 6K 25
Fairlawn Av. W4 . . . . .1K 5
Fair Lawn Cl. KT10: Clay 3A 28
Fairlawn Cl. KT2: King T 3K 17
TW13: Hanw 1E 14
Fairlawn Ct. W4 . . . . .1K 5
Fairlawn Gro. W4 . . . . .1K 5
Fairlawn Rd. SW19 . . . . .4J 19
Fairlawns TW1: Twick 3D 10
Fairlight TW12: Hamp H 2G 15
Fairlight Cl. KT4: Wor Pk 7F 25
Fairmead KT5: Surb 5J 23
Fairmead Cl. KT3: N Mald 7A 18
Fairmead Ct. TW9: Rich 6J 5
Fairmile Ho. TW11: Tedd 1B 16
Fairmile La. KT11: Cobh 7C 26
Fairoak Cl. KT22: Oxs 7J 27
Fairoak La. KT9: Chess 7J 27
KT22: Oxs 7J 27
Fairs Rd. KT22: Lea 7B 32
Fair St. TW3: Houn 1H 9
Fairview KT17: Ewe 7F 31
Fairview Rd. KT17: Ewe 7C 30
Fairwater Ho. TW11: Tedd 1B 16
Fairway SW20 . . . . .7F 19
Fairway, The KT3: N Mald 5A 18
KT8: W Mole 7G 15
KT22: Lea 7B 32
Fairway Cl. KT19: Ewe 1K 29
TW4: Houn 2B 8
(Green La.)
TW4: Houn 2C 8
(Staines Rd.)
Fairways TW11: Tedd 4E 16
Falcon Cl. W4 . . . . .3K 5
Falcon Rd. TW12: Hamp 4E 14
Falconry Ct. KT1: King T 5D 36
Falcon Way TW14: Felt 2A 8
Falkland Ho. *W14* *2J 7*
(off Edith Vs.)
Falmouth Ho. *KT2: King T* *2B 36*
(off Skerne Rd.)
Falmouth Rd. KT12: Hers 1B 26
Falstaff M. *TW12: Hamp H* *2J 15*
(off Parkside)
Fane St. W14 . . . . .3J 7
Fanshawe Rd. TW10: Ham 1D 16
Fanthorpe St. SW15 . . . . .7F 7
Faraday Mans. *W14* *3H 7*
(off Queen's Club Gdns.)
Faraday Pl. KT8: W Mole 1F 21
Faraday Rd. KT8: W Mole 1F 21
SW19 . . . . .3K 19
Fareham Rd. TW14: Felt 4B 8
Farlington Pl. SW15 . . . . .4E 12
Farlow Rd. SW15 . . . . .7G 7
Farm Cl. SW6 . . . . .4K 7
Farm La. KT21: Asht 6H 33
SW6 . . . . .3K 7
(not continuous)
Farm La. Trad. Est. SW6 . . . . .3K 7
Farm Rd. KT10: Esh 5G 21
TW4: Houn 5D 8
Farmstead KT19: Eps 5H 29
Farm Way KT4: Wor Pk 7F 25
Farnborough Ho. SW15 . . . . .5D 12
Farnell M. SW5 . . . . .2K 7
Farnell Rd. TW7: Isle 1J 9
Farnham Ct. SM3: Cheam 3H 31
Farnham Gdns. SW20 . . . . .6E 18
Faroe Rd. W14 . . . . .1G 7
Farquhar Rd. SW19 . . . . .7K 13
Farrer Ct. TW1: Twick 4E 10
Farrier Pl. SM1: Sutt 7K 25
Farriers Cl. KT17: Eps 1B 34
Farriers Rd. KT17: Eps 1B 34
Farringdon Ho. TW9: Kew 4J 5
Farthings, The KT2: King T 5H 17
Fassett Rd.
KT1: King T 7C 36 (1F 23)
Fauconberg Ct. *W4* *3K 5*
(off Fauconberg Rd.)

Garth Rd.—Grosvenor Rd.

Garth Rd. KT2: King T 2G **17**
SM4: Mord 3F **25**
W4 2A **6**
Garth Rd. Ind. Est.
SM4: Mord 5G **25**
Garthside TW10: Ham 2F **17**
Gartmoor Gdns. SW19 5J **13**
Gastein Rd. W6 3G **7**
Gaston Bell Cl. TW9: Rich 7G **5**
Gate Cen., The TW8: Bford 4B **4**
Gatehouse Cl. KT2: King T 4K **17**
Gateways *KT6: Surb 2F 23*
(off Surbiton Hill Rd.)
Gateways, The *TW9: Rich 1E 10*
(off Park La.)
Gatfield Gro. TW13: Hanw 6F **9**
Gatfield Ho. TW13: Hanw 6E **8**
Gatley Av. KT19: Ewe 2J **29**
Gatwick Rd. SW18 4J **13**
Gayfere Rd. KT17: Ewe 2D **30**
Gay St. SW15 7G **7**
Gayton Cl. KT21: Asht 7F **33**
Gaywood Rd. KT21: Asht 7G **33**
Geneva Rd.
KT1: King T 7D **36** (1F **23**)
Genoa Av. SW15 2F **13**
George Lindgren Ho.
SW6 4J 7
(off Clem Attlee Ct.)
George Rd. KT2: King T 4J **17**
(not continuous)
KT3: N Mald 1C **24**
George Sq. SW19 7K **19**
George's Sq. *SW6 3J 7*
(off Nth. End Rd.)
George St. TW9: Rich 2E **10**
George Wyver Cl.
SW19 4H **13**
Georgia Rd. KT3: N Mald 1K **23**
Geraldine Rd. W4 3H **5**
Gerald's Gro. SM7: Bans 3G **35**
Gerard Av. TW4: Houn 4F **9**
Gerard Rd. SW13 5C **6**
Gerrards Mead SM7: Bans 5J **35**
Gibbon Rd.
KT2: King T 1D **36** (5F **17**)
Gibbon Wlk. SW15 1D **12**
Gibbs Grn. W14 2J **7**
(not continuous)
Gibbs Grn. Cl. W14 2J **7**
Gibraltar Cres. KT19: Ewe 6B **30**
Gibson Cl. KT9: Chess 2D **28**
TW7: Isle 1K **9**
Gibson Ct. KT10: Hin W 6A **22**
Gibson Ho. SM1: Sutt 7K **25**
Gibson M. TW1: Twick 3D **10**
Gibson Rd. SM1: Sutt 2K **31**
GIGGSHILL 4B **22**
Giggshill Gdns. KT7: T Ditt 5B **22**
Giggshill Rd. KT7: T Ditt 4B **22**
Gilbert Ho. *SW13 4E 6*
(off Trinity Chu. Rd.)
Gilbert Scott SW18 3H **13**
Gilberts Lodge KT17: Eps 1B **34**
Gilders Rd. KT9: Chess 4G **29**
Gilesmead *KT18: Eps 3B 34*
(off Downside)
Gilhams Av. SM7: Bans 1G **35**
GILLETTE CORNER 4B **4**
Gillian Pk. Rd. SM3: Sutt 5J **25**
Gilpin Av. SW14 1A **12**
Gilpin Cres. TW2: Whit 4G **9**
Gipsy La. SW15 7E **6**
Girdler's Rd. W14 1G **7**
Girdwood Rd. SW18 4H **13**
Gironde Rd. SW6 4J **7**
Glade, The KT17: Ewe 3D **30**
SM2: Cheam 5H **31**
Glade Cl. KT6: Surb 6E **22**
Glades, The KT6: Surb 4F **23**
Gladeside Cl. KT9: Chess 4E **28**
Gladioli Cl. TW12: Hamp 3F **15**
Gladsmuir Cl. KT12: Walt T 6B **20**
Gladstone Av. TW2: Twick 5J **9**
TW14: Felt 3A **8**
Gladstone Pl. KT8: E Mos 2K **21**
Gladstone Rd. KT1: King T 7H **17**
KT6: Surb 6E **22**
KT21: Asht 7E **32**
SW19 4K **19**
W4 1A **6**
Gladwyn Rd. SW15 7G **7**
Glamorgan Rd.
KT1: Hamp W 1A **36** (4D **16**)
Glasbrook Av. TW2: Whit 5E **8**
Glastonbury Rd. SM4: Mord 4K **25**
Glazbury Rd. W14 1H **7**
Glazebrook Rd. TW11: Tedd 4A **16**
Glebe, The KT4: Wor Pk 5C **24**
Glebe Cl. W4 2B **6**
Glebe Cotts. *TW13: Hanw 7F 9*
(off Twickenham Rd.)
Glebe Gdns. KT3: N Mald 4B **24**
Glebelands KT8: W Mole 2G **21**
KT10: Clay 5A **28**
Glebe Rd. KT21: Asht 7E **32**
SM2: Cheam 5H **31**
SW13 6D **6**
Glebe Side TW1: Twick 3A **10**
Glebe St. W4 2B **6**
Glebe Ter. W4 2B **6**
Glebe Way TW13: Hanw 7F **9**
Gledstanes Rd. W14 2H **7**
Glegg Pl. SW15 1G **13**
Glen Albyn Rd. SW19 6G **13**
Glenallan Ho. *W14 1J 7*
(off Nth. End Cres.)
Glenavon Cl. KT10: Clay 3B **28**
Glenavon Ct. KT4: Wor Pk 6E **24**
Glenbuck Ct. KT6: Surb 3F **23**
Glenbuck Rd. KT6: Surb 3E **22**
Glendale Dr. SW19 2J **19**
Glendarvon St. SW15 7G **7**
Glendower Gdns. SW14 7A **6**
Glendower Rd. SW14 7A **6**
Glenfield Rd. SM7: Bans 4K **35**
Glenhurst Rd. TW8: Bford 3D **4**
Glenmill TW12: Hamp 2E **14**
Glen Rd. KT9: Chess 1G **29**
Glentham Gdns. SW13 3E **6**
Glentham Rd. SW13 3D **6**
Glenthorne Cl. SM3: Sutt 5K **25**
Glenthorne Gdns. SM3: Sutt 5K **25**
Glenthorne M. W6 1E **6**
Glenthorne Rd.
KT1: King T 7E **36** (1G **23**)
W6 1E **6**
Glenthorpe Av. SW15 1D **12**
Glenthorpe Rd. SM4: Mord 2G **25**
Glenvern Ct. *TW7: Isle 6B 4*
(off White Lodge Cl.)
Glenville M. SW18 4K **13**
Glenville M. Ind. Est. SW18 4K **13**
Glenville Rd. KT2: King T 5H **17**
Glen Wlk. TW7: Isle 2J **9**
(not continuous)
Glenwood Rd. KT17: Ewe 3D **30**
Gliddon Rd. W14 1H **7**
Gloster Rd. KT3: N Mald 1B **24**
Gloucester Cl. KT7: T Ditt 5B **22**
Gloucester Ct. TW9: Kew 4H **5**
Gloucester Ho. TW10: Rich 2H **11**
Gloucester Rd. KT1: King T 6H **17**
TW2: Twick 5H **9**
TW4: Houn 1D **8**
TW9: Kew 4H **5**
TW11: Tedd 2K **15**
TW12: Hamp 4G **15**
TW13: Felt 5B **8**
Gloxinia Wlk. TW12: Hamp 3F **15**
Glyn Cl. KT17: Ewe 5D **30**
Glyndale Grange SM2: Sutt 3K **31**
Glyn Rd. KT4: Wor Pk 6G **25**
Goater's All. *SW6 4J 7*
(off Dawes Rd.)
Goat Wharf TW8: Bford 3F **5**
Godfrey Av. TW2: Whit 4J **9**
Godfrey Way TW4: Houn 4D **8**
Godolphin Cl. SM2: Cheam 7J **31**
Godstone Rd. TW1: Twick 3C **10**
Godwin Cl. KT19: Ewe 3K **29**
Goldcliff Cl. SM4: Mord 4K **25**
Golden Ct. TW9: Rich 2E **10**
Goldhawk Rd. W6 1C **6**
Golding Cl. KT9: Chess 3D **28**
Golf Club Dr. KT2: King T 4A **18**
Golf Side SM2: Cheam 7H **31**
TW2: Twick 7J **9**
Golfside Cl. KT3: N Mald 6B **18**
Gomer Gdns. TW11: Tedd 3B **16**
Gomer Pl. TW11: Tedd 3B **16**
Gomshall Rd. SM2: Cheam 6F **31**
Gonston Cl. SW19 6H **13**
Gonville St. SW6 7H **7**
Goodenough Rd. SW19 4J **19**
Gooding Cl. KT3: N Mald 1K **23**
Goodwood Cl. SM4: Mord 1K **25**
Gordon Av. SW14 1B **12**
TW1: Twick 2B **10**
Gordondale Rd. SW19 6K **13**
Gordon Rd.
KT2: King T 2E **36** (5G **17**)
KT5: Surb 4G **23**
KT10: Clay 4K **27**
TW3: Houn 1H **9**
TW9: Rich 6G **5**
W4 3J **5**
Gore Rd. SW20 6F **19**
Gorleston St. W14 1H **7**
(not continuous)
Gosbury Hill KT9: Chess 1F **29**
Gosfield Rd. KT19: Eps 1A **34**
Gostling Rd. TW2: Whit 5F **9**
Gothic Rd. TW2: Twick 6J **9**
Gough Ho. KT1: King T 3C **36**
Gould Rd. TW2: Twick 5K **9**
Gowan Av. SW6 5H **7**
Gower Rd. TW7: Isle 3A **4**
Graburn Way KT8: E Mos 7J **15**
Graemesdyke Av. SW14 7J **5**
Grafton Cl. KT4: Wor Pk 7B **24**
TW4: Houn 5D **8**
Grafton Pk. Rd. KT4: Wor Pk 6B **24**
Grafton Rd. KT3: N Mald 7B **18**
KT4: Wor Pk 7A **24**
Grafton Way KT8: W Mole 1E **20**
Graham Gdns. KT6: Surb 5F **23**
Graham Rd. SW19 4J **19**
TW12: Hamp H 1F **15**
Grainger Rd. TW7: Isle 6A **4**
Granard Av. SW15 2E **12**
Grand Av. KT5: Surb 2J **23**
Grand Dr. SW20 6F **19**
Grandfield Ct. W4 3A **6**
Grandison Rd. KT4: Wor Pk 6F **25**
Grand Pde. KT6: Surb 5H **23**
SW14 1K 11
(off Up. Richmond Rd. W.)
Grand Pde. M. SW15 2H **13**
Grandstand Rd. KT17: Eps D 6C **34**
Grange, The KT3: N Mald 2C **24**
KT4: Wor Pk 7A **24**
KT12: Walt T 6A **20**
SW19 3G **19**
W4 2J **5**
W14 1J **7**
Grange Av. TW2: Twick 6K **9**
Grange Cl. KT8: W Mole 1G **21**
Grange Lodge SW19 3G **19**
Grange Mans. KT17: Ewe 4C **30**
Grange Pk. Pl. SW20 4E **18**
Grange Pl. KT12: Walt T 6A **20**
Grange Rd.
KT1: King T 5C **36** (7F **17**)
KT8: W Mole 1G **21**
KT9: Chess 1F **29**
KT12: Hers 1D **26**
SM2: Sutt 4K **31**
SW13 5D **6**
W4 2J **5**
Grantchester *KT1: King T 6H 17*
(off St Peters Rd.)
Grantham Ct. KT2: King T 2E **16**
Grantham Rd. W4 4B **6**
Grantley Pl. KT10: Esh 2G **27**
Grant Way TW7: Isle 3B **4**
Granville Av. TW3: Houn 2F **9**
Granville Rd. SW18 4J **13**
SW19 4K **19**
Grapsome Cl. KT9: Chess 4D **28**
Grasmere Av. SW15 1A **18**
SW19 7K **19**
TW3: Houn 3G **9**
Grasmere Ct. *SW13 3D 6*
(off Verdun Rd.)
Gratton Rd. W14 1H **7**
Gravel Rd. TW2: Twick 5K **9**
Grayham Cres. KT3: N Mald 1A **24**
Grayham Rd. KT3: N Mald 1A **24**
Gray's La. KT21: Asht 7G **33**
Grayswood Gdns. SW20 6E **18**
Grayswood Point SW15 5D **12**
GREAT BURGH 6F **35**
Gt. Chertsey Rd. TW2: Twick 7E **8**
TW13: Hanw, Twick 7E **8**
W4 6K **5**
Great Chu. La. W6 1G **7**
Great Ellshams SM7: Bans 5K **35**
Greatham Wlk. SW15 5D **12**
Great Tattenhams
KT18: Tatt C 7E **34**
Great W. Rd. TW7: Bford, Isle 4A **4**
TW8: Bford 4A **4**
W4 2C **6**
W6 2C **6**
Great W. Trad. Est. TW8: Bford 3C **4**
Grebe Ct. SM1: Sutt 2J **31**
Grebe Ter.
KT1: King T 5C **36** (7F **17**)
Green, The KT3: N Mald 7A **18**
KT10: Clay 3A **28**
KT12: Hers 2C **26**
KT17: Ewe 7D **30**
KT20: Tad 7H **35**
SM1: Sutt 7K **25**
SM4: Mord 1H **25**
SW19 2G **19**
TW2: Twick 5K **9**
TW9: Rich 2E **10**
TW13: Felt 6A **8**
Green Cl. TW13: Hanw 2D **14**
Green Curve SM7: Bans 3J **35**
Grn. Dragon La. TW8: Bford 2F **5**
Green End KT9: Chess 1F **29**
Greenfield Av. KT5: Surb 4J **23**
Greenfield Ho. SW19 5G **13**
Greenford Rd. SM1: Sutt 1K **31**
(not continuous)
Greenhayes Av. SM7: Bans 3K **35**
Greenhayes Gdns.
SM7: Bans 4K **35**
Green Hedge TW1: Twick 2D **10**
Greenlands KT19: Ewe 2J **29**
Green La. KT3: N Mald 2K **23**
KT4: Wor Pk 5D **24**
KT8: W Mole 2G **21**
KT9: Chess 5E **28**
KT11: Cobh 7D **26**
KT12: Hers 3A **26**
KT21: Asht 6D **32**
SM4: Mord 3K **25**
(Central Rd.)
SM4: Mord 4F **25**
(Lwr. Morden La.)
TW4: Houn 1A **8**
TW13: Hanw 2D **14**
Green La. Av. KT12: Hers 2B **26**
Green Lanes KT19: Ewe 5B **30**
(not continuous)
Greenlaw Gdns. KT3: N Mald 4C **24**
Grn. Lawn La. TW8 1E **4**
Green Leas KT1: King T 5D **36**
Grn. Man La. TW14: Felt 1A **8**
(not continuous)
Green Mead KT10: Esh 3E **26**
Greenoak Way SW19 1G **19**
Greenock Rd. W3 1J **5**
Green Pde. TW3: Houn 2G **9**
Greenside Dr. KT21: Asht 7C **32**
Greenslade Av. KT21: Asht 7J **33**
Greenstead Gdns.
SW15 2E **12**
Green St. TW16: Sun 7A **14**
Green Vw. KT9: Chess 4G **29**
Green Wlk. TW12: Hamp 3E **14**
Greenway SW20 1F **25**
Greenway, The KT18: Eps 3H **33**
TW4: Houn 1E **8**
Greenways KT10: Hin W 7K **21**
Greenways, The TW1: Twick 3B **10**
Greenwood Cl. KT7: T Ditt 5B **22**
SM4: Mord 1H **25**
Greenwood La.
TW12: Hamp H 2G **15**
Greenwood Pk. KT2: King T 4B **18**
Greenwood Rd. KT7: T Ditt 5B **22**
TW7: Isle 7A **4**
Grena Gdns. TW9: Rich 1G **11**
Grena Rd. TW9: Rich 1G **11**
Grenville Cl. KT5: Surb 5K **23**
Grenville M. TW12: Hamp H 2G **15**
Gresham Rd. TW12: Hamp 3F **15**
Gresham Way SW19 7K **13**
Gressenhall Rd. SW18 3J **13**
Greswell St. SW6 5G **7**
Greville Cl. KT21: Asht 7F **33**
TW1: Twick 4C **10**
Greville Ct. KT21: Asht 7F **33**
Greville Pk. Av. KT21: Asht 7F **33**
Greville Pk. Rd. KT21: Asht 7F **33**
Greville Rd. TW10: Rich 3G **11**
Grey Alders SM7: Bans 3F **35**
Greyhound Mans. *W6 3H 7*
(off Greyhound Rd.)
Greyhound Rd. W6 3G **7**
W14 3G **7**
Griffin Cen. TW14: Felt 2A **8**
Griffin Cen., The KT1: King T 4B **36**
Griffin Ct. TW8: Bford 3F **5**
W4 2C **6**
Griffin Ho. *W6 1G 7*
(off Hammersmith Rd.)
Griffin Pk. 3E **4**
Griffiths Cl. KT4: Wor Pk 6E **24**
Griffiths Rd. SW19 4K **19**
Grimston Rd. SW6 6J **7**
Grimwood Rd. TW1: Twick 4A **10**
Grogan Cl. TW12: Hamp 3E **14**
Groombridge Cl. KT12: Hers 2A **26**
Grosse Way SW15 3E **12**
Grosvenor Av. SW14 7B **6**
TW10: Rich 2F **11**
Grosvenor Ct. SM4: Mord 1K **25**
TW11: Tedd 3B **16**
Grosvenor Gdns. KT2: King T 3E **16**
SW14 7B **6**
Grosvenor Hill SW19 3H **19**
Grosvenor Rd. KT18: Eps D 7A **34**
TW1: Twick 5B **10**
TW4: Houn 1E **8**

Grosvenor Rd.—Heathfield Gdns.

Grosvenor Rd. TW8: Bford .3E 4
TW10: Rich .2F 11
W4 .2J 5
Grotto Rd. TW1: Twick .6A 10
Grove, The KT12: Walt T .4A 20
KT17: Eps .2B 34
KT17: Ewe .6C 30
TW1: Twick .3C 10
TW7: Isle .5A 4
TW11: Tedd .1B 16
Grove Av. KT17: Eps .2B 34
SM1: Sutt .3K 31
TW1: Twick .5A 10
Grove Cl.
KT1: King T .7E 36 (1G 23)
KT19: Eps .6H 29
TW13: Hanw .1D 14
Grove Cotts. W4 .3B 6
Grove Ct. KT1: King T .6C 36
KT8: E Mos .1J 21
TW3: Houn .1F 9
Grove Cres.
KT1: King T .6C 36 (7F 17)
KT12: Walt T .4A 20
TW13: Hanw .1D 14
Grove End La. KT10: Esh .5J 21
Grove Footpath
KT5: Surb .7D 36 (1F 23)
Grove Gdns. TW10: Rich .3G 11
TW11: Tedd .1B 16
Grove Ho. *KT12: Walt T .4A 20*
(off Grove, The)
Grovelands *KT1: King T .1E 22*
(off Palace Rd.)
KT8: W Mole .1F 21
Groveland Way KT3: N Mald .2K 23
Grove La.
KT1: King T .7D 36 (1F 23)
GROVE PARK .5K 5
Grove Pk. Bri. W4 .4K 5
Grove Pk. Gdns. W4 .4J 5
Grove Pk. M. W4 .4K 5
Grove Pk. Rd. W4 .4J 5
Grove Pk. Ter. W4 .4J 5
(not continuous)
Grove Rd. KT6: Surb .2E 22
KT8: E Mos .1J 21
KT17: Eps .2B 34
KT21: Asht .7G 33
SM1: Sutt .3K 31
SW13 .6C 6
TW2: Twick .7J 9
TW3: Houn .1F 9
TW7: Isle .5A 4
TW8: Bford .2D 4
TW10: Rich .3G 11
Grove Ter. TW11: Tedd .1B 16
Grove Way KT10: Esh .4H 21
Grovewood TW9: Kew .5H 5
Guilford Av. KT5: Surb .2G 23
Guinness Trust Bldgs.
W6 .2G 7
(off Fulham Pal. Rd.)
Guion Rd. SW6 .6J 7
Gumleigh Rd. W5 .1D 4
Gumley Gdns. TW7: Isle .7B 4
GUNNERSBURY .2J 5
Gunnersbury Av. W3 .1H 5
W4 .1H 5
Gunnersbury Cl. W4 .2J 5
Gunnersbury M. W4 .2J 5
Gunnersbury Station (Rail & Tube) .2J 5
Gunnersbury Triangle Nature Reserve .1K 5
Gunters Mead KT22: Oxs .7H 27
Gunterstone Rd. W14 .1H 7
Gwalior Rd. SW15 .1G 13
Gwendolen Av. SW15 .1G 13
Gwendolen Cl. SW15 .2G 13
Gwendwr Rd. W14 .2H 7
Gwynne Cl. W4 .3C 6

H

Haarlem Rd. W14 .1G 7
Haddon Cl. KT3: N Mald .2C 24
Haddon Rd. SM1: Sutt .1K 31
(not continuous)
Hadleigh Cl. SW20 .6J 19
Hadleigh Dr. SM2: Sutt .5K 31
Hadley Gdns. W4 .2A 6
Hadrian Ct. SM2: Sutt .4K 31
Haggard Rd. TW1: Twick .4C 10
Haig Pl. SM4: Mord .3K 25
Hailsham Cl. KT6: Surb .4E 22
Haining Cl. W4 .2H 5
Haldane Rd. SW6 .4J 7
Haldon Rd. SW18 .3J 13
Halesowen Rd. SM4: Mord .4K 25
Half Acre TW8: Bford .3E 4
Halford Rd. SW6 .3K 7
TW10: Rich .2F 11
Halfway Grn. KT12: Walt T .7A 20
Haliburton Rd. TW1: Twick .2B 10
Halifax Cl. TW11: Tedd .3K 15
Hallam Rd. SW13 .7E 6
Hall Ct. TW11: Tedd .2A 16
Hall Farm Dr. TW2: Whit .4J 9
Halliford Rd. TW16: Sun .1A 20
Hallmead Rd. SM1: Sutt .7K 25
Hall Rd. TW7: Isle .2J 9
HAM .7D 10
Ham, The TW8: Bford .4D 4
Hambledon Hill KT18: Eps .5K 33
Hambledon Rd. SW18 .4J 13
Hambledon Va. KT18: Eps .5K 33
Hambleton Cl. KT4: Wor Pk .6F 25
Ham Cl. TW10: Ham .7D 10
(not continuous)
Ham Comn. TW10: Ham .7E 10
Ham Farm Rd. TW10: Ham .1E 16
Ham Ga. Av. TW10: Ham .7E 10
Ham House .5D 10
Hamilton Av. KT6: Surb .6H 23
SM3: Cheam .6H 25
Hamilton Cl. KT19: Eps .1K 33
Hamilton Ct. SW15 .7H 7
Hamilton Cres. TW3: Houn .2G 9
Hamilton Ho. W4 .3B 6
Hamilton M. SW18 .5K 13
SW19 .4K 19
Hamilton Pl. TW16: Sun .4A 14
Hamilton Rd. TW2: Twick .5K 9
TW8: Bford .3E 4
Ham Lands Nature Reserve .6B 10
Hamlet Ct. W6 .1D 6
Hamlet Gdns. W6 .1D 6
HAMMERSMITH .1F 7
Hammersmith Bri. W6 .3E 6
Hammersmith Bri. Rd.
W6 .2F 7
HAMMERSMITH BROADWAY .1F 7
Hammersmith B'way. W6 .1F 7
HAMMERSMITH FLYOVER .2F 7
Hammersmith Flyover
W6 .2F 7
Hammersmith Gro. W6 .1F 7
Hammersmith Ind. Est.
W6 .3F 7
Hammersmith Rd. W6 .1G 7
W14 .1G 7
Hammersmith Station (Tube) .1F 7
Hammersmith Ter. W6 .2D 6
Hammond Cl. TW12: Hamp .5F 15
Hampden Rd. KT1: King T .7H 17
Hampshire Hog La. W6 .2E 6
HAMPTON .5G 15
Hampton & Richmond Borough FC .5G 15
Hampton Cl. SW20 .4F 19
HAMPTON COURT .1K 21
HAMPTON COURT .7K 15
Hampton Ct. Av. KT8: E Mos .3J 21
Hampton Ct. Bri. KT8: E Mos .1K 21
Hampton Ct. Cres.
KT8: E Mos .7J 15
Hampton Ct. Est. KT7: E Mos .1K 21
Hampton Court Palace .1A 22
Hampton Ct. Pde.
KT8: E Mos .1K 21
Hampton Ct. Rd.
KT1: Hamp W .7A 16
KT8: E Mos .3A 36 (7A 16)
TW12: Hamp .6H 15
Hampton Court Station (Rail) .1K 21
Hampton Ct. Way KT7: T Ditt .6K 21
KT8: E Mos .6K 21
Hampton Farm Ind. Est.
TW13: Hanw .7D 8
Hampton Gro. KT17: Ewe .7C 30
HAMPTON HILL .2H 15
Hampton Hill Playhouse Theatre .2H 15
Hampton La. TW13: Hanw .1D 14
Hampton Open Air Pool .4H 15
Hampton Rd. KT4: Wor Pk .6D 24
TW2: Twick .7J 9
TW11: Tedd .2J 15
TW12: Tedd .2J 15
Hampton Rd. E. TW13: Hanw .1E 14
Hampton Rd. W. TW13: Hanw .7D 8
Hampton Sport, Arts & Fitness Cen. .2F 15
Hampton Station (Rail) .5F 15
HAMPTON WICK .1A 36 (5D 16)
Hampton Wick Station (Rail) .2A 36 (5D 16)
Hampton Youth Project .3E 14
Ham Ridings TW10: Ham .2G 17
Ham St. TW10: Ham .5C 10
Hanah Ct. SW19 .4G 19
Handel Mans. SW13 .4F 7
Handside Cl. KT4: Wor Pk .5G 25
Hanford Cl. SW18 .5K 13
Hanford Row SW19 .3F 19
Hannell Rd. SW6 .4H 7
Hanover Cl. SM3: Cheam .7H 25
TW9: Kew .4H 5
Hanover Ct. SW15 .1C 12
Hanover Ter. TW7: Isle .5B 4
Hansler Gro. KT8: E Mos .1J 21
Hanson Cl. SW14 .7K 5
HANWORTH .2D 14
Hanworth Rd. TW3: Houn .5D 8
TW4: Houn .5D 8
TW12: Hamp .1E 14
TW13: Felt .5A 8
TW16: Sun .4A 14
(not continuous)
Hanworth Ter. TW3: Houn .1G 9
Hanworth Trad. Est.
TW13: Hanw .7D 8
Harbledown Rd. SW6 .5K 7
Harbord St. SW6 .5G 7
Harbourfield Rd. SM7: Bans .4K 35
Harbridge Av. SW15 .4C 12
Harcourt Cl. TW7: Isle .7B 4
Harcourt Rd. SW19 .4K 19
Harding Ho. *SW13 .3E 6*
(off Wyatt Dr.)
Harding Rd. KT18: Eps D .7B 34
Harding's Cl.
KT2: King T .1E 36 (5G 17)
Hardman Rd.
KT2: King T .3D 36 (6F 17)
Hardwicke Rd. TW10: Ham .1D 16
W4 .1A 6
Hardwicks Way SW18 .2K 13
Hardy's M. KT8: E Mos .1K 21
Harefield KT10: Hin W .7K 21
Harefield Av. SM2: Cheam .5H 31
Hare La. KT10: Clay .2J 27
Harewood Rd. TW7: Isle .4A 4
Harfield Rd. TW16: Sun .6C 14
Harkness Cl. KT17: Eps D .5F 35
Harlequin Av. TW8: Bford .3B 4
Harlequin Cl. TW7: Isle .2K 9
Harlequin Rd. TW11: Tedd .4C 16
Harlequins RUFC .4K 9
Harlington Rd. E. TW13: Felt .4A 8
TW14: Felt .4A 8
Harlington Rd. W. TW14: Felt .3A 8
Harold Wilson Ho. *SW6 .3J 7*
(off Clem Attlee Ct.)
Harriott's La. KT21: Asht .7D 32
Harrow Cl. KT9: Chess .4E 28
Harrowdene Gdns.
TW11: Tedd .3B 16
Hartfield Cres. SW19 .4J 19
Hartfield Rd. KT9: Chess .2E 28
SW19 .4J 19
Hartford Rd. KT19: Ewe .3J 29
Hartham Cl. TW7: Isle .5B 4
Hartham Rd. TW7: Isle .5A 4
Hartington Ct. W4 .4J 5
Hartington Rd. TW1: Twick .4C 10
W4 .4J 5
Hartismere Rd. SW6 .4J 7
Hartland Rd. SM4: Mord .4K 25
TW7: Isle .7B 4
TW12: Hamp H .1G 15
Hartland Way SM4: Mord .4J 25
Hartop Point *SW6 .4H 7*
(off Pellant Rd.)
Hartswood Gdns. W12 .1C 6
Harvard Hill W4 .3J 5
Harvard La. W4 .2K 5
Harvard Rd. W4 .2J 5
Harvest Ct. KT10: Esh .6F 21
Harvester Rd. KT19: Eps .6A 30
Harvesters Cl. TW7: Isle .2J 9
Harvest La. KT7: T Ditt .3B 22
Harvey Ct. KT19: Eps .5J 29
Harvey Dr. TW12: Hamp .5G 15
Harvey Ho. TW8: Bford .2F 5
Harvey Rd. TW4: Houn .4E 8
Harwood Ct. SW15 .1F 13
Harwood M. SW6 .4K 7
Harwood Rd. SW6 .4K 7
Haslam Av. SM3: Sutt .5H 25
Haslemere Av. SW18 .6K 13
W7 .1B 4
W13 .1B 4
Haslemere Cl. TW12: Hamp .2E 14
Hastings Ct. TW11: Tedd .2J 15
Hastings Dr. KT6: Surb .3D 22
Hatch Pl. KT2: King T .2G 17
Hatfield Cl. SM2: Sutt .5K 31
Hatfield Mead SM4: Mord .2K 25
Hatfield Rd. KT21: Asht .7G 33
Hatherleigh Cl. KT9: Chess .2E 28
SM4: Mord .1K 25
Hatherley Rd. TW9: Kew .5G 5
Hatherop Rd. TW12: Hamp .4E 14
Hatton Ho. *KT1: King T .6G 17*
(off Victoria Rd.)
Hauteville Ct. Gdns. *W6 .1C 6*
(off South Side)
Havana Rd. SW19 .6K 13
Haven, The TW9: Rich .7H 5
Haven Cl. SW19 .7G 13
Haven Ct. KT5: Surb .3G 23
KT10: Hin W .6K 21
Haven Pl. KT10: Hin W .6K 21
Haverfield Gdns. TW9: Kew .4H 5
Havers Av. KT12: Hers .2C 26
Haversham Cl. TW1: Twick .3E 10
Hawker Ct. *KT1: King T .6G 17*
(off Church Rd.)
Hawkesbury Rd. SW15 .2E 12
Hawkesley Cl. TW1: Twick .1B 16
Hawkewood Rd. TW16: Sun .7A 14
Hawkfield Ct. TW7: Isle .6A 4
Hawkhurst Gdns.
KT9: Chess .1F 29
Hawkhurst Way KT3: N Mald .2A 24
Hawkins Rd. TW11: Tedd .3C 16
Hawkshill Cl. KT10: Esh .3F 27
Hawkshill Pl. KT10: Esh .3F 27
Hawkshill Way KT10: Esh .3E 26
Hawksmoor St. W6 .3G 7
Hawks Pas. KT1: King T .3E 36
Hawks Rd. KT1: King T .6G 17
Hawley Cl. TW12: Hamp .3E 14
Hawthorn Cl. SM7: Bans .3H 35
TW12: Hamp .2F 15
Hawthorn Ct. TW9: Kew .5J 5
Hawthorne Ct. KT12: Walt T .5C 20
Hawthorne Pl. KT17: Eps .1B 34
Hawthorn Gdns. W5 .1E 4
Hawthorn Hatch TW8: Bford .4C 4
Hawthorn Rd. TW8: Bford .4C 4
TW13: Felt .5A 8
Hawthorns, The KT17: Ewe .4C 30
Haycroft Rd. KT6: Surb .6E 22
Haydon Pk. Rd. SW19 .2K 19
Hayes Cres. SM3: Cheam .7G 25
Haygarth Pl. SW19 .2G 19
Haygreen Cl. KT2: King T .3J 17
Haylett Gdns. KT1: King T .1E 22
Hayling Ct. SM3: Cheam .7F 25
Haymeads Dr. KT10: Esh .3H 27
Haymer Gdns. KT4: Wor Pk .7D 24
Haynt Wlk. SW20 .7H 19
Hays Wlk. SM2: Cheam .6G 31
Hayward Gdns. SW15 .3F 13
Hayward Rd. KT7: T Ditt .5A 22
Hazelbank KT5: Surb .5K 23
Hazelbury Cl. SW19 .6K 19
Hazel Cl. TW2: Whit .4H 9
TW8: Bford .4C 4
Hazel La. TW10: Ham .6F 11
Hazel Mead KT17: Ewe .6D 30
Hazelwood Ct. KT6: Surb .3F 23
Hazledene Rd. W4 .3K 5
Hazlemere Gdns.
KT4: Wor Pk .5D 24
Hazlewell Rd. SW15 .2F 13
Hazlitt Cl. TW13: Hanw .1D 14
Hazlitt M. W14 .1H 7
Hazlitt Rd. W14 .1H 7
Hazon Way KT19: Eps .1K 33
Headley Cl. KT19: Ewe .3H 29
Headley Rd.
KT18: Eps, Eps D .7J 33
Headway, The KT17: Ewe .5C 30
Headway Cl. TW10: Ham .1D 16
Hearne Rd. W4 .3H 5
Heatham Pk. TW2: Twick .4A 10
Heath Bus. Cen. TW3: Houn .1H 9
Heathcote Rd. KT18: Eps .3A 34
TW1: Twick .3C 10
Heath Ct. TW4: Houn .1E 8
Heathdale Av. TW4: Houn .1D 8
Heathdene KT20: Tad .7H 35
Heath Dr. SW20 .1F 25
Heatherbank Cl. KT11: Cobh .7C 26
Heather Cl. TW7: Isle .2J 9
TW12: Hamp .5E 14
Heatherdale Cl. KT2: King T .3H 17
Heather Gdns. SM2: Sutt .3K 31
Heather Pl. KT10: Esh .1G 27
Heatherset Cl. KT10: Esh .2H 27
Heatherside Rd. KT19: Ewe .4A 30
Heather Wlk. *TW2: Whit .4F 9*
(off Stephenson Rd.)
Heathfield Ct. W4 .2A 6
Heathfield Gdns. W4 .2K 5

Heathfield Nth. TW2: Twick 4K 9
Heathfield Rd. KT12: Hers 7D 20
Heathfields Cl. KT21: Asht 7D 32
Heathfields Ct. TW4: Houn 2D 8
Heathfield Sth. TW2: Twick 4A 10
Heathfield Ter. W4 ......2K 5
Heath Gdns. TW1: Twick 5A 10
Heathlands Cl. TW1: Twick 6A 10
Heathlands Way TW4: Houn 2D 8
Heathmans Rd. SW6 ......5J 7
Heath Mead SW19 ......7G 13
Heath Ri. SW15 ......3G 13
Heath Rd. KT22: Oxs 7H 27
TW1: Twick 5A 10
TW2: Twick 5A 10
TW3: Houn, Isle 1G 9
Heathrow C'way. Cen.
TW4: Houn 1A 8
Heathrow Gateway
TW4: Houn 4D 8
Heathrow Intl. Trad. Est.
TW4: Houn 1A 8
Heath Royal SW15 ......3G 13
Heathside KT10: Hin W 7K 21
TW4: Houn 4K 8
Heathside Cl. KT10: Hin W 7K 21
Heathside Pl. KT18: Tatt C 7G 35
Heathview Gdns. SW15 ......4F 13
Heber Mans. W14 ......3H 7
(off Queen's Club Gdns.)
Hebron Rd. W6 ......1F 7
Heckets Cl. KT10: Esh 6H 27
Heckfield Pl. SW6 ......4K 7
Heddon Cl. TW7: Isle 1B 18
Hedingham Ho.
KT2: King T 2C 36 (5F 17)
Hedley Rd. TW2: Whit 4F 9
Heidegger Cres. SW13 ......4E 6
Heights Cl. SM7: Bans 5H 35
SW20 ......4E 18
Heldmann Cl. TW3: Isle 1J 9
Helen Av. TW14: Felt 4A 8
Helen Cl. KT8: W Mole 1G 21
Helm Cl. KT19: Eps 1H 33
Helme Cl. SW19 ......2J 19
Hemingford Rd. SM3: Cheam 1F 31
Hemming Cl. TW12: Hamp 5F 15
Hemmings Mead KT19: Ewe 3K 29
Hemsby Rd. KT9: Chess 3G 29
HENDERSON HOSPITAL 5K 31
Hendon Gro. KT19: Eps 5K 29
Henfield Rd. SW19 ......5J 19
Henley Av. SM3: Cheam 7H 25
Henley Cl. TW7: Isle 5A 4
Henley Dr. KT2: King T 4C 18
Henley Way TW13: Hanw 2C 14
Henlow Pl. TW10: Ham 6E 10
Henrietta Ct. TW1: Twick 4D 10
(off Richmond Rd.)
Henrietta Ho. W6 ......2F 7
(off Queen Caroline St.)
Henry Jackson Rd.
SW15 ......7G 7
Henry Lodge KT12: Hers 3B 26
Henry Macaulay Av.
KT2: King T 2B 36 (5E 16)
Henry Peters Dr. TW11: Tedd 2K 15
(off Somerset Gdns.)
Henty Wlk. SW15 ......2E 12
Hepple Cl. TW7: Isle 6C 4
Hepplestone Cl. SW15 ......3E 12
Hepworth Ct. SM3: Sutt 5K 25
Herbert Gdns. W4 ......3J 5
Herbert Morrison Ho.
SW6 ......3J 7
(off Clem Attlee Ct.)
Herbert Rd.
KT1: King T 6E 36 (7G 17)
SW19 ......4J 19
(not continuous)
Hereford Cl. KT18: Eps 2A 34
Hereford Ct. SM2: Sutt 4K 31
Hereford Gdns. TW2: Twick 5H 9
Hereford Rd. TW13: Felt 5B 8
W5 ......1D 4
Hereford Way KT9: Chess 2D 28
Hermitage, The
KT1: King T 7B 36 (1E 22)
SW13 ......5C 6
TW10: Rich 2F 11
Hermitage Ct. KT10: Clay 3B 28
Hermitage Vs. SW6 ......3J 7
(off Lillie Rd.)
Herne Rd. KT6: Surb 6E 22
Heron Cl. SM1: Sutt 2J 31
Heron Ct. KT1: King T 6C 36 (7F 17)
KT17: Eps 3D 34
Heronry, The KT12: Hers 3A 26
Heron's Pl. TW7: Isle 7C 4

Heron Sq. TW9: Rich 2E 10
Heron Vw. TW8: Bford 4D 4
(off Commerce Rd.)
Heron Way TW14: Felt 1A 8
HERSHAM 2B 26
Hersham By-Pass KT12: Hers 2A 26
Hersham Cl. SW15 ......4D 12
Hersham Ct. KT12: Hers 7A 20
HERSHAM GREEN 2C 26
Hersham Grn. Shop. Cen.
KT12: Hers 2C 26
Hersham Pl. KT12: Hers 2C 26
Hersham Rd.
KT12: Hers, Walt T 5A 20
Hersham Station (Rail) 7D 20
Hersham Trad. Est.
KT12: Walt T 6D 20
Hershell Ct. SW14 ......1J 11
Hertford Av. SW14 ......2A 12
Hessle Gro. KT17: Ewe 7C 30
Hestercombe Av. SW6 ......6H 7
Hester Ter. TW9: Rich 7H 5
Hexham Gdns. TW7: Isle 4B 4
Hexham Rd. SM4: Mord 5K 25
Heybridge Av. SW20 ......7J 19
Heythorp St. SW18 ......5J 13
Hibernia Gdns. TW3: Houn 1F 9
Hibernia Rd. TW3: Houn 1F 9
Hickey's Almshouses
TW9: Rich 1G 11
Hidcote Gdns. SW20 ......7E 18
Higgins Wlk. TW12: Hamp 3D 14
(off Abbott Cl.)
High Ashton KT2: King T 4J 17
High Beeches SM7: Bans 3F 35
Highbury Cl. KT3: N Mald 1K 23
Highbury Rd. SW19 ......2H 19
High Cedar Dr. SW20 ......4F 19
Highclere Rd. KT3: N Mald 7A 18
Highcliffe Dr. SW15 ......3C 12
(not continuous)
High Coombe Pl. KT2: King T 3A 18
Highcross Way SW15 ......5D 12
Highdown KT4: Wor Pk 6B 24
Highdown Rd. SW15 ......3E 12
High Dr. KT3: N Mald 5K 17
Higher Dr. SM7: Bans 1G 35
Higher Grn. KT17: Eps 2D 34
Highfield Cl. KT6: Surb 5D 22
KT22: Oxs 7J 27
Highfield Dr. KT19: Ewe 2C 30
Highfield Rd. KT5: Surb 4K 23
KT12: Walt T 5A 20
TW7: Isle 5A 4
TW13: Felt 6A 8
Highfields KT21: Asht 7E 32
SM1: Sutt 6K 25
High Foleys KT10: Clay 4C 28
High Gth. KT19: Eps 3H 27
Highgrove Ct. SM1: Sutt 3K 31
Highlands Heath SW15 ......4F 13
High Pk. Av. TW9: Kew 5H 5
High Pk. Rd. TW9: Kew 5H 5
Highridge Cl. KT18: Eps 3B 34
High St.
KT1: Hamp W 2A 36 (5D 16)
KT1: King T 5B 36 (7E 16)
KT3: N Mald 1B 24
KT7: T Ditt 3B 22
KT8: W Mole 1F 21
KT10: Clay 3A 28
KT10: Esh 1G 27
KT17: Eps 2A 34
KT17: Ewe 5C 30
KT19: Ewe 2A 34
SM3: Cheam 3H 31
SM7: Bans 4K 35
SW19 ......2G 19
TW2: Whit 4H 9
TW3: Houn 1G 9
(not continuous)
TW8: Bford 4D 4
TW11: Tedd 2A 16
TW12: Hamp, Hamp H 5H 15
TW13: Felt 6A 8
High St. M. SW19 ......2H 19
Highview SM2: Cheam 7J 31
Highview Path SM7: Bans 4K 35
Hilbert Rd. SM3: Cheam 7G 25
Hilda Ct. KT6: Surb 4E 22
Hilderley Ho. KT1: King T 5E 36
Hilders, The KT21: Asht 6J 33
Hildyard Rd. SW6 ......3K 7
Hillary Cres. KT12: Walt T 5B 20
Hillary Dr. TW7: Isle 2A 10
Hillbrow KT3: N Mald 7C 18
Hillbrow Rd. KT10: Esh 7H 21
Hill Cl. KT11: Cobh 7F 27
Hill Cres. KT4: Wor Pk 6F 25
KT5: Surb 2G 23

Hill Crest KT6: Surb 4F 23
Hillcrest Cl. KT18: Eps 4C 34
Hillcrest Gdns. KT10: Hin W 7A 22
Hillcross Av. SM4: Mord 3G 25
Hilldale Rd. SM1: Sutt 1J 31
Hillersdon Av. SW13 ......6D 6
Hillfield Ct. KT10: Esh 2G 27
Hill Fld. Rd. TW12: Hamp 4E 14
Hill Gro. TW13: Hanw 6E 8
Hill Ho. Dr. TW12: Hamp 5F 15
Hillier Lodge TW11: Tedd 2J 15
Hillier Pl. KT9: Chess 3E 28
Hillmont Rd. KT10: Hin W 7K 21
Hill Ri. KT10: Hin W 6C 22
TW10: Rich 2E 10
Hillside KT10: Esh 2G 27
SM7: Bans 4H 35
SW19 ......3G 19
Hillside Cl. SM4: Mord 1H 25
SM7: Bans 5H 35
Hillside Rd. KT5: Surb 1G 23
KT17: Ewe 6F 31
KT21: Asht 6G 33
SM2: Sutt 4J 31
Hill St. TW9: Rich 2E 10
Hill Top SM3: Sutt 4J 25
SM4: Mord 3K 25
Hillview SW20 ......4E 18
Hill Vw. Rd. KT10: Clay 4B 28
TW1: Twick 3B 10
Hilsea Point SW15 ......5E 12
Hinchley Cl. KT10: Hin W 1A 28
Hinchley Dr. KT10: Hin W 7A 22
Hinchley Mnr. KT10: Hin W 7A 22
Hinchley Way KT10: Hin W 7B 22
HINCHLEY WOOD 7A 22
Hinchley Wood Station (Rail) 7A 22
Hindhead Point SW15 ......5E 12
Hinton Av. TW4: Houn 1C 8
Hobart Pl. TW10: Rich 4G 11
Hobart Rd. KT4: Wor Pk 7E 24
Hobbes Wlk. SW15 ......2E 12
Hobill Wlk. KT5: Surb 3G 23
Hogarth Bus. Pk. W4 ......3B 6
Hogarth La. W4 ......3B 6
Hogarth Pl. SW5 ......1K 7
(off Hogarth Rd.)
Hogarth Rd. SW5 ......1K 7
HOGARTH RDBT. 3B 6
Hogarth's House 3B 6
(off Hogarth La.)
Hogarth Ter. W4 ......3B 6
Hogarth Way TW12: Hamp 5H 15
Hogsmill Ho. KT1: King T 5E 36
Hogsmill Wlk. KT1: King T 5E 36
Hogsmill Way KT19: Ewe 2K 29
Holbrooke Pl. TW10: Rich 2E 10
Holcombe St. W6 ......1E 6
Holdernesse Cl. TW7: Isle 5B 4
Holland Av. SM2: Sutt 5K 31
SW20 ......5C 18
Holland Cl. KT6: Surb 4E 22
Holland Rd. W14 ......1J 7
Hollands, The KT4: Wor Pk 5C 24
TW13: Hanw 1C 14
Holles Cl. TW12: Hamp 3F 15
Hollies Cl. TW1: Twick 6A 10
Hollies Rd. W5 ......1D 4
Hollingsworth Ct. KT6: Surb 4E 22
Hollington Cres.
KT3: N Mald 3C 24
Hollingworth Cl.
KT8: W Mole 1E 20
Hollows, The TW8: Bford 3G 5
Holly Av. KT12: Walt T 5C 20
Hollybank Cl. TW12: Hamp 2F 15
Hollybush La. TW12: Hamp 4E 14
Hollybush Rd. KT2: King T 2F 17
Holly Cl. TW13: Hanw 2D 14
Holly Ct. SM2: Sutt 4K 31
Hollyfield Rd. KT5: Surb 4G 23
Hollygrove Cl. TW3: Houn 1E 8
Holly Hill Dr. SM7: Bans 5K 35
Holly Hill Pk. SM7: Bans 6K 35
Holly Ho. TW8: Bford 3D 4
Holly La. SM7: Bans 5K 35
Holly La. E. SM7: Bans 5K 35
Holly La. W. SM7: Bans 6K 35
Hollymoor La. KT19: Ewe 6A 30
Holly Rd. TW1: Twick 5A 10
TW3: Houn 1G 9
TW12: Hamp H 3H 15
W4 ......1A 6
Holly Tree Cl. SW19 ......5G 13
Holly Vs. W6 ......1E 6
(off Wellesley Av.)
Holman Ct. KT17: Ewe 5D 30
Holman Hunt Ho. W6 ......2H 7
(off Field Rd.)
Holman Rd. KT19: Ewe 2K 29

Holmbush Rd. SW15 ......3H 13
Holme Ct. TW7: Isle 7B 4
Holmesdale Av. SW14 ......7J 5
Holmesdale Rd. TW9: Kew 5G 5
TW11: Tedd 4D 16
Holmes Place Health Club
Hammersmith 1G 7
(off Hammersmith Rd.)
Holmes Rd. TW1: Twick 6A 10
Holmeswood SM2: Sutt 3K 31
Holmoak Cl. SW15 ......3J 13
Holmsley Cl. KT3: N Mald 3C 24
Holmsley Ho. SW15 ......4C 12
(off Tangley Gro.)
Holmwood Cl. SM2: Cheam 5G 31
Holmwood Rd. KT9: Chess 2E 28
SM2: Cheam 5F 31
Holne Chase SM4: Mord 3J 25
Holroyd Cl. KT10: Clay 5A 28
Holroyd Rd. KT10: Clay 5A 28
SW15 ......1F 13
Holst Mans. SW13 ......3F 7
Holsworthy Way KT9: Chess 2D 28
Holt, The SM4: Mord 1K 25
Holybourne Av. SW15 ......4D 12
Holyhead Ct. KT1: King T 7B 36
Holyport Rd. SW6 ......4G 7
Home Ct. KT6: Surb 2E 22
Home Farm Cl. KT7: T Ditt 4A 22
KT10: Esh 3G 27
KT18: Tad 6G 35
Home Farm Gdns.
KT12: Walt T 6B 20
Homefield SM4: Mord 1K 25
Homefield Av. KT12: Hers 1C 26
Homefield Rd. KT12: Walt T 4D 20
SW19 ......3G 19
W4 ......2C 6
Homeland Dr. SM2: Sutt 5K 31
Home Mdw. SM7: Bans 5K 35
Home Pk. Ct. KT1: King T 1E 22
(off Palace Rd.)
Home Pk. Pde.
KT1: Hamp W 3A 36
Home Pk. Rd. SW19 ......1J 19
Home Pk. Ter. KT1: Hamp W 3A 36
Home Pk. Wlk. KT1: King T 1E 22
Homersham Rd. KT1: King T 6H 17
Homestead Gdns. KT10: Clay 2K 27
Homestead Rd. SW6 ......4J 7
Homewater Ho. KT17: Eps 2B 34
Homewood Cl. TW12: Hamp 3E 14
Honeywood Rd. TW7: Isle 1B 10
Hood Av. SW14 ......2K 11
Hood Rd. SW20 ......4C 18
HOOK 2E 28
Hookfield KT19: Eps 2K 33
Hookfield M. KT19: Eps 2K 33
HOOK JUNC. 7F 23
Hook Ri. Nth. KT6: Surb 7F 23
Hook Ri. Sth. KT6: Surb 7F 23
Hook Ri. Sth. Ind. Pk.
KT6: Surb 7G 23
Hook Rd. KT6: Surb 6F 23
KT9: Chess 2E 28
KT19: Eps, Ewe 4K 29
Hope Cl. TW8: Bford 2F 5
Hoppingwood Av.
KT3: N Mald 7B 18
Hopton Gdns. KT3: N Mald 3D 24
Horace Rd.
KT1: King T 6E 36 (7G 17)
Horatio Ho. W6 ......2G 7
(off Fulham Pal. Rd.)
Horatio Pl. SW19 ......5K 19
Horder Rd. SW6 ......5H 7
Horizon Ho. KT17: Eps 2B 34
Hornbeam Cres. TW8: Bford 4C 4
Hornbeam Wlk. TW10: Rich 6G 11
Hornchurch Cl. KT2: King T 1E 16
Horndean Cl. SW15 ......5D 12
Horne Way SW15 ......6F 7
Horsecroft SM7: Bans 6J 35
Horsecroft Mdws. SM7: Bans 5J 35
Horse Fair
KT1: King T 3A 36 (6E 16)
Horseshoe, The SM7: Bans 4J 35
Horsley Cl. KT19: Eps 2A 34
Horsley Dr. KT2: King T 2E 16
Horticultural Pl. W4 ......2A 6
HORTON 7K 29
Horton Country Pk. 6G 29
Horton Footpath KT19: Eps 7K 29
Horton Hill KT19: Eps 7K 29
Horton Ho. W6 ......2H 7
(off Field Rd.)
Horton La. KT19: Eps 7H 29
Horton Pk. Children's Farm 6H 29

Lavender Ct. KT8: W Mole 7G 15
TW14: Felt 3A 8
Lavender Ho. TW9: Kew 5J 5
Lavender Rd. KT19: Ewe 2J 29
Lavenham Rd. SW18 ....6J 13
Laverstoke Gdns.
SW15 ....4C 12
Lawford Rd. W4 ....4K 5
Lawley Ho. TW1: Twick 3E 10
Lawn Cl. KT3: N Mald 6B 18
Lawn Cres. TW9: Kew 6H 5
Lawns, The SM2: Cheam 4H 31
SW19 ....2J 19
Lawrence Av. KT3: N Mald ...3A 24
Lawrence Est. TW4: Houn 1B 8
Lawrence Pde. TW7: Isle 7C 4
(off Lower Sq.)
Lawrence Rd. TW4: Houn 1B 8
TW10: Ham 1D 16
TW12: Hamp 4E 14
W5 ....1E 4
Lawrence Weaver Cl.
SM4: Mord 3K 25
Lawson Cl. SW19 ....7G 13
Lawson Ct. KT6: Surb 4E 22
Layton Ct. TW8: Bford 2E 4
Layton Pl. TW9: Kew 5H 5
Layton Rd. TW3: Houn 1G 9
TW8: Bford 2E 4
Lea Cl. TW2: Whit 4E 8
Leaf Cl. KT7: T Ditt 2K 21
Leafield Rd. SM1: Sutt 6K 25
SW20 ....7J 19
Leamington Av.
SM4: Mord 1H 25
Leamington Cl. TW3: Houn 2H 9
Leamore St. W6 ....1F 7
Leander Ct. KT6: Surb 4E 22
Leas Cl. KT9: Chess 4G 29
LEATHERHEAD COMMON 7B 32
Leatherhead Rd. KT9: Chess ..3C 32
KT21: Asht 7F 33
Lebanon Av. TW13: Hanw 2C 14
Lebanon Gdns. SW18 ....3K 13
Lebanon Pk. TW1: Twick 4C 10
Lebanon Rd. SW18 ....2K 13
Leconfield Av. SW13 ....7C 6
Leeson Ho. TW1: Twick 4C 10
Leeward Gdns. SW19 ....2H 19
Leeways, The SM3: Cheam 3H 31
Legion Ct. SM4: Mord 3K 25
Leicester Cl. KT4: Wor Pk 7F 25
Leicester Ct. TW1: Twick 3E 10
(off Clevedon Rd.)
Leigh, The KT2: King T 4B 18
Leigham Dr. TW7: Isle 4A 4
Leigh Cl. KT3: N Mald 1K 23
Leigh Cl. Ind. Est.
KT3: N Mald 1A 24
Leigh Pl. TW13: Felt 5B 8
Leigh Rd. TW3: Houn 1J 9
Leighton Mans. W14 ....3H 7
Leighton Way KT18: Eps 3A 34
Leinster Av. SW14 ....7K 5
Leisure W. TW13: Felt 6A 8
Leith Rd. KT17: Eps 1B 34
Lemon Gro. TW13: Felt 5A 8
(off Highfield Rd.)
Lena Gdns. W6 ....1F 7
Lenelby Rd. KT6: Surb 5H 23
Len Freeman Pl. SW6 ....3J 7
Lennox Ho. TW1: Twick 3E 10
(off Clevedon Rd.)
Lenton Ri. TW9: Rich 7F 5
Leo Ct. TW8: Bford 4E 4
Leopold Av. SW19 ....2J 19
Leopold Rd. SW19 ....1J 19
Leopold Ter. SW19 ....2J 19
Lerry Cl. W14 ....3J 7
Leslie Gdns. SM2: Sutt 3K 31
Letterstone Rd. SW6 ....4J 7
Lettice St. SW6 ....5J 7
Levana Cl. SW19 ....5H 13
Lewesdon Cl. SW19 ....5G 13
Lewin Rd. SW14 ....7A 6
Lewins Rd. KT18: Eps 3J 33
Lewis Rd. TW10: Rich 2E 10
Lewiston Cl. KT4: Wor Pk 4E 24
Lexham Gdns. W8 ....1K 7
Lexham M. W8 ....1K 7
Leyborne Pk. TW9: Kew 5H 5
Leyfield KT4: Wor Pk 5B 24
Leylands SW18 ....3J 13
Leys, The KT12: Hers 1E 26
Library Way TW2: Whit 4H 9
Lichfield Cl. KT6: Surb 2F 23
(off Claremont Rd.)
TW9: Rich 1F 11
Lichfield Gdns. TW9: Rich 1F 11

Lichfield Rd. TW4: Houn 1B 8
TW9: Kew 5G 5
Lichfield Ter. TW9: Rich 2F 11
(off Sheen Rd.)
Lickey Ho. W14 ....3J 7
(off Nth. End Rd.)
Liffords Pl. SW13 ....6C 6
Lifford St. SW15 ....1G 13
Lightermans Wlk.
SW18 ....1K 13
Lilac Ct. TW11: Tedd 1A 16
Lillian Rd. SW13 ....3D 6
Lillie Mans. SW6 ....3J 7
(off Lillie Rd.)
Lillie Rd. SW6 ....3H 7
Lillie Yd. SW6 ....3K 7
Lilliot's La. KT22: Lea 7B 32
Lily Cl. W14 ....1G 7
(not continuous)
Lilyville Rd. SW6 ....5J 7
Lime Cres. TW16: Sun 6B 14
Limecroft Cl. KT19: Ewe 4A 30
Lime Gro. KT3: N Mald 7A 18
TW1: Twick 3A 10
Lime Ho. TW9: Kew 5J 5
Lime Rd. TW9: Rich 1G 11
Limes, The KT8: W Mole 1G 21
SW18 ....3K 13
Limes Av. SW13 ....6C 6
Limes Fld. Rd. SW14 ....7B 6
Limes Rd. TW9: Rich 3K 13
Lime Tree Av.
KT10: Esh, T Ditt 5J 21
Lime Tree Cl. KT21: Asht 7F 33
Lime Wlk. KT8: E Mos 1A 22
Limpsfield Av. SW19 ....6G 13
Linacre Ct. W6 ....2G 7
Lincoln Av. SW19 ....7G 13
TW2: Twick 6H 9
Lincoln Rd. KT3: N Mald 7K 17
KT4: Wor Pk 5E 24
TW13: Hanw 7E 8
Lincoln Wlk. KT19: Ewe 6A 30
(not continuous)
Linden Av. TW3: Houn 2G 9
Linden Cl. KT7: T Ditt 4A 22
Linden Cres. KT1: King T 6G 17
Linden Gdns. W4 ....2B 6
Linden Gro. KT3: N Mald 7B 18
TW11: Tedd 2A 16
Linden Ho. TW12: Hamp 3F 15
Linden Pl. KT17: Eps 1B 34
Linden Rd. TW12: Hamp 4F 15
Lindens, The W4 ....5K 5
Lindisfarne Rd. SW20 ....4D 18
Lindley Ct. KT1: Hamp W 5D 16
Lindley Pl. TW9: Kew 5H 5
Lindley Rd. KT12: Walt T 7C 20
Lindsay Cl. KT9: Chess 4F 29
KT19: Eps 2K 33
Lindsay Rd. KT4: Wor Pk 6E 24
TW12: Hamp 1G 15
Lindsey Ho. W5 ....1E 4
Lindum Rd. TW11: Tedd 4D 16
Linfield Cl. KT12: Hers 2A 26
Lingfield Av.
KT1: King T ...7D 36 (1F 23)
Lingfield Rd. KT4: Wor Pk ...7F 25
SW19 ....2G 19
Link, The TW11: Tedd 3A 16
Linkenholt Mans. W6 ....1C 6
(off Stamford Brook Av.)
Linkfield KT8: W Mole 7G 15
Linkfield Rd. TW7: Isle 6A 4
Links Av. SM4: Mord 1K 25
(not continuous)
Links Cl. KT21: Asht 6D 32
Linkside KT3: N Mald 6B 18
Links Pl. KT21: Asht 6E 32
Links Rd. KT17: Eps 2D 34
KT21: Asht 7D 32
Links Vw. Ct. TW12: Hamp H ..1J 15
Links Vw. Rd.
TW12: Hamp H 2H 15
Linkway SW20 ....7E 18
TW10: Ham 6C 10
Linslade Cl. TW4: Houn 2D 8
Linstead Way SW18 ....4H 13
Lintaine Cl. W6 ....3H 7
Lintons La. KT17: Eps 1B 34
Linver Rd. SW6 ....6K 7
Lion Av. TW1: Twick 5A 10
Lionel Mans. W14 ....1G 7
(off Haarlem Rd.)
Lionel Rd. Nth. TW8: Bford ...1F 5
Lionel Rd. Sth. TW8: Bford ...2G 5
Lion Ga. Gdns. TW9: Rich 7G 5
Lion Gate M. KT8: W Mole ...7A 16

Lion Pk. Av. KT9: Chess 1H 29
Lion Rd. TW1: Twick 5A 10
Lion Way TW8: Bford 4E 4
Lion Wharf Rd. TW7: Isle 7C 4
Lloyds Lanes Raynes Pk. 7G 19
Lisbon Av. TW2: Twick 6H 9
Lisgar Ter. W14 ....1J 7
Lismore SW19 ....2J 19
(off Woodside)
Lismore Cl. TW7: Isle 6B 4
Lissant Cl. KT6: Surb 4E 22
Listergate Ct. SW15 ....1F 13
Litchfield Av. SM4: Mord 4J 25
Littlecombe Cl. SW15 ....3G 13
Littlecote Cl. SW19 ....4H 13
LITTLE EALING 1E 4
Lit. Ealing La. W5 ....1D 4
Lit. Ferry Rd. TW1: Twick 5C 10
Littlefield Cl.
KT1: King T 4D 36 (6F 17)
Littlefield Ho. KT1: King T ...4C 36
Little Grn. TW9: Rich 1E 10
Littlemead KT10: Esh 1J 27
Little Orchards KT18: Eps 3B 34
(off Worple Rd.)
Little Pk. Dr. TW13: Felt 6D 8
Lit. Queen's Rd. TW11: Tedd ..3A 16
Lit. St Leonard's SW14 ......7K 5
Lit. Warkworth Ho. TW7: Isle ..6C 4
Littlewood Cl. W13 ....1C 4
Lit. Wood St.
KT1: King T 3B 36 (6E 16)
Littleworth Av. KT10: Esh 2J 27
Littleworth Comn. Rd.
KT10: Esh 7J 21
Littleworth La. KT10: Esh 1J 27
Littleworth Pl. KT10: Esh 7J 21
Littleworth Rd. KT10: Esh 2J 27
Liverpool Rd. KT2: King T ...4H 17
Livesey Cl.
KT1: King T 5E 36 (7G 17)
Livingstone Mans. W14 .....3H 7
(off Queen's Club Gdns.)
Livingstone Rd. TW3: Houn ...1H 9
Lloyd Rd. KT4: Wor Pk 7F 25
Lochaline St. W6 ....3F 7
Lockesley Sq. KT6: Surb 3E 22
Lock Rd. TW10: Ham 1D 16
Locksmeade Rd.
TW10: Ham 1D 16
Lockwood Way KT9: Chess ..2H 29
Lockyer Ho. SW15 ....7G 7
Locomotive Dr. TW14: Felt ...5A 8
Lodge Av. SW14 ....7B 6
Lodge Cl. KT17: Ewe 6F 31
TW7: Isle 5C 4
Loft Ho. Pl. KT9: Chess 3D 28
Logan Cl. TW4: Houn 1E 8
Logan M. W8 ....1K 7
Logan Pl. W8 ....1K 7
London Academy of Music &
Dramatic Art 1K 7
(off Cromwell Rd.)
London Apollo 2F 7
London Broncos Rugby League
Football Club 3E 4
London Butterfly House 5C 4
London Rd.
KT2: King T 3E 36 (6G 17)
(not continuous)
KT17: Ewe 5C 30
SM3: Cheam 7G 25
SM4: Mord 2K 25
TW1: Twick 4B 10
TW7: Bford, Isle 6A 4
TW7: Isle, Twick 2B 10
TW8: Bford 6A 4
LONDON ROAD RDBT. 3B 10
London Scottish & Richmond RUFC
...................7E 4
London Stile W4 ....2H 5
London Welsh RUFC 7F 5
London Wetland Cen. 5E 6
LONG DITTON 5D 22
Longdown La. Nth.
KT17: Eps 3D 34
Longdown La. Sth.
KT17: Eps, Eps D 3D 34
Longdown Rd. KT17: Eps 3D 34
Longfellow Rd.
KT4: Wor Pk 6D 24
Longfield Dr. SW14 ....2J 11
Longfield St. SW18 ....4K 13
Longford Cl. TW12: Hamp H ..1F 15
TW13: Hanw 7G 8
Longford Ho. TW12: Hamp H ..1F 15
Longford Rd. TW2: Whit 5F 9
Long Gro. Rd. KT19: Eps 6J 29
Long Lodge Dr. KT12: Walt T ..7B 20

Longmead Bus. Cen.
KT19: Eps 7A 30
Longmead Rd. KT7: T Ditt ...4K 21
KT19: Eps, Ewe 7A 30
Longmoor Point SW15 ......5E 12
(off Norley Vale)
Longmore Rd. KT12: Hers ...1D 26
Longridge Rd. SW5 ....1K 7
Longs Cl. TW9: Rich 1G 11
Longshott Ct. SW5 ....1K 7
(off W. Cromwell Rd.)
Longstaff Cres. SW18 ......3K 13
Longstaff Rd. SW18 ....3K 13
Longthorpe Ct. W6 ....1D 6
(off Invermead Cl.)
Long Wlk. KT3: N Mald 7K 17
KT18: Tatt C 7F 35
SW13 ....6B 6
Longwater Ho. KT1: King T ...6B 36
Longwood Dr. SW15 ....3D 12
Lonsdale Cl. KT6: Surb 4E 22
Lonsdale M. TW9: Kew 5H 5
Lonsdale Rd. SW13 ....5C 6
W4 ....1C 6
Loop Rd. KT18: Eps 5K 33
Lorac Ct. SM2: Sutt 4K 31
Loraine Gdns. KT21: Asht ...6F 33
Loraine Rd. W4 ....3J 5
Lord Chancellor Wlk.
KT2: King T 5K 17
Lordell Pl. SW19 ....3F 19
Lord Napier Pl. W6 ....2D 6
Lord Roberts M. SW6 ......4K 7
Lords Cl. TW13: Hanw 6D 8
Loring Rd. TW7: Isle 6A 4
Lorne Rd. TW10: Rich 2G 11
Loseberry Rd. KT10: Clay ...2J 27
Louisa Cl. TW2: Twick 6K 9
Lovekyn Cl.
KT2: King T 3E 36 (6F 17)
Lovelace Gdns. KT6: Surb ...4E 22
KT12: Hers 2B 26
Lovelace Rd. KT6: Surb 4D 22
Lovelace Vs. KT7: T Ditt 4C 22
(off Portsmouth Rd.)
Love La. KT6: Surb 6D 22
SM1: Sutt 3J 31
SM3: Cheam, Sutt 3H 31
SM4: Mord 4K 25
Lovell Rd. TW10: Ham 7D 10
LOWER ASHTEAD 7E 32
Lower Comn. Sth. SW15 ....7E 6
Lower Ct. Rd. KT19: Eps 7K 29
Lwr. Downs Rd. SW20 ......5G 19
Lower Dunnymans
SM7: Bans 3J 35
Lwr. George St. TW9: Rich ...2E 10
LOWER GREEN 6G 21
Lower Grn. Gdns.
KT4: Wor Pk 5D 24
Lwr. Grn. Rd. KT10: Esh 6G 21
Lwr. Gro. Rd. TW10: Rich ...3G 11
Lwr. Hampton Rd.
TW16: Sun 7B 14
Lwr. Ham Rd.
KT2: King T 1C 36 (2E 16)
Lwr. Hill Rd. KT19: Eps 1J 33
Lwr. King's Rd.
KT2: King T 1C 36 (5F 17)
Lower Mall W6 ....2E 6
Lwr. Marsh La.
KT1: King T 7E 36 (1G 23)
(not continuous)
Lower Mill KT17: Ewe 4C 30
Lwr. Morden La. SM4: Mord ..3F 25
Lwr. Mortlake Rd. TW9: Rich ..1F 11
Lwr. Northfield SM7: Bans ...3J 35
Lwr. Richmond Rd.
SW14 ....7J 5
SW15 ....7E 6
TW9: Rich 7H 5
Lwr. Sand Hills KT6: Surb ...4D 22
Lwr. Sawleywood SM7: Bans ..3J 35
Lower Sq. TW7: Isle 7C 4
Lwr. Sunbury Rd.
TW12: Hamp 6E 14
Lwr. Teddington Rd.
KT1: Hamp W 1A 36 (5E 16)
Lwr. Wood Rd. KT10: Clay ...3C 28
Lowther Rd. KT2: King T 5G 17
SW13 ....5C 6

Meadow Wlk.—Nassau Rd.

Meadow Wlk. KT17: Ewe 4C 30
KT19: Ewe 3B 30
(not continuous)
Meadow Way KT9: Chess 2F 29
KT20: Tad 6H 35
Mead Rd. KT12: Hers 7D 20
TW10: Ham 7D 10
Meads, The SM3: Cheam 7H 25
Meadside *KT18: Eps* 3A 34
(off South St.)
Meadway KT5: Surb 5K 23
KT10: Esh 5G 27
KT19: Eps 1K 33
SW20 1F 25
TW2: Twick 5J 9
Meadway Ct. TW11: Tedd 2D 16
Mecca Bingo
Fulham Broadway 4K 7
(off Vanston Pl.)
Medcroft Gdns. SW14 1K 11
Medfield St. SW15 4D 12
Medina Av. KT10: Hin W 7K 21
Medina Sq. KT19: Eps 5H 29
Medway Ho.
KT2: King T 1B 36 (5E 16)
Megabowl
Feltham 6A 8
Melancholy Wlk.
TW10: Ham 6D 10
Melbourne Mans. *W14* 3H 7
(off Musard Rd.)
Melbourne Rd. SW19 5K 19
TW11: Tedd 3D 16
Melbourne Ter. *SW6* 4K 7
(off Moore Pk. Rd.)
Melbray M. SW6 6J 7
Melbury Cl. KT10: Clay 3C 28
Melbury Gdns. SW20 5E 18
Meldone Cl. KT5: Surb 4J 23
Melford Cl. KT9: Chess 2G 29
Melina Ct. SW15 7D 6
Melliss Av. TW9: Kew 5J 5
Mellor Cl. KT12: Walt T 4E 20
Melrose Av. SW19 6J 13
TW2: Whit 4G 9
Melrose Gdns. KT3: N Mald 7A 18
KT12: Hers 2B 26
Melrose Rd. SW13 6C 6
SW18 3J 13
SW19 6K 19
Melton Flds. KT19: Ewe 5A 30
Melton Pl. KT19: Ewe 5A 30
Melville Av. SW20 4D 18
Melville Rd. SW13 5D 6
Mendip Cl. KT4: Wor Pk 5F 25
Mendora Rd. SW6 4H 7
Mercer Cl. KT7: T Ditt 4A 22
Mercers Pl. W6 1G 7
Mercier Rd. SW15 2H 13
Mercury Cen. TW14: Felt 2A 8
Mercury Ho. *TW8: Bford* 3D 4
(off Glenhurst Rd.)
Mercury Rd. TW8: Bford 3D 4
Mere Cl. SW15 4G 13
Meredyth Rd. SW13 6D 6
Mereway Rd. TW2: Twick 5J 9
Merivale Rd. SW15 1H 13
Merland Ri. KT18: Tatt C 7F 35
Merling Cl. KT9: Chess 2D 28
Merrilands Rd. KT4: Wor Pk 5F 25
Merrilyn Cl. KT10: Clay 3B 28
Merrington Rd. SW6 3K 7
Merritt Gdns. KT9: Chess 3D 28
(not continuous)
Merrow Rd. SM2: Cheam 5G 31
Merryweather Ct.
KT3: N Mald 2B 24
Mersey Ct.
KT2: King T 1B 36 (5E 16)
Merthyr Ter. SW13 3E 6
Merton Av. W4 1C 6
Merton Hall Gdns.
SW20 5H 19
Merton Hall Rd. SW19 4H 19
Merton Mans. SW20 6G 19
MERTON PARK 6K 19
Merton Pk. Pde. SW19 5J 19
Merton Park Stop (CT) 5K 19
Merton Rd. SW18 3K 13
Merton Wlk. KT22: Lea 7B 32
Merton Way KT8: W Mole 1G 21
KT22: Lea 7B 32
Metcalf Wlk. TW13: Hanw 1D 14
Metro Ind. Cen. TW7: Isle 6A 4
Metropolitan Sta. Bldgs.
W6 1F 7
(off Beadon Rd.)
Mews, The TW1: Twick 3C 10
Mexfield Rd. SW15 2J 13
Michaelmas Cl. SW20 7F 19
Michael Stewart Ho.
SW6 3J 7
(off Clem Attlee Ct.)
Michelham Gdns.
TW1: Twick 7A 10
Michelsdale Dr. TW9: Rich 1F 11
Michel's Row *TW9: Rich* 1F 11
(off Michelsdale Dr.)
Mickleham Gdns.
SM3: Cheam 3H 31
Micklethwaite Rd. SW6 3K 7
Midas Metropolitan Ind. Est.
SM4: Mord 4F 25
Middle Cl. KT17: Eps 1B 34
Middle Grn. Cl. KT5: Surb 3G 23
Middle La. KT17: Eps 1B 34
TW11: Tedd 3A 16
Middle Mill Hall
KT1: King T 6D 36 (7G 17)
Middlesex Ct. W4 1C 6
Middleton Rd. KT3: N Mald 7K 17
KT19: Ewe 6A 30
SM4: Mord 3K 25
Midhurst Rd. W13 1C 4
Midmoor Rd. SW19 5G 19
Midsummer Av. TW4: Houn 1E 8
Midway KT12: Walt T 6A 20
SM3: Sutt 4J 25
Miena Way KT21: Asht 6E 32
Milbourne La. KT10: Esh 3H 27
Milbrook KT10: Esh 3H 27
Milburn Wlk. KT18: Eps 4B 34
Miles Pl. KT5: Surb 7E 36 (1G 23)
Miles Rd. KT19: Eps 1A 34
MILESTONE GREEN 1K 11
Milestone Ho. KT1: King T 6B 36
Millais Cres. KT19: Ewe 2B 30
Millais Rd. KT3: N Mald 4B 24
Millais Way KT19: Ewe 1K 29
Millbourne Rd. TW13: Hanw 1D 14
Mill Farm Bus. Pk.
TW4: Houn 4D 8
Mill Farm Cres. TW4: Houn 5D 8
Millfield KT1: King T 5E 36 (7G 17)
Millfield Rd. TW4: Houn 5D 8
Mill Hill SW13 6D 6
Mill Hill Rd. SW13 6D 6
Milliners Ho. SW18 1K 13
Mill La. KT17: Ewe 5C 30
Millmead KT10: Esh 6F 21
Mill Pl. KT1: King T 5D 36 (7G 17)
Mill Plat TW7: Isle 6B 4
(not continuous)
Mill Plat Av. TW7: Isle 6B 4
Mill Rd. KT10: Esh 6F 21
KT17: Eps 1C 34
TW2: Twick 6H 9
Millshot Cl. SW6 5F 7
Millside Pl. TW7: Isle 6C 4
Mills Rd. KT12: Hers 2B 26
Mills Row W4 1A 6
Mill St. KT1: King T 5D 36 (7F 17)
Mill Vw. Cl. KT17: Ewe 4C 30
Mill Way TW14: Felt 2A 8
Millwood Rd. TW3: Houn 2H 9
Milner Dr. KT11: Cobh 7E 26
TW2: Whit 4J 9
Milner Rd.
KT1: King T 6B 36 (7E 16)
SW19 5K 19
Milnthorpe Rd. W4 3A 6
Milton Ct. SW18 2K 13
TW2: Twick 7K 9
Milton Gdns. KT18: Eps 3B 34
Milton Ho. SM1: Sutt 7K 25
Milton Lodge TW2: Twick 4A 10
Milton Mans. *W14* 3H 7
(off Queen's Club Gdns.)
Milton Rd. KT12: Walt T 7C 20
SM1: Sutt 7K 25
SW14 7A 6
TW12: Hamp 4F 15
Mimosa St. SW6 5J 7
Mina Rd. SW19 5K 19
Minden Rd. SM3: Sutt 6J 25
Minerva Rd.
KT1: King T 3E 36 (6G 17)
Minniedale KT5: Surb 2G 23
Minstead Gdns. SW15 4C 12
Minstead Way KT3: N Mald 3B 24
Minster Av. SM1: Sutt 6K 25
Minster Gdns. KT8: W Mole 1E 20
Minstrel Gdns. KT5: Surb 1G 23
Mirabel Rd. SW6 4J 7
Mission Sq. TW8: Bford 3F 5
Misty's Fld. KT12: Walt T 5B 20
Mitford Cl. KT9: Chess 3D 28
Moat, The KT3: N Mald 5B 18
Moat Ct. KT21: Asht 6F 33
Moat La. KT8: E Mos 7A 16
Moat Side TW13: Hanw 1B 14
Modder Pl. SW15 1G 13
Model Cotts. SW14 1K 11
Moffat Ct. SW19 2K 19
Mogden La. TW7: Isle 2A 10
Mole Abbey Gdns.
KT8: W Mole 7G 15
Mole Ct. KT19: Ewe 1K 29
Molember Ct. KT8: E Mos 1K 21
Molember Rd. KT8: E Mos 2K 21
Mole Rd. KT12: Hers 2C 26
Molesey Av. KT8: W Mole 2E 20
Molesey Cl. KT12: Hers 7D 20
Molesey Dr. SM3: Cheam 6H 25
MOLESEY HOSPITAL 2F 21
Molesey Pk. Av.
KT8: W Mole 2G 21
Molesey Pk. Cl. KT8: E Mos 2H 21
Molesey Pk. Rd.
KT8: W Mole, E Moss 2G 21
Molesey Rd. KT8: W Mole 4D 20
KT12: Hers, Walt T, W Mole
2C 26
Molesford Rd. SW6 5K 7
Molesham Cl. KT8: W Mole 7G 15
Molesham Way
KT8: W Mole 7G 15
Moles Hill KT22: Oxs 7J 27
Monaveen Gdns.
KT8: W Mole 7G 15
Moncks Row SW18 3J 13
Mongers La. KT17: Ewe 6C 30
(not continuous)
Monkleigh Rd. SM4: Mord 7H 19
Monks Av. KT8: W Mole 2E 20
Monks Cres. KT12: Walt T 5A 20
Monks Rd. SM7: Bans 6K 35
Monmouth Av.
KT1: Hamp W 1A 36 (4D 16)
Monmouth Cl. W4 1K 5
Monmouth Gro. TW8 1F 5
Mono La. TW13: Felt 6A 8
Monroe Dr. SW14 2J 11
Monro Pl. KT19: Eps 5H 29
Montague Cl. KT12: Walt T 4A 20
Montague Rd. SW19 4K 19
TW3: Houn 1G 9
TW10: Rich 3F 11
Montana Rd. SW20 5F 19
Montem Rd. KT3: N Mald 1B 24
Montford Rd. TW16: Sun 1A 20
Montfort Pl. SW19 5G 13
Montgomery Av.
KT10: Hin W 6K 21
Montgomery Ct. W4 4K 5
Montgomery Rd. W4 1K 5
Montolieu Gdns. SW15 2E 12
Montpelier Row TW1: Twick 4D 10
Montpellier Ct. KT12: Walt T 3A 20
Montrose Av. TW2: Whit 4G 9
Montrose Gdns. KT22: Oxs 7J 27
Montrouge Cres.
KT17: Eps D 5F 35
Montserrat Rd. SW15 1H 13
Moore Cl. SW14 7K 5
Moore Pk. Rd. SW6 4K 7
Moore Way SM2: Sutt 5K 31
Moorfield Rd. KT9: Chess 2F 29
Moorings Ho. TW8: Bford 4D 4
Moorland Cl. TW2: Whit 4F 9
Moorlands *KT12: Walt T* 7A 20
(off Ashley Pk. Rd.)
Moor La. KT9: Chess 1F 29
Moormead Dr. KT19: Ewe 2B 30
Moor Mead Rd. TW1: Twick 3B 10
Moor Pk. Gdns. KT2: King T 4B 18
Morden Ct. SM4: Mord 1K 25
Morden Ct. Pde. SM4: Mord 1K 25
Morden Ho. SM4: Mord 1K 25
MORDEN PARK 3H 25
Morden Pk. Pool 3J 25
Morden South Station (Rail) 2K 25
Morden Station (Tube) 7K 19
Morden Way SM3: Sutt 4K 25
More Cl. W14 1G 7
Morecoombe Cl. KT2: King T 4J 17
More La. KT10: Esh 7G 21
Moresby Av. KT5: Surb 4J 23
Moreton Rd. KT4: Wor Pk 6D 24
Morgan Rd. TW11: Tedd 3K 15
Morland Cl. TW12: Hamp 2E 14
Morley Rd. SM3: Sutt 5J 25
TW1: Twick 3E 10
Morningside Rd.
KT4: Wor Pk 6E 24
Mornington Av. W14 1J 7
Mornington Wlk. TW10: Ham 1D 16
Morris Gdns. SW18 4K 13
Morris Rd. TW7: Isle 7A 4
Mortimer Cres. KT4: Wor Pk 7A 24
Mortimer Ho. *W14* 1H 7
(off Nth. End Rd.)
MORTLAKE 7A 6
Mortlake Crematorium
TW9: Rich 6J 5
Mortlake High St.
SW14 7A 6
Mortlake Rd. TW9: Kew, Rich 4H 5
Mortlake Station (Rail) 7K 5
Mortlake Ter. *TW9: Kew* 4H 5
(off Mortlake Rd.)
Mospey Cres. KT17: Eps 4C 34
Mossville Gdns. SM4: Mord 7J 19
Mostyn Rd. SW19 5J 19
MOTSPUR PARK 3D 24
Motspur Pk. KT3: N Mald 3C 24
Motspur Park Station (Rail) 2E 24
Mount, The KT3: N Mald 7C 18
KT4: Wor Pk 1E 30
KT10: Esh 3F 27
KT17: Ewe 6C 30
Mt. Angelus Rd. SW15 4C 12
Mt. Ararat Rd. TW10: Rich 2F 11
Mountcombe Cl. KT6: Surb 4F 23
Mount Ct. SW15 7H 7
Mount M. TW12: Hamp 5G 15
Mount Pleasant KT17: Ewe 6C 30
Mt. Pleasant Rd.
KT3: N Mald 7K 17
Mount Rd. KT3: N Mald 7A 18
KT9: Chess 2G 29
SW19 6K 13
TW13: Hanw 7D 8
Mount Vw. Rd. KT10: Clay 4C 28
Mount Wood KT8: W Mole 7G 15
Mowat Ct. *KT4: Wor Pk* 6C 24
(off Avenue, The)
Mowbray Rd. TW10: Ham 7D 10
Moylan Rd. W6 3H 7
Muirdown Av. SW14 1A 12
Mulberry Ct. KT6: Surb 4E 22
TW1: Twick 7A 10
Mulberry Cres. TW8: Bford 4C 4
Mulberry Ga. SM7: Bans 5J 35
Mulberry Pl. W6 2D 6
Mulgrave Rd. SM2: Sutt 4J 31
SW6 3J 7
Mullins Path SW14 7A 6
Munden St. W14 1H 7
Mund St. W14 2J 7
Munnings Gdns. TW7: Isle 2J 9
Munro Ho. KT11: Cobh 7C 26
Munster Av. TW4: Houn 2D 8
Munster Ct. SW6 6J 7
TW11: Tedd 3D 16
Munster M. SW6 4H 7
Munster Rd. SW6 4H 7
TW11: Tedd 3C 16
Murfett Cl. SW19 6H 13
Murray Av. TW3: Houn 2G 9
Murray Ct. TW2: Twick 6J 9
Murray Rd. SW19 3G 19
TW10: Ham 6C 10
W5 1D 4
Murray Ter. W5 1E 4
Murreys, The KT21: Asht 7D 32
Murreys Ct. KT21: Asht 7E 32
Musard Rd. W6 3H 7
W14 3H 7
Muscal *W6* 3H 7
(off Field Rd.)
Mus. of Richmond 2E 10
(off Whittaker Av.)
Mus. of Rugby, The 3K 9
Musgrave Cres. SW6 4K 7
Musgrave Rd. TW7: Isle 5A 4
Mustow Pl. SW6 6J 7
Muybridge Rd. KT3: N Mald 6K 17
Mylne Cl. W6 2D 6
Mynn's Cl. KT18: Eps 3J 33
Myrtle Gro. KT3: N Mald 6K 17
Myrtle Rd. TW12: Hamp H 3H 15

N

Nailhead Rd. TW13: Hanw 2B 14
Napier Av. SW6 7J 7
Napier Ct. *SW6* 7J 7
(off Ranelagh Gdns.)
Napier Pl. W14 1J 7
Napier Rd. TW7: Isle 1B 10
W14 1J 7
Napoleon Rd. TW1: Twick 4C 10
Narborough St. SW6 6K 7
Narwhal Inuit Art Gallery 1A 6
Naseby Cl. TW7: Isle 5A 4
Naseby Ct. KT12: Walt T 6B 20
Nasmyth St. W6 1E 6
Nassau Rd. SW13 5C 6

Natalie M.—Old Lodge Pl.

Natalie M. TW2: Twick 7J 9
NHS WALK-IN CENTRE
(CHARING CROSS) *2G 7*
(in Charing Cross Hospital)
NHS WALK-IN CENTRE
(PARSONS GREEN) 5K 7
NHS WALK-IN CENTRE
(TEDDINGTON) *3K 15*
(in Teddington Memorial Hospital)
National Walks TW4: Houn 1E 8
Nella Rd. W6 . . . . .3G 7
Nell Gwynne Cl. KT19: Eps 7H 29
Nelson Cl. KT12: Walt T 5A 20
Nelson Gdns. TW3: Houn 3F 9
NELSON HOSPITAL 6J 19
Nelson Rd. KT3: N Mald 2A 24
TW2: Whit 4G 9
TW3: Houn 3F 9
Nelson Wlk. KT19: Eps 5H 29
Nene Gdns. TW13: Hanw 6E 8
Nepean St. SW15 . . . . .3D 12
Nero Ct. TW8: Bford 4E 4
Nescot Sports Cen. 7D 30
Netheravon Rd. W4 . . . . .1C 6
Netheravon Rd. Sth. W4 . . . . .2C 6
Netherbury Rd. W5 . . . . .1E 4
Netherton Rd. TW1: Twick 2B 10
Netley Cl. SM3: Cheam 2G 31
Netley Dr. KT12: Walt T 4E 20
Netley Rd. TW8: Bford 3F 5
Nevada Cl. KT3: N Mald 1K 23
Nevern Pl. SW5 . . . . .1K 7
Nevern Rd. SW5 . . . . .1K 7
Nevern Sq. SW5 . . . . .1K 7
Neville Av. KT3: N Mald 5A 18
Neville Cl. KT10: Esh 3E 26
SM7: Bans 3K 35
Neville Gill Cl. SW18 . . . . .3K 13
Neville Ho. Yd.
KT1: King T 3C 36 (6F 17)
Neville Rd. KT1: King T 6H 17
TW10: Ham 7D 10
Newark Ct. KT12: Walt T 5B 20
New Berry La. KT12: Hers 2C 26
Newbolt Av. SM3: Cheam 2F 31
Newborough Grn.
KT3: N Mald 1A 24
New B'way. TW12: Hamp H 2J 15
Newbury Gdns. KT19: Ewe 7C 24
New Chapel Sq. TW13: Felt 5A 8
New Chiswick Pool 4B 6
New Cl. TW13: Hanw 2D 14
Newcombe Gdns. TW4: Houn 1E 8
NEW EPSOM & EWELL COTTAGE
HOSPITAL, THE 7F 29
Newfield Cl. TW12: Hamp 5F 15
Newgate Cl. TW13: Hanw 6D 8
Newhall Gdns. KT12: Walt T 6B 20
New Horizons Ct. TW8: Bford 3B 4
Newhouse Cl. KT3: N Mald 4B 24
New Kelvin Av. TW11: Tedd 3K 15
New Kings Rd. SW6 . . . . .6J 7
Newlands, The KT7: T Ditt 5K 21
Newlands Av. KT7: T Ditt 5K 21
Newlands Cl. KT12: Hers 1D 26
Newlands Way KT9: Chess 2D 28
NEW MALDEN **1B 24**
New Malden Station (Rail) **7B 18**
Newmans La. KT6: Surb 3E 22
Newnes Path SW15 . . . . .1E 12
Newport Rd. SW13 . . . . .5D 6
New Rd. KT2: King T 4H 17
KT8: W Mole 1F 21
KT10: Esh 7H 21
KT22: Oxs 7A 28
TW3: Houn 1G 9
TW8: Bford 3E 4
TW10: Ham 1D 16
TW13: Hanw 2D 14
TW14: Felt 5A 8
Newry Rd. TW1: Twick 2B 10
Newstead Way SW19 . . . . .1G 19
Newton Gro. W4 . . . . .1B 6
Newton Mans. *W14* *3H 7*
(off Queen's Club Gdns.)
Newton Rd. SW19 . . . . .4H 19
TW7: Isle 6A 4
Newton's Yd. SW18 . . . . .2K 13
Newton Wood Rd.
KT21: Asht 5G 33
NEW VICTORIA HOSPITAL 5B 18
Niagara Av. W5 . . . . .1D 4
Nicholas Ct. *W4* *3B 6*
(off Corney Reach Way)
Nicholas Lodge KT10: Esh 6F 21
Nicholas M. W4 . . . . .3B 6
Nicholes Rd. TW3: Houn 1F 9
Nichols Cl. KT9: Chess 3D 28
Nicholson M.
KT1: King T 7D 36 (1F 23)
Nickols Wlk. SW18 . . . . .1K 13
Nicol Cl. TW1: Twick 3C 10
Nigel Fisher Way KT9: Chess 4D 28
Nigel Playfair Av. W6 . . . . .1E 6
Nightingale Cl. KT11: Cobh 7C 26
KT19: Eps 1H 33
W4 . . . . .3K 5
Nightingale Dr. KT19: Ewe 3J 29
Nightingale Ho. KT17: Eps 1B 34
Nightingale La. TW10: Rich 4F 11
Nightingale M. KT1: King T 5B 36
Nightingale Rd. KT8: W Mole 2G 21
KT10: Esh 2E 26
KT12: Walt T 4B 20
TW12: Hamp 2F 15
Nimbus Rd. KT19: Eps 6A 30
Niton Rd. TW9: Rich 7H 5
Niton St. SW6 . . . . .4G 7
Noble St. KT12: Walt T 7B 20
Nonsuch Ct. Av. KT17: Ewe 6E 30
Nonsuch Pl. *SM3: Cheam* *4G 31*
(off Ewell Rd.)
Nonsuch Trad. Est.
KT17: Eps 7B 30
Nonsuch Wlk. SM2: Cheam 6F 31
NORBITON **6H 17**
Norbiton Av. KT1: King T 5H 17
Norbiton Comn. Rd.
KT1: King T 7J 17
Norbiton Hall KT2: King T 6G 17
Norbiton Station (Rail) **5H 17**
Norbury Av. TW3: Houn 1J 9
Norcutt Rd. TW2: Twick 5K 9
Norfolk Cl. TW1: Twick 3C 10
Norfolk Gdns. TW4: Houn 2E 8
Norfolk Rd. KT10: Clay 2K 27
TW13: Felt 5B 8
Norfolk Ter. W6 . . . . .2H 7
NORK **4G 35**
Nork Gdns. SM7: Bans 3H 35
Nork Ri. SM7: Bans 5G 35
Nork Way SM7: Bans 5F 35
Norley Va. SW15 . . . . .5D 12
Norman Av. KT17: Eps 1C 34
TW1: Twick 4D 10
TW13: Hanw 6D 8
Normanby Cl. SW15 . . . . .2J 13
Norman Colyer Ct. KT19: Eps 6A 30
Normand Gdns. *W14* *3H 7*
(off Greyhound Rd.)
Normand M. W14 . . . . .3H 7
Normand Rd. W14 . . . . .3J 7
Norman Ho. *TW13: Hanw* *6E 8*
(off Watermill Way)
Normanhurst Dr. TW1: Twick 2B 10
Normanhurst Rd.
KT12: Walt T 6C 20
Norman Rd. SM1: Sutt 2K 31
Normansfield Av.
TW11: Tedd 4D 16
Normanton Av. SW19 . . . . .6K 13
Norroy Rd. SW15 . . . . .1G 13
Norstead Pl. SW15 . . . . .6D 12
North Acre SM7: Bans 5J 35
North Av. TW9: Kew 5H 5
NORTH CHEAM **7F 25**
North Cheam Sports Club 7G 25
Northcliffe Cl. KT4: Wor Pk 7B 24
North Cl. SM4: Mord 1H 25
Northcote Av. KT5: Surb 4J 23
TW7: Isle 2B 10
Northcote Rd. KT3: N Mald 7K 17
TW1: Twick 2B 10
Northcroft Rd. KT19: Ewe 4B 30
Northdown Rd. SM2: Sutt 6K 31
North E. Surrey Crematorium
SM4: Mord 3F 25
Nth. End Cres. W14 . . . . .1J 7
Nth. End Ho. W14 . . . . .1H 7
Nth. End Pde. *W14* *1H 7*
(off Nth. End Rd.)
Nth. End Rd. SW6 . . . . .1H 7
W14 .1H 7
Northernhay Wlk.
SM4: Mord 1H 25
Northey Av. SM2: Cheam 6G 31
Nth. Eyot Gdns. W6 . . . . .2C 6
NORTH FELTHAM **3A 8**
Nth. Feltham Trad. Est.
TW14: Felt 2A 8
Northfield Av. W5 . . . . .1D 4
Northfield Cres.
SM3: Cheam 1H 31
NORTHFIELDS **1C 4**
Northfields KT17: Eps 7B 30
KT21: Asht 7F 33
(not continuous)
SW18 . . . . .1K 13
Northfields Prospect Bus. Cen.
SW18 . . . . .1K 13
Northfields Station (Tube) **1D 4**
North La. TW11: Tedd 3A 16
Nth. Lodge Cl. SW15 . . . . .2G 13
NORTH LOOE **2F 35**
North Mall *SW18* *2K 13*
(off Buckhold Rd.)
North Pde. KT9: Chess 2G 29
North Pas. SW18 . . . . .2K 13
North Pl. TW11: Tedd 3A 16
North Rd. KT6: Surb 3E 22
KT12: Hers 2B 26
TW8: Bford 3F 5
TW9: Kew 5H 5
TW9: Rich 7H 5
W5 . . . . .1E 4
NORTH SHEEN **7H 5**
North Sheen Station (Rail) **1H 11**
Northspur Rd. SM1: Sutt 7K 25
North St. TW7: Isle 7B 4
Northumberland Av. TW7: Isle 5A 4
Northumberland Gdns.
TW7: Isle 4B 4
Northumberland Pl.
TW10: Rich 2E 10
Northumberland Row
TW2: Twick 5K 9
Nth. Verbena Gdns.
W6 . . . . .2D 6
North Vw. SW19 . . . . .2F 19
North Vw. Cres. KT18: Tatt C 6E 34
Northway SM4: Mord 7H 19
Northweald La. KT2: King T 2E 16
Nth. Weylands Ind. Est.
KT12: Walt T 6D 20
Nth. Worple Way SW14 . . . . .7A 6
Norton Av. KT5: Surb 4J 23
Norwood Cl. TW2: Twick 6J 9
Norwood Farm La.
KT11: Cobh 7A 26
Nottingham Rd. TW7: Isle 6A 4
Nova M. SM3: Sutt 5H 25
Novello St. SW6 . . . . .5K 7
Nowell Rd. SW13 . . . . .3D 6
Numa Ct. TW8: Bford 4E 4
Nursery Cl. KT17: Ewe 6B 30
SW15 . . . . .1G 13
TW14: Felt 4A 8
(not continuous)
Nursery Gdns. TW4: Houn 2E 8
TW12: Hamp 1E 14
Nursery Rd. SW19 . . . . .4H 19
Nye Bevan Ho. *SW6* *4J 7*
(off St Thomas's Way)
Nylands Av. TW9: Kew 5H 5
Nymans Gdns. SW20 . . . . .7E 18

O

Oak Av. TW12: Hamp 2D 14
Oakbank Av. KT12: Walt T 4E 20
Oakbark Ho. *TW8: Bford* *4D 4*
(off High St.)
Oakcombe Cl. KT3: N Mald 5B 18
Oakcroft Bus. Cen.
KT9: Chess 1G 29
Oakcroft Rd. KT9: Chess 1G 29
Oakcroft Vs. KT9: Chess 1G 29
Oakdale Rd. KT19: Ewe 5A 30
Oakdene Av. KT7: T Ditt 5B 22
Oakdene Ct. KT12: Walt T 7A 20
Oakdene Dr. KT5: Surb 4K 23
Oakdene M. SM3: Sutt 5J 25
Oake Ct. SW15 . . . . .2H 13
Oakeford Ho. *W14* *1H 7*
(off Russell Rd.)
Oaken Dr. KT10: Clay 3A 28
Oaken La. KT10: Clay 1K 27
Oakenshaw Cl. KT6: Surb 4F 23
Oakfield Cl. KT3: N Mald 2C 24
Oakfield Rd. KT21: Asht 6E 32
SW19 . . . . .7G 13
Oakfields KT12: Walt T 5A 20
Oak Glade KT19: Eps 1H 33
Oak Gro. TW16: Sun 4A 14
Oak Hill KT6: Surb 4F 23
KT18: Eps 5A 34
Oakhill KT10: Clay 3B 28
Oakhill Cl. KT21: Asht 7D 32
Oakhill Ct. SW19 . . . . .4G 19
Oak Hill Cres. KT6: Surb 4F 23
Oakhill Dr. KT6: Surb 4F 23
Oak Hill Gro. KT6: Surb 3F 23
Oak Hill Path KT6: Surb 3F 23
Oakhill Pl. SW15 . . . . .2K 13
Oak Hill Rd. KT6: Surb 3F 23
Oakhill Rd. KT21: Asht 7D 32
SW15 . . . . .2J 13
Oak Ho. TW9: Kew 5J 5
Oakhurst Cl. TW11: Tedd 2K 15
Oakhurst Rd. KT19: Ewe 3K 29
Oakington Dr. TW16: Sun 6B 14
Oaklands Av. KT10: Esh 5J 21
TW7: Isle 3A 4
Oaklands Cl. KT9: Chess 1D 28
Oaklands Dr. TW2: Whit 4H 9
Oaklands Rd. SW14 . . . . .7A 6
Oakland Way KT19: Ewe 3B 30
Oak La. TW1: Twick 4B 10
TW7: Isle 1K 9
Oaklawn Rd. KT22: Lea 6A 32
Oak Leaf Cl. KT19: Eps 1K 33
Oaklea Pas.
KT1: King T 5B 36 (7E 16)
Oakleigh KT18: Eps 3B 34
Oakleigh Av. KT6: Surb 5H 23
Oakleigh Way KT6: Surb 5H 23
Oakley Gdns. SM7: Bans 4K 35
Oakley Wlk. W6 . . . . .3G 7
Oak Lodge Cl. KT12: Hers 2B 26
Oakman Ho. SW19 . . . . .5G 13
Oakmead Grn. KT18: Eps 4K 33
Oak Pk. Gdns. SW19 . . . . .5G 13
Oak Rd. KT3: N Mald 6A 18
KT22: Lea 7B 32
Oaks, The KT18: Eps 3C 34
SM4: Mord 1H 25
Oaks Av. KT4: Wor Pk 7E 24
TW13: Felt 6D 8
Oaks Cvn. Pk., The
KT9: Chess 7D 22
Oaks Sq., The *KT19: Eps* *2A 34*
(off High St.)
Oaks Way KT18: Tatt C 7E 34
Oaksway KT6: Surb 5E 22
Oak Way KT21: Asht 5H 33
Oakway SW20 . . . . .1F 25
Oakwood *KT18: Eps* *3B 34*
(off Worple Rd.)
Oakwood Av. KT19: Eps 5H 29
Oakwood Gdns. SM1: Sutt 6K 25
Oakwood Rd. SW20 . . . . .5D 18
Oarsman Pl. KT8: E Mos 1K 21
Oast Lodge *W4* *4B 6*
(off Corney Reach Way)
Observatory Rd. SW14 . . . . .1K 11
Occupation La. W5 . . . . .1E 4
Occupation Rd. KT19: Ewe 4A 30
Octavia Rd. TW7: Isle 7A 4
Odard Rd. KT8: W Mole 1F 21
Odeon Cinema
Epsom 2B 34
Esher 7G 21
Putney 7H 7
Richmond 2E 10
Wimbledon 3J 19
Offers Ct.
KT1: King T 5E 36 (7G 17)
Office Pk., The KT22: Lea 7A 32
Ogden Ho. TW13: Hanw 7D 8
Oil Mill La. W6 . . . . .2D 6
Old Barn Cl. SM2: Cheam 4H 31
Old Barn Rd. KT18: Eps 6K 33
OLD BRENTFORD **4E 4**
Old Bri. St.
KT1: Hamp W 3A 36 (6E 16)
Old Brompton Rd. SW5 . . . . .2K 7
Old Chestnut Av. KT10: Esh 3F 27
Old Chiswick Yd. *W4* *3B 6*
(off Pumping Sta. Rd.)
Old Chu. Path KT10: Esh 1H 27
Old Claygate La. KT10: Clay 3B 28
Old Comn. Rd. KT11: Cobh 7A 26
Old Deer Pk. 6D 4
Old Deer Pk. Gdns.
TW9: Rich 7F 5
Old Dock Cl. TW9: Kew 3H 5
Old Esher Cl. KT12: Hers 2C 26
Old Esher Rd. KT12: Hers 2C 26
Old Farm Cl. TW4: Houn 1E 8
Old Farm Pas. TW12: Hamp 5H 15
Old Farm Rd. TW12: Hamp 3E 14
(not continuous)
Oldfield Ct. *KT5: Surb* *1G 23*
(off Cranes Pk. Cres.)
Oldfield Gdns. KT21: Asht 7E 32
Oldfield Ho. *W4* *2B 6*
(off Devonshire Rd.)
Oldfield Rd. SW19 . . . . .3H 19
TW12: Hamp 5E 14
Oldfields Rd. SM1: Sutt 7J 25
Oldfields Trad. Est.
SM1: Sutt 7K 25
Old Ho. Cl. KT17: Ewe 6C 30
SW19 . . . . .2H 19
Old Ho. Gdns. TW1: Twick 3D 10
OLD ISLEWORTH **7C 4**
Old Kingston Rd.
KT4: Wor Pk 6K 23
Old Lodge Pl. TW1: Twick 3C 10

A-Z Richmond & Kingston 57

Old London Rd.—Pemberley Chase

Old London Rd.
KT2: King T 3D **36** (6F **17**)
KT18: Eps D 7D **34**
(not continuous)
OLD MALDEN 5B **24**
Old Malden La. KT4: Wor Pk 6A **24**
Old Mnr. Dr. TW7: Isle 3H **9**
Old Mnr. Yd. SW5 1K **7**
Old Oak Cl. KT9: Chess 1G **29**
Old Orchard TW16: Sun 6B **14**
Old Pal. La. TW9: Rich 2D **10**
Old Pal. Ter. TW9: Rich 2E **10**
Old Pal. Yd. TW9: Rich 2D **10**
Old Pound Cl. TW7: Isle 5B **4**
Old Rope Wlk. TW16: Sun 7A **14**
Old School Cl. SW19 6K **19**
Old Schools La. KT17: Ewe 5C **30**
Old School Sq. KT7: T Ditt 3A **22**
Old School Ter. SM3: Cheam 4G **31**
Old Sta. Gdns. *TW11: Tedd* *3B 16*
(off Victoria Rd.)
Oliver Cl. W4 3J **5**
Olive Rd. W5 1E **4**
Oliver Rd. KT3: N Mald 6K **17**
Olivette St. SW15 7G **7**
Olympia 1H **7**
Olympia Way W14 1H **7**
Ongar Rd. SW6 3K **7**
Onslow Av. SM2: Cheam 6J **31**
TW10: Rich 2F **11**
Onslow Cl. KT7: T Ditt 5K **21**
Onslow Gdns. KT7: T Ditt 5K **21**
Onslow Ho. KT2: King T 1E **36**
Onslow Rd. KT3: N Mald 1D **24**
KT12: Hers 3A **26**
TW10: Rich 2F **11**
Onslow Way KT7: T Ditt 5K **21**
Ophelia Ho. *W6* *2G 7*
(off Fulham Pal. Rd.)
Orangery, The TW10: Ham 6D **10**
Orange Tree Theatre 1F **11**
Orbain Rd. SW6 4H **7**
Orchard, The KT17: Ewe 4C **30**
(Meadow Wlk.)
KT17: Ewe 6C **30**
(Tayles Hill Dr.)
SM7: Bans 4K **35**
W4 1A **6**
Orchard Av. KT3: N Mald 6B **18**
KT7: T Ditt 5B **22**
Orchard Cl. KT6: T Ditt 5C **22**
KT12: Walt T 4A **20**
KT19: Ewe 3J **29**
SW20 1F **25**
Orchard Cotts. KT2: King T 5G **17**
Orchard Ct. KT4: Wor Pk 5D **24**
TW2: Twick 6J **9**
Orchard Gdns. KT9: Chess 1F **29**
KT18: Eps 3K **33**
SM1: Sutt 2K **31**
Orchard Ga. KT10: Esh 5J **21**
Orchard Ho. *SW6* *4J 7*
(off Varna Rd.)
Orchard La. KT8: E Mos 3J **21**
SW20 5E **18**
Orchard Ri. KT2: King T 5K **17**
TW10: Rich 1J **11**
Orchard Rd.
KT1: King T 4C **36** (6F **17**)
KT9: Chess 1F **29**
SM1: Sutt 2K **31**
TW1: Twick 2B **10**
TW4: Houn 2E **8**
TW8: Bford 3D **4**
TW9: Rich 7H **5**
TW12: Hamp 4E **14**
TW16: Sun 4A **14**
Orchard Sq. W14 2J **7**
Orchard Studios *W6* *1G 7*
(off Brook Grn.)
Orchard Way KT10: Esh 3H **27**
Orchid Cl. KT9: Chess 4D **28**
Orchid Gdns. TW3: Houn 1E **8**
Ordnance Cl. TW13: Felt 6A **8**
Oregon Cl. KT3: N Mald 1K **23**
Orford Gdns. TW1: Twick 6A **10**
ORGAN CROSSROADS 4D **30**
Oriel Dr. SW13 3F **7**
Orlando Gdns. KT19: Ewe 6A **30**
Orleans Cl. KT10: Esh 6J **21**
Orleans Ct. KT12: Walt T 6B **20**
TW1: Twick 4C **10**
Orleans House Gallery 5C **10**
Orleans Pk. School Sports Cen.
4C **10**
Orleans Rd. TW1: Twick 4C **10**
Orme Rd. KT1: King T 6J **17**
Ormond Av. TW10: Rich 2E **10**
TW12: Hamp 5G **15**
Ormond Cres. TW12: Hamp 5G **15**
Ormond Dr. TW12: Hamp 4G **15**
Ormonde Av. KT19: Ewe 6A **30**
Ormonde Ct. SW15 1F **13**
Ormonde Rd. SW14 7K **5**
Ormond Rd. TW10: Rich 2E **10**
Orpwood Cl. TW12: Hamp 3E **14**
Osborne Cl. TW13: Hanw 2C **14**
Osborne Rd. KT2: King T 4F **17**
KT12: Walt T 5A **20**
TW3: Houn 1E **8**
Osborne Way *KT9: Chess* *2G 29*
(off Bridge Rd.)
Osbourne Ho. TW2: Twick 6H **9**
Osier Ct. *TW8: Bford* *3F 5*
(off Ealing Rd.)
Osier M. W4 3B **6**
Osiers Ct. KT1: King T 2B **36**
Osiers Est., The SW18 1K **13**
Osiers Rd. SW18 1K **13**
Osier Way SM7: Bans 3H **35**
Osprey Cl. SM1: Sutt 2J **31**
Osram Ct. W6 1F **7**
Osterley Cres. TW7: Isle 5A **4**
Otho Ct. TW8: Bford 4E **4**
Otterburn Gdns. TW7: Isle 4B **4**
Ottway's Av. KT21: Asht 7F **33**
Oval, The SM7: Bans 3K **35**
Overdale KT21: Asht 4F **33**
Overdale Av. KT3: N Mald 6K **17**
Overstone Rd. W6 1F **7**
Overton Cl. TW7: Isle 5A **4**
Overton Ct. SM2: Sutt 4K **31**
Overton Ho. *SW15* *4C 12*
(off Tangley Gro.)
Overton Rd. SM2: Sutt 3K **31**
Owen Ho. TW1: Twick 4C **10**
Owen Mans. *W14* *3H 7*
(off Queen's Club Gdns.)
Oxberry Av. SW6 6H **7**
Oxford Av. SW20 6H **19**
Oxford Ct. KT18: Eps 3B **34**
TW13: Hanw 1C **14**
W4 2J **5**
Oxford Cres. KT3: N Mald 3A **24**
Oxford Gdns. W4 2H **5**
Oxford Ga. W6 1G **7**
Oxford Rd. SW15 1H **13**
TW11: Tedd 2J **15**
Oxford Rd. Nth. W4 2J **5**
Oxford Rd. Sth. W4 2H **5**
Oxford Way TW13: Hanw 1C **14**
Ox La. KT17: Ewe 5D **30**
Oxleigh Cl. KT3: N Mald 2B **24**
OXSHOTT 7K **27**
Oxshott Rd. KT22: Lea 5A **32**

P

Pachesham Dr. KT22: Lea 5A **32**
PACHESHAM PARK 5A **32**
Pachesham Pk. KT22: Lea 5B **32**
Packham Ct. KT4: Wor Pk 7F **25**
Paddenswick Rd. W6 1D **6**
Paddock Cl. KT4: Wor Pk 5B **24**
Paddocks, The *W5* *1E 4*
(off Popes La.)
Paddocks Cl. KT21: Asht 7F **33**
Paddocks Way KT21: Asht 7F **33**
Paddock Way KT17: Ewe 7F **31**
SW15 4F **13**
Padley Cl. KT9: Chess 2G **29**
Page Cl. TW12: Hamp 3D **14**
Pages Yd. W4 3C **6**
Paget Cl. TW12: Hamp H 1J **15**
Paget La. TW7: Isle 1J **9**
Paget Pl. KT2: King T 3K **17**
KT7: T Ditt 5A **22**
Pagoda Av. TW9: Rich 7G **5**
Palace Mans. *KT1: King T* *1E 22*
(off Palace Rd.)
W14 *1H 7*
(off Hammersmith Rd.)
Palace M. SW6 4K **7**
Palace Rd. KT1: King T 1E **22**
KT8: E Mos 7H **15**
Palace Wharf *W6* *4F 7*
(off Rainville Rd.)
Palemead Cl. SW6 5G **7**
Palewell Comn. Dr.
SW14 2A **12**
Palewell Pk. SW14 2A **12**
Palgrave Ho. TW2: Whit 4H **9**
Palgrave Rd. W12 1C **6**
Palliser Ct. *W14* *2H 7*
(off Palliser Rd.)
Palliser Rd. W14 2H **7**
Palmer Av. SM3: Cheam 1F **31**
Palmer Cres.
KT1: King T 5C **36** (7F **17**)
Palmersfield Rd. SM7: Bans 3K **35**
Palmers Gro. KT8: W Mole 1F **21**
Palmers Pas. *SW14* *7K 5*
(off Palmers Rd.)
Palmers Rd. SW14 7K **5**
Palmerston Ct. KT6: Surb 4E **22**
Palmerston Gro. SW19 4K **19**
Palmerston Mans. *W14* *3H 7*
(off Queen's Club Gdns.)
Palmerston Rd. SW14 1K **11**
SW19 4K **19**
TW2: Twick 3K **9**
Pams Way KT19: Ewe 2A **30**
Pankhurst Cl. TW7: Isle 7A **4**
Pankhurst Rd. KT12: Walt T 4B **20**
Panmuir Rd. SW20 5E **18**
Parade, The KT2: King T 3D **36**
KT4: Wor Pk 7C **24**
KT10: Clay 3K **27**
KT18: Eps *3H 33*
(off Spa Dr.)
KT18: Eps 2A **34**
(Parade, The)
KT20: Tad 7H **35**
SM1: Sutt 7J **25**
TW12: Tedd 2J **15**
Paradise Rd. TW9: Rich 2E **10**
Paragon Gro. KT5: Surb 3G **23**
Paragon Pl. KT5: Surb 3G **23**
Parbury Ri. KT9: Chess 3F **29**
Parfrey St. W6 3F **7**
Parish Ct. KT6: Surb 2F **23**
Park and Ride
Kingston upon Thames
(November-mid January)
5D **28**
Park Av. SW14 1A **12**
TW3: Houn 3G **9**
Park Av. E. KT17: Ewe 3D **30**
Park Av. W. KT17: Ewe 3D **30**
Park Cl. KT2: King T 5H **17**
KT10: Esh 3F **27**
TW3: Houn 2H **9**
TW12: Hamp 5H **15**
W4 3A **6**
Park Ct. KT1: Hamp W 5D **16**
KT3: N Mald 1A **24**
W6 1D **6**
Park Cres. TW2: Twick 5J **9**
Parkdale Cres. KT4: Wor Pk 7A **24**
Park Dr. KT21: Asht 7H **33**
SW14 2A **12**
W3 1H **5**
Parke Rd. SW13 5D **6**
TW16: Sun 1A **20**
Parker's Cl. KT21: Asht 7F **33**
Parker's La. KT21: Asht 7F **33**
Park Farm Rd. KT2: King T 4F **17**
Parkfield Av. SW14 1B **12**
TW13: Felt 7A **8**
Parkfield Cres. TW13: Felt 7A **8**
Parkfield Rd. TW13: Felt 7A **8**
Parkfields KT22: Oxs 7J **27**
SW15 1F **13**
Parkfields Av. SW20 5E **18**
Parkfields Rd. KT2: King T 2G **17**
Park Gdns. KT2: King T 2G **17**
Park Ga. Cl. KT2: King T 3J **17**
Park Ga. Ct. TW12: Hamp H 3H **15**
Parkgate Gdns. SW14 2A **12**
Park Hill TW10: Rich 3G **11**
Parkhill Rd. KT17: Ewe 7C **30**
Park Ho. Gdns. TW1: Twick 2D **10**
Parkhurst KT19: Eps 6K **29**
Parkland Gdns. SW19 5G **13**
Parklands KT5: Surb 2G **23**
Parklands Cl. SW14 2K **11**
Parklands Gro. TW7: Isle 5A **4**
Parklands Way KT4: Wor Pk 6B **24**
Park La. KT21: Asht 7G **33**
SM3: Cheam 3H **31**
TW9: Rich 1E **10**
TW11: Tedd 3A **16**
Parklawn Av. KT18: Eps 2J **33**
Parkleys TW10: Ham 1E **16**
Parkleys Pde. TW10: King T 1E **16**
Parkmead SW15 3E **12**
Park Pl. TW12: Hamp H 3H **15**
W3 1H **5**
Park Pl. Dr. W3 1H **5**
Park Rd.
KT1: Hamp W 2A **36** (5D **16**)
KT2: King T 2G **17**
KT3: N Mald 1A **24**
KT5: Surb 3G **23**
KT8: E Mos 1H **21**
KT10: Esh 1G **27**
KT21: Asht 7F **33**
SM3: Cheam 3H **31**
TW1: Twick 3D **10**
Park Rd. TW3: Houn 2G **9**
TW7: Isle 5C **4**
TW10: Rich 3G **11**
TW11: Tedd 3A **16**
TW12: Hamp H 1G **15**
TW13: Hanw 1C **14**
TW16: Sun 4A **14**
W4 4K **5**
Park Rd. Ho. KT2: King T 4H **17**
Park Rd. Nth. W4 2A **6**
Parkshot TW9: Rich 1E **10**
Parkside SM3: Cheam 3H **31**
SW19 7G **13**
TW12: Hamp H 2J **15**
Parkside Av. SW19 2G **19**
Parkside Cres. KT5: Surb 3K **23**
Parkside Gdns. SW19 1G **19**
PARKSIDE HOSPITAL 7G **13**
Parkside Rd. TW3: Houn 2G **9**
Park Sq. KT10: Esh 1G **27**
Parkstead Rd. SW15 2D **12**
Park St. TW11: Tedd 3K **15**
Park Ter. KT4: Wor Pk 5D **24**
Park Vw. KT3: N Mald 7C **18**
Parkview Ct. SW6 6H **7**
SW18 3K **13**
Parkville Rd. SW6 4J **7**
Park Wlk. KT21: Asht 7G **33**
Park Way KT8: W Mole 7G **15**
TW14: Felt 4A **8**
W3 1H **5**
Parkway SW20 1G **25**
Parkwood Av. KT10: Esh 5H **21**
Park Wood Cl. SM7: Bans 4G **35**
Park Wood Rd. SM7: Bans 4G **35**
Parkwood Rd. SW19 2J **19**
TW7: Isle 5A **4**
Park Wood Vw. SM7: Bans 5F **35**
Parliament M. SW14 6K **5**
Parr Av. KT17: Ewe 5E **30**
Parr Ct. TW13: Hanw 1B **14**
Parrs Pl. TW12: Hamp 4F **15**
Parry Cl. KT17: Ewe 4E **30**
Parsonsfield Cl. SM7: Bans 4G **35**
Parsonsfield Rd. SM7: Bans 5G **35**
PARSONS GREEN 6J **7**
Parson's Grn. SW6 5K **7**
Parson's Grn. La. SW6 5K **7**
Parsons Green Station (Tube) 5K **7**
Parsons Mead KT8: E Mos 7H **15**
Parthenia Rd. SW6 5K **7**
Partridge Mead SM7: Bans 4F **35**
Partridge Rd. TW12: Hamp 3E **14**
Passage, The TW9: Rich 2F **11**
Passfields *W14* *2J 7*
(off Star St.)
Patricia Gdns. SM2: Sutt 7K **31**
Patten All. TW10: Rich 2E **10**
Pauline Cres. TW2: Whit 5H **9**
Paul Robeson Theatre, The 1G **9**
Paul's Pl. KT21: Asht 7J **33**
Paul Vanson Ct. KT12: Hers 3C **26**
Paved Ct. TW9: Rich 2E **10**
Pavement, The *TW7: Isle* *7B 4*
(off South St.)
W5 1F **5**
Pavilion Sports & Fitness Club, The
7H **15**
Paxton Cl. KT12: Walt T 4B **20**
TW9: Kew 6G **5**
Paxton Rd. W4 3B **6**
Paynesfield Av. SW14 7A **6**
Paynes Wlk. W6 3H **7**
Peabody Est. *SW6* *3K 7*
(off Lillie Rd.)
W6 2F **7**
Peaches Cl. SM2: Cheam 4H **31**
Pearce Rd. KT8: W Mole 7G **15**
Pears Rd. TW3: Houn 1H **9**
Pear Tree Cl. KT9: Chess 2H **29**
Peek Cres. SW19 2G **19**
Peel Cen. Ind. Est.
KT17: Eps 7B **30**
Pegasus Ct.
KT1: King T 6B **36** (7E **16**)
KT10: Clay 3A **28**
SM7: Bans 4K **35**
TW8: Bford 2G **5**
Pegasus Pl. SW6 5K **7**
Pelabon Ho. *TW1: Twick* *3E 10*
(off Clevedon Rd.)
Peldon Ct. TW9: Rich 1G **11**
Peldon Pas. TW10: Rich 1G **11**
Pelham Ho. *W14* *1J 7*
(off Mornington Av.)
Pelham Rd. SW19 4K **19**
Pelham's Cl. KT10: Esh 1F **27**
Pelham's Wlk. KT10: Esh 7F **21**
Pellant Rd. SW6 4H **7**
Pemberley Chase KT19: Ewe 2J **29**

Pemberley Cl.—Quarry Ri.

Pemberley Cl. KT19: Ewe 2J **29**
Pemberley Ho. *KT19: Ewe* *2J **29***
(off Pemberley Chase)
Pemberton Pl. KT10: Esh 7H **21**
Pemberton Rd. KT8: E Mos 1H **21**
Pembridge Av. TW2: Whit 5E **8**
Pembridge Pl. SW15 . . . . 2K **13**
Pembroke Av. KT5: Surb 2J **23**
KT12: Hers 1C **26**
Pembroke Cl. SM7: Bans 5K **35**
Pembroke Cotts. *W8* *1K **7***
(off Pembroke Sq.)
Pembroke Gdns. W8 . . . . 1J **7**
Pembroke Gdns. Cl. W8 . . . . 1K **7**
Pembroke M. W8 . . . . 1K **7**
Pembroke Pl. W8 . . . . 1K **7**
Pembroke Rd. W8 . . . . 1J **7**
Pembroke Sq. W8 . . . . 1K **7**
Pembroke Studios W8 . . . . 1J **7**
Pembroke Vs. TW9: Rich 1E **10**
W8 . . . . 1K **7**
Pembroke Wlk. W8 . . . . 1K **7**
Pembury Av. KT4: Wor Pk 5D **24**
Penates KT10: Esh 7J **21**
Pendarves Rd. SW20 . . . . 5F **19**
Penderel Rd. TW3: Houn 2F **9**
Pendlebury Ct. *KT5: Surb* *1F **23***
(off Cranes Pk.)
Pennant M. W8 . . . . 1K **7**
Pennards, The TW16: Sun 7B **14**
Penner Cl. SW19 . . . . 6H **13**
Penners Gdns. KT6: Surb 4F **23**
Pennington Lodge
KT5: Surb *2F **23***
(off Cranes Dr.)
Penrhyn Cres. SW14 . . . . 1K **11**
Penrhyn Gdns.
KT1: King T 7B **36** (1E **22**)
Penrhyn Rd.
KT1: King T 7C **36** (1F **23**)
Penrith Cl. SW15 . . . . 2H **13**
Penrith Rd. KT3: N Mald 1A **24**
Penrose Dr. KT19: Eps 7H **29**
Pensford Av. TW9: Kew 6H **5**
Penshurst Way SM2: Sutt 4K **31**
Pentlow St. SW15 . . . . 7F **7**
Pentney Rd. SW19 . . . . 5H **19**
Penwith Rd. SW18 . . . . 6K **13**
Penwood Ho. SW15 . . . . 3C **12**
Penywern Rd. SW5 . . . . 2K **7**
Pepys Cl. KT21: Asht 6H **33**
Pepys Rd. SW20 . . . . 5F **19**
Percheron Cl. TW7: Isle 7A **4**
Percival Cl. KT22: Oxs 7G **27**
Percival Rd. SW14 . . . . 1K **11**
Percival Way KT19: Ewe 1A **30**
Percy Gdns. KT4: Wor Pk 5B **24**
TW7: Isle 7B **4**
Percy Laurie Ho. *SW15* *1G **13***
(off Nursery Cl.)
Percy Rd. TW2: Whit 5G **9**
TW7: Isle 1B **10**
TW12: Hamp 4F **15**
Percy Way TW2: Whit 5H **9**
Peregrine Way SW19 . . . . 4F **19**
Perham Rd. W14 . . . . 2H **7**
Perkin Cl. TW3: Houn 1F **9**
Perran Wlk. TW8: Bford 2F **5**
Perrers Rd. W6 . . . . 1E **6**
Perryfield Way TW10: Ham 7C **10**
Perry How KT4: Wor Pk 5C **24**
Perrymead St. SW6 . . . . 5K **7**
Perryn Ct. TW1: Twick 3B **10**
Perseverance Pl. TW9: Rich 1F **11**
Persfield Cl. KT17: Ewe 6C **30**
Persfield M. KT17: Ewe 6C **30**
Perth Cl. SW20 . . . . 6C **18**
Petavel Rd. TW11: Tedd 3K **15**
Peterborough M. SW6 . . . . 6K **7**
Peterborough Rd. SW6 . . . . 6K **7**
Peterborough Vs. SW6 . . . . 5K **7**
Peter Scott Vis. Cen., The 5E **6**
Petersfield Ri. SW15 . . . . 5E **12**
PETERSHAM 5F **11**
Petersham Cl. SM1: Sutt 2J **31**
TW10: Ham 6E **10**
Petersham Rd.
TW10: Rich, Ham 3E **10**
Peterstow Cl. SW19 . . . . 6H **13**
Petley Rd. W6 . . . . 3G **7**
Petters Rd. KT21: Asht 5G **33**
Pettiward Cl. SW15 . . . . 1F **13**
Petworth Gdns. SW20 . . . . 7E **18**
Pevensey Rd. TW13: Felt 5D **8**
Peveril Dr. TW11: Tedd 2J **15**
Philbeach Gdns. SW5 . . . . 2K **7**
Phoenix Cl. KT19: Eps 1H **33**
Phoenix Ct. KT3: N Mald 7C **18**
KT17: Eps *2B **34***
(off Church St.)
Phoenix Ct. TW4: Houn 2C **8**
TW8: Bford 2F **5**
Phoenix Lodge Mans.
W6 . . . . *1G **7***
(off Brook Grn.)
Phoenix Trad. Pk. TW8: Bford 2E **4**
Phyllis Av. KT3: N Mald 2E **24**
Pickering Ho. *W5* *1D **4***
(off Windmill Rd.)
Pickwick Cl. TW4: Houn 2D **8**
Picquets Way SM7: Bans 5H **35**
Picton Pl. KT6: Surb 5H **23**
Pier Rd. TW14: Felt 2A **8**
Pigeon La. TW12: Hamp 1F **15**
Pikemans Ct. *SW5* *1K **7***
(off W. Cromwell Rd.)
Pikes Hill KT17: Eps 2B **34**
Pilsden Cl. SW19 . . . . 5G **13**
Pine Gdns. KT5: Surb 3H **23**
Pine Gro. SW19 . . . . 2J **19**
Pine Hill KT18: Eps 4A **34**
Pine Pl. SM7: Bans 3G **35**
Pines, The KT9: Chess 7F **23**
TW16: Sun 7A **14**
Pine Wlk. KT5: Surb 3H **23**
Pine Wood TW16: Sun 5A **14**
Pinewood Pl. KT19: Ewe 1A **30**
Pinewood Rd. TW13: Felt 7A **8**
Pinkcoat Cl. TW13: Felt 7A **8**
Pinkham Mans. W4 . . . . 2H **5**
Piper Rd. KT1: King T 7H **17**
Pirbright Rd. SW18 . . . . 5J **13**
Pitt Cres. SW19 . . . . 1K **19**
Pitt Pl. KT17: Eps 3B **34**
Pitt Rd. KT17: Eps 3B **34**
Planetree Ct. *W6* *1G **7***
(off Brook Grn.)
Plane Tree Cres. TW13: Felt 7A **8**
Plantagenet Cl. KT4: Wor Pk 7A **24**
Platt, The SW15 . . . . 7G **7**
Playfair Mans. *W14* *3H **7***
(off Queen's Club Gdns.)
Playfair St. W6 . . . . 2F **7**
Pleasance, The SW15 . . . . 1E **12**
Pleasance Rd. SW15 . . . . 2E **12**
Pleasant Pl. KT12: Hers 3B **26**
Pleasure Pit Rd. KT21: Asht 7J **33**
Plevna Rd. TW12: Hamp 5G **15**
Pleydell Av. W6 . . . . 1C **6**
Plough La. TW11: Tedd 2B **16**
Ploughmans End
TW7: Isle 2J **9**
Plough Rd. KT19: Ewe 5A **30**
Plum Gth. TW8: Bford 1E **4**
Plymen Ho. KT8: W Mole 2F **21**
Plymouth Ct. *KT5: Surb* *1F **23***
(off Cranes Pk. Av.)
Pocklington Ct. SW15 . . . . 5D **12**
Pointers Cotts. TW10: Ham 6D **10**
Point Pleasant SW18 . . . . 1K **13**
Point Wharf TW8: Bford 4F **5**
Point Wharf La. TW8: Bford 4E **4**
Polehamptons, The
TW12: Hamp 5H **15**
Polesden Gdns. SW20 . . . . 6E **18**
Police Sta. Rd. KT12: Hers 3B **26**
Pollard Ho. KT4: Wor Pk 7F **25**
Pomeroy Cl. TW1: Twick 1C **10**
Pond Hill Gdns. SM3: Cheam 3H **31**
Pond Pl. KT21: Asht 6F **33**
Pond Way TW11: Tedd 3D **16**
Ponsonby Rd. SW15 . . . . 4E **12**
Pool Cl. KT8: W Mole 2E **20**
Poole Rd. KT19: Ewe 3A **30**
Pooles Cotts. TW10: Ham 6E **10**
Pool Rd. KT8: W Mole 2E **20**
Pools on the Pk. 1E **10**
Popes Av. TW2: Twick 6K **9**
Popes Ct. TW2: Twick 6K **9**
Popes Gro. TW1: Twick 6A **10**
TW2: Twick 6A **10**
Popes La. W5 . . . . 1E **4**
Popham Cl. TW13: Hanw 7E **8**
Popham Gdns. TW9: Rich 7H **5**
Popinjays Row *SM3: Cheam* *2G **31***
(off Netley Cl.)
Poplar Ct. SW19 . . . . 2K **19**
TW1: Twick 3D **10**
Poplar Cres. KT19: Ewe 3K **29**
Poplar Dr. SM7: Bans 3G **35**
Poplar Farm Cl. KT19: Ewe 3K **29**
Poplar Gdns. KT3: N Mald 6A **18**
Poplar Gro. KT3: N Mald 6A **18**
Poplar Rd. SM3: Sutt 5J **25**
SW19 . . . . 6K **19**
Poplar Rd. Sth. SW19 . . . . 7K **19**
Poplar Way TW13: Felt 7A **8**
Porchester Rd. KT1: King T 6J **17**
Porten Ho's. *W14* *1H **7***
(off Porten Rd.)
Porten Rd. W14 . . . . 1H **7**
Portinscale Rd. SW15 . . . . 2H **13**
Portland Av. KT3: N Mald 4C **24**
Portland Cl. KT4: Wor Pk 4E **24**
Portland Pl. KT17: Eps 1B **34**
Portland Rd.
KT1: King T 6D **36** (7F **17**)
Portland Ter. TW9: Rich 1E **10**
Portman Av. SW14 . . . . 7A **6**
Portman Rd. KT1: King T 6G **17**
Porton Ct. KT6: Surb 3D **22**
Portsmouth Av. KT7: T Ditt 4B **22**
Portsmouth Rd. KT1: King T 4B **22**
KT6: Surb 4B **22**
KT7: T Ditt 7B **36** (4B **22**)
KT10: Esh 3F **27**
(Old Chestnut Av.)
KT10: Esh 7H **21**
(Sandown Rd.)
KT11: Cobh 7C **26**
SW15 . . . . 4E **12**
Portswood Pl. SW15 . . . . 3C **12**
Portugal Gdns. TW2: Twick 6H **9**
Portway KT17: Ewe 5D **30**
Portway Cres. KT17: Ewe 5D **30**
Post La. TW2: Twick 5J **9**
Post Office All. TW12: Hamp 6G **15**
W4 . . . . *3J **5***
(off Thames Rd.)
Potterne Cl. SW19 . . . . 4G **13**
Potters Gro. KT3: N Mald 1K **23**
Pottery Rd. TW8: Bford 3F **5**
Poulett Gdns. TW1: Twick 5B **10**
Pound Cl. KT6: Surb 5D **22**
Pound Ct. KT21: Asht 7G **33**
Pound Farm Cl. KT10: Esh 5J **21**
Pound La. KT19: Eps 1K **33**
Pound Rd. SM7: Bans 6J **35**
Powder Mill La. TW2: Whit 4E **8**
Powell Cl. KT9: Chess 2E **28**
Powell's Wlk. W4 . . . . 3B **6**
Power Rd. W4 . . . . 1H **5**
Powers Ct. TW1: Twick 4E **10**
Pownall Gdns. TW3: Houn 1G **9**
Pownall Rd. TW3: Houn 1G **9**
Pratts La. KT12: Hers 1C **26**
Pratts Pas.
KT1: King T 4C **36** (6F **17**)
Prebend Gdns. W4 . . . . 1C **6**
W6 . . . . 1C **6**
(not continuous)
Prebend Mans. *W4* *1C **6***
(off Chiswick High Rd.)
Precinct, The KT8: W Mole 7G **15**
Precincts, The SM4: Mord 3K **25**
Premier Pl. SW15 . . . . 1H **13**
Prentice Ct. SW19 . . . . 2J **19**
Presburg Rd. KT3: N Mald 2B **24**
Preston Cl. TW2: Twick 7K **9**
Preston Ct. KT12: Walt T 5B **20**
Preston Dr. KT19: Ewe 3B **30**
Preston Gro. KT21: Asht 6D **32**
Preston Pl. TW10: Rich 2F **11**
Preston Rd. SW20 . . . . 4C **18**
Price Way TW12: Hamp 3D **14**
Priest's Bri. SW14 . . . . 7B **6**
Primrose Pl. TW7: Isle 6A **4**
Primrose Rd. KT12: Hers 2B **26**
Primrose Wlk. KT17: Ewe 4C **30**
Prince George's Av.
SW20 . . . . 6F **19**
Prince of Wales Ter.
W4 . . . . 2B **6**
Princes Av. KT6: Surb 5H **23**
W3 . . . . 1H **5**
Prince's Cl. TW11: Tedd 1J **15**
Prince's Dr. KT22: Oxs 7K **27**
Princes M. TW3: Houn 1F **9**
W6 . . . . *2E **6***
(off Down Pl.)
Princes Rd. KT2: King T 4H **17**
SW14 . . . . 7A **6**
SW19 . . . . 3K **19**
TW9: Kew 5G **5**
TW10: Rich 2G **11**
TW11: Tedd 1J **15**
PRINCESS ALICE HOSPICE 2F **27**
Princess Ct. KT1: King T 6E **36**
Princess M.
KT1: King T 6E **36** (7G **17**)
Princes St. TW9: Rich 1F **11**
Princes Way SW19 . . . . 4G **13**
W3 . . . . 1H **5**
Princeton Ct. SW15 . . . . 7G **7**
Princeton M. KT2: King T 5H **17**
Priors Wood KT10: Hin W 6A **22**
Priory Av. SM3: Cheam 1G **31**
W4 . . . . 1B **6**
Priory Cl. TW12: Hamp 5E **14**
TW16: Sun 4A **14**
Priory Ct. KT1: King T 5C **36**
KT17: Ewe 5C **30**
SM3: Cheam 1H **31**
Priory Cres. SM3: Cheam 1G **31**
Priory Gdns. SW13 . . . . 7C **6**
TW12: Hamp 4E **14**
W4 . . . . 1B **6**
Priory La. KT8: W Mole 1G **21**
SW15 . . . . 3B **12**
TW9: Kew 4H **5**
Priory Pl. KT12: Walt T 7A **20**
Priory Rd. KT9: Chess 7F **23**
SM3: Cheam 1G **31**
TW3: Houn 2H **9**
TW9: Kew 3H **5**
TW12: Hamp 4E **14**
W4 . . . . 1A **6**
Priory Ter. TW16: Sun 4A **14**
Profumo Rd. KT12: Hers 2C **26**
Prologis Pk. TW4: Houn 1B **8**
Promenade, The W4 . . . . 6B **6**
Promenade App. Rd. W4 . . . . 4B **6**
Prospect Cotts. SW18 . . . . 1K **13**
Prospect Cres. TW2: Whit 3H **9**
Prospect Ho. KT19: Eps 5J **29**
Prospect Pl. KT17: Eps 1B **34**
SW20 . . . . 4E **18**
W4 . . . . 2A **6**
Prospect Quay *SW18* *1K **13***
(off Lightermans Wlk.)
Prospect Rd. KT6: Surb 3D **22**
Prothero Rd. SW6 . . . . 4H **7**
Providence Pl. KT17: Eps 1B **34**
Public Record Office 4H **5**
Pulborough Rd. SW18 . . . . 4J **13**
Pulborough Way TW4: Houn 1B **8**
Pullman Gdns. SW15 . . . . 3F **13**
Pulteney Cl. TW7: Isle 7B **4**
Pulton Pl. SW6 . . . . 4K **7**
Pump All. TW8: Bford 4E **4**
Pumping Sta. Rd. W4 . . . . 4B **6**
Purbeck Av. KT3: N Mald 3C **24**
Purberry Gro. KT17: Ewe 6C **30**
Purcell Cres. SW6 . . . . 4G **7**
(not continuous)
Purcell Mans. *W14* *3H **7***
(off Queen's Club Gdns.)
Purcell's Cl. KT21: Asht 7G **33**
Purdy Ct. KT4: Wor Pk 6D **24**
Pursers Cross Rd. SW6 . . . . 5J **7**
(not continuous)
PUTNEY 1G **13**
Putney Arts Theatre 1G **13**
Putney Bri. SW6 . . . . 7H **7**
SW15 . . . . 7H **7**
Putney Bri. App. SW6 . . . . 7H **7**
Putney Bri. Rd. SW15 . . . . 1H **13**
SW18 . . . . 1H **13**
Putney Bridge Station (Tube) 7J **7**
Putney Comn. SW15 . . . . 7F **7**
Putney Exchange Shop. Cen.
SW15 . . . . 1G **13**
PUTNEY HEATH 3F **13**
Putney Heath SW15 . . . . 4E **12**
Putney Heath La. SW15 . . . . 3G **13**
Putney High St. SW15 . . . . 1G **13**
Putney Hill SW15 . . . . 4G **13**
(not continuous)
Putney Leisure Cen. 1F **13**
Putney Pk. Av. SW15 . . . . 1D **12**
Putney Pk. La. SW15 . . . . 1E **12**
(not continuous)
Putney Station (Rail) 1H **13**
PUTNEY VALE 7D **12**
Putney Va. Crematorium
SW15 . . . . 6D **12**
Putney Wharf SW15 . . . . 7H **7**
Pylbrook Rd. SM1: Sutt 7K **25**
Pyne Rd. KT6: Surb 5H **23**
Pyramid Ct. *KT1: King T* *6G **17***
(off Cambridge Rd.)
Pyrland Rd. TW10: Rich 3G **11**
Pyrmont Rd. W4 . . . . 3H **5**

Q

Quadrangle, The SW6 . . . . 4H **7**
Quadrant, The KT17: Eps 2B **34**
SW20 . . . . 5H **19**
TW9: Rich 1E **10**
Quadrant Rd. TW9: Rich 1E **10**
Quain Mans. *W14* *3H **7***
(off Queen's Club Gdns.)
Quakers La. TW7: Isle 4B **4**
(not continuous)
Quantock Dr. KT4: Wor Pk 6F **25**
Quarrendon St. SW6 . . . . 6K **7**
Quarry Pk. Rd. SM1: Sutt 3J **31**
Quarry Ri. SM1: Sutt 3J **31**

Rivermead Cl.—St James Rd.

Rivermead Cl. TW11: Tedd 2C 16
Rivermead Ct. SW6 . . . . .7J 7
Rivermead Ho. TW16: Sun 7B 14
(off Thames St.)
River Meads Av. TW2: Twick 7F 9
River Mole Bus. Pk.
KT10: Esh 6F 21
Rivernook Cl. KT12: Walt T 2B 20
River Reach TW11: Tedd 2D 16
Riversdale Rd. KT7: T Ditt 2B 22
Rivers Ho. W4 . . . . .2H 5
(off Chiswick High Rd.)
Riverside TW1: Twick 5C 10
TW9: Rich 2E 10
TW16: Sun 7C 14
Riverside, The KT8: E Mos 7J 15
Riverside Av. KT8: E Mos 2J 21
Riverside Bus. Cen.
SW18 . . . . .5K 13
Riverside Cl.
KT1: King T 7B 36 (1E 22)
Riverside Ct. TW7: Isle 6A 4
(off Woodlands Rd.)
Riverside Dr. KT10: Esh 1F 27
TW10: Ham 7C 10
W4 . . . . .4A 6
Riverside Gdns. W6 . . . . .2E 6
Riverside Rd. KT12: Hers 1D 26
Riverside Studios 2F 7
(off River Ter.)
Riverside Vs. KT6: Surb 3D 22
Riverside Wlk.
KT1: King T 3A 36 (7E 16)
SW6 .7H 7
TW7: Isle 7A 4
W4 . . . . .3C 6
(off Chiswick Wharf)
Riverstone Ct.
KT2: King T 2E 36 (5G 17)
River Ter. W6 . . . . .2F 7
River Vw. Gdns. TW1: Twick 6A 10
Riverview Gdns. SW13 . . . . .3E 6
Riverview Gro. W4 . . . . .3J 5
Riverview Rd. KT19: Ewe 1K 29
W4 . . . . .4J 5
River Wlk. KT12: Walt T 3A 20
W6 . . . . .4F 7
River Way KT19: Ewe 2A 30
TW2: Twick 6G 9
Robert Cl. KT12: Hers 2A 26
Robert Gentry Ho. W14 . . . . .2H 7
(off Gledstanes Rd.)
Robert Owen Ho. SW6 . . . . .5G 7
Roberts Cl. SM3: Cheam 4G 31
Roberts Ct. KT9: Chess 2E 28
Robin Cl. TW12: Hamp 2D 14
Robin Gro. TW8: Bford 3D 4
ROBIN HOOD 7B 12
Robin Hood La. SM1: Sutt 2K 31
SW15 . . . . .7B 12
Robin Hood Rd. SW19 . . . . .2D 18
Robin Hood Way SW15 . . . . .7B 12
SW20 . . . . .1B 18
Robinsway KT12: Hers 1B 26
Robinwood Pl. SW15 . . . . .1A 18
Rochester M. W5 . . . . .1D 4
Rock Av. SW14 . . . . .7A 6
Rockingham Cl. SW15 . . . . .1C 12
Rockland Rd. SW15 . . . . .1H 13
Rocks La. SW13 . . . . .5D 6
Rocque Ho. SW6 . . . . .4J 7
(off Estcourt Rd.)
Rodney Cl. KT3: N Mald 2B 24
KT12: Walt T 5B 20
Rodney Grn. KT12: Walt T 6B 20
Rodney Rd. KT3: N Mald 2B 24
KT12: Walt T 6B 20
TW2: Whit 3F 9
Rodway Rd. SW15 . . . . .4D 12
Rodwell Ct. KT12: Walt T 7A 20
Roebuck Cl. TW13: Felt 1A 14
Roebuck Rd. KT9: Chess 2H 29
Roedean Cres. SW15 . . . . .3B 12
ROEHAMPTON 4D 12
Roehampton Cl. SW15 . . . . .1D 12
Roehampton Ga. SW15 . . . . .3B 12
Roehampton High St.
SW15 . . . . .4D 12
ROEHAMPTON HUNTERCOMBE
HOSPITAL 4D 12
ROEHAMPTON LANE 5E 12
Roehampton La. SW15 . . . . .1D 12
ROEHAMPTON PRIORY HOSPITAL
. . . . .1C 12
Roehampton Recreation Cen.
. . . . .4D 12
Roehampton Va. SW15 . . . . .7C 12
Rokeby Pl. SW20 . . . . .4E 18
Roland Way KT4: Wor Pk 6C 24
Rollesby Rd. KT9: Chess 3H 29
Rollit Cres. TW3: Houn 2F 9
Roman Cl. TW14: Felt 2B 8
Roman Rd. W4 . . . . .1B 6
Romany Gdns. SM3: Sutt 4K 25
Roma Read Cl. SW15 . . . . .4E 12
Romily Ct. SW6 . . . . .6J 7
Romney Cl. KT9: Chess 1F 29
Romney Rd. KT3: N Mald 3A 24
Romulus Ct. TW8: Bford 4E 4
Ronelean Rd. KT6: Surb 6G 23
Rookeries Cl. TW13: Felt 7A 8
Rookery Hill KT21: Asht 7H 33
Rookwood Av. KT3: N Mald 1D 24
Rope Wlk. TW16: Sun 7B 14
Rosaline Rd. SW6 . . . . .4H 7
Rosaline Ter. SW6 . . . . .4H 7
(off Rosaline Rd.)
Rosaville Rd. SW6 . . . . .4J 7
Rose & Crown Pas.
TW7: Isle 5B 4
Rosebank KT18: Eps 3K 33
SW6 . . . . .4F 7
Rosebank Cl. TW11: Tedd 3B 16
Rosebery Av. KT3: N Mald 6C 18
KT17: Eps 3B 34
Rosebery Cl. SM4: Mord 3G 25
Rosebery Rd. KT1: King T 6J 17
KT18: Eps D 7A 34
SM1: Sutt 3J 31
TW3: Houn 2H 9
Rosebery Sq. KT1: King T 6J 17
Rosebine Av. TW2: Twick 4J 9
Rosebriars KT10: Esh 2H 27
(not continuous)
Rosebushes KT17: Eps D 5E 34
Rosecroft Gdns. TW2: Twick 5J 9
Rosedale KT21: Asht 7D 32
Rosedale Rd. KT17: Ewe 2D 30
TW9: Rich 7F 5
Rosedale Ter. W6 . . . . .1E 6
(off Dalling Rd.)
Rosedene Av. SM4: Mord 2K 25
Rosedew Rd. W6 . . . . .3G 7
Rose End KT4: Wor Pk 5G 25
Roseheath Rd. TW4: Houn 2E 8
Rosehill KT10: Clay 3B 28
TW12: Hamp 5F 15
Roseleigh Cl. TW1: Twick 3E 10
Rosemary Av. KT8: W Mole 7F 15
Rosemary Gdns. KT9: Chess 1F 29
SW14 .7K 5
Rosemary Ga. KT10: Esh 2H 27
Rosemary La. SW14 . . . . .7K 5
Rosemont Rd. KT3: N Mald 7K 17
TW10: Rich 3F 11
Roseville Av. TW3: Houn 2F 9
Rosevine Rd. SW20 . . . . .5F 19
Rose Wlk. KT5: Surb 2J 23
Rosewood KT7: T Ditt 6B 22
Roskell Rd. SW15 . . . . .7G 7
Ross Ct. SW15 . . . . .4G 13
Rossdale Rd. SW15 . . . . .1F 13
Rossindel Rd. TW3: Houn 2F 9
Rosslyn Av. SW13 . . . . .7B 6
TW14: Felt 3A 8
Rosslyn Pk. RUFC 1C 12
Rosslyn Rd. TW1: Twick 3D 10
Ross Rd. TW2: Whit 5G 9
Rostrevor M. SW6 . . . . .5J 7
Rostrevor Rd. SW6 . . . . .5J 7
SW19 . . . . .2K 19
Rothbury Gdns. TW7: Isle 4B 4
Rotherwood Cl. SW20 . . . . .5H 19
Rotherwood Rd. SW15 . . . . .7G 7
Rothesay Av. SW20 . . . . .6H 19
TW10: Rich 1J 11
Rothschild Rd. W4 . . . . .1K 5
Rotunda Cen., The 3D 36 (6F 17)
Rougemont Av. SM4: Mord 3K 25
Roundacre SW19 . . . . .6G 13
Roundhill Way KT11: Cobh 7G 27
Roundway, The KT10: Clay 3A 28
Roundwood Vw. SM7: Bans 4G 35
Roundwood Way
SM7: Bans 4G 35
Roupell Ho. KT2: King T 4G 17
(off Florence Rd.)
Rowallan Rd. SW6 . . . . .4H 7
Rowan Cl. KT3: N Mald 6B 18
Rowan Rd. TW8: Bford 4C 4
W6 . . . . .1G 7
Rowan Ter. W6 . . . . .1G 7
Rowberry Cl. SW6 . . . . .4F 7
Rowden Rd. KT19: Ewe 1J 29
Rowhurst Av. KT22: Lea 6A 32
Rowlls Rd. KT1: King T 7G 17
Rowntree Rd. TW2: Twick 5K 9
Roxborough Av. TW7: Isle 4A 4
Roxby Pl. SW6 . . . . .3K 7
Royal Av. KT4: Wor Pk 6B 24
Royal Botanic Gardens 5F 5
Royal Cl. KT4: Wor Pk 6B 24
SW19 . . . . .7G 13
Royal Dr. KT18: Tatt C 7E 34
Royal Gdns. W7 . . . . .1B 4
ROYAL HOSPITAL FOR
NEURO-DISABILITY 3H 13
Royal Mid Surrey Golf Course
. . . . .7E 4
Royal Orchard Cl.
SW18 . . . . .4H 13
Royal Pde. SW6 . . . . .4H 7
TW9: Kew 5H 5
(off Layton Pl.)
Royal Rd. TW11: Tedd 2J 15
Roydon Ct. KT12: Hers 7A 20
Roy Gro. TW12: Hamp 3G 15
Roymount Ct. TW2: Twick 7K 9
Royston Cl. KT12: Walt T 5A 20
Royston Ct. KT10: Hin W 6A 22
TW9: Kew 5G 5
Royston Rd. TW10: Rich 2F 11
Roystons, The KT5: Surb 2J 23
Rq33 SW18 . . . . .1K 13
Ruden Way KT17: Eps D 5E 34
Ruffetts Way KT20: Tad 7H 35
Rugby La. SM2: Cheam 5G 31
Rugby Mans. W14 . . . . .1H 7
(off Bishop King's Rd.)
Rugby Rd. TW1: Twick 2K 9
Rumsey Cl. TW12: Hamp 3E 14
Running Horse Yd.
TW8: Bford 3F 5
Runnymede Cl. TW2: Whit 3G 9
Runnymede Ct. SW15 . . . . .5D 12
Runnymede Gdns. TW2: Whit 3G 9
Runnymede Rd. TW2: Whit 3G 9
Rupert Ct. KT8: W Mole 1F 21
(off St Peters Rd.)
Rupert Rd. W4 . . . . .1B 6
Rush, The SW19 . . . . .5J 19
(off Kingston Rd.)
Rushbury Ct. TW12: Hamp 5F 15
Rushett Cl. KT7: T Ditt 5C 22
Rushett La. KT9: Chess 7D 28
Rushett Rd. KT7: T Ditt 4C 22
Rushey Cl. KT3: N Mald 1A 24
Rushmead TW10: Ham 7C 10
Rushmere Ct. KT4: Wor Pk 6D 24
Rushmere Pl. SW19 . . . . .2G 19
Rushmon Gdns.
KT12: Walt T 7A 20
Rushmon Pl. SM3: Cheam 3H 31
Rushmon Vs. KT3: N Mald 1C 24
Rushmore Ho. SW15 . . . . .4D 12
W14 .1H 7
(off Russell Rd.)
Rusholme Rd. SW15 . . . . .3G 13
Ruskin Av. TW9: Kew 4H 5
(not continuous)
Ruskin Dr. KT4: Wor Pk 6E 24
Ruskin Mans. W14 . . . . .3H 7
(off Queen's Club Gdns.)
Ruskin Rd. TW7: Isle 7A 4
Russell Cl. W4 . . . . .3C 6
Russell Gdns. TW10: Ham 6D 10
Russell Kerr Cl. W4 . . . . .4K 5
Russell Rd. KT12: Walt T 3A 20
SW19 . . . . .4K 19
TW2: Twick 3A 10
Russell Wlk. TW10: Rich 3G 11
Russell Way SM1: Sutt 2K 31
Russell Yd. SW15 . . . . .1H 13
Russet Cl. KT12: Hers 7C 20
Rusthall Av. W4 . . . . .1A 6
Rustington Wlk. SM4: Mord 4J 25
Ruston Av. KT5: Surb 4J 23
Ruthen Cl. KT18: Eps 3J 33
Rutherwyke Cl. KT17: Ewe 3D 30
Rutland Cl. KT9: Chess 3G 29
KT19: Ewe 6A 30
KT21: Asht 6F 33
SW14 . . . . .7J 5
Rutland Ct. KT1: King T 1E 22
(off Palace Rd.)
Rutland Dr. SM4: Mord 3J 25
TW10: Ham 5E 10
Rutland Gro. W6 . . . . .2E 6
Rutland Rd. TW2: Twick 6J 9
Rutlish Rd. SW19 . . . . .5K 19
Ruvigny Gdns. SW15 . . . . .7G 7
Ruxley Cl. KT19: Ewe 2J 29
Ruxley Ct. KT19: Ewe 2K 29
Ruxley Cres. KT10: Clay 3C 28
Ruxley La. KT19: Ewe 3J 29
Ruxley M. KT19: Ewe 2J 29
Ruxley Ridge KT10: Clay 4B 28
Ruxley Towers KT10: Clay 4B 28
Ryan Dr. TW8: Bford 3B 4
Rybrook Dr. KT12: Walt T 6B 20
Rydal Gdns. SW15 . . . . .2B 18
TW3: Houn 3G 9
RYDENS 7B 20
Rydens Av. KT12: Walt T 6A 20
Rydens Cl. KT12: Walt T 6B 20
Rydens Gro. KT12: Hers 1C 26
Rydens Pk. KT12: Walt T 6C 20
Rydens Rd. KT12: Walt T 7A 20
Ryde Pl. TW1: Twick 3E 10
Rydon M. SW19 . . . . .4F 19
Ryebridge Cl. KT22: Lea 7B 32
Ryebrook Rd. KT22: Lea 7B 32
Ryecroft Av. TW2: Whit 4G 9
Ryecroft St. SW6 . . . . .5K 7
Rye Fld. KT21: Asht 5E 32
Ryefield Path SW15 . . . . .5D 12
Ryelands Ct. KT22: Lea 7B 32
Rye Wlk. SW15 . . . . .2G 13
Ryfold Rd. SW19 . . . . .7K 13
Rylston Rd. SW6 . . . . .3J 7
Rythe, The KT10: Esh 6G 27
Rythe Cl. KT9: Chess 4D 28
Rythe Ct. KT7: T Ditt 4B 22
Rythe Rd. KT10: Clay 2J 27

S

Sackville Rd. SM2: Sutt 4K 31
Saddlers Ct. KT18: Eps 2K 33
Saddlers M.
KT1: Hamp W 2A 36 (5D 16)
Sadlers Ride KT8: W Mole 6H 15
Saffron M. SW19 . . . . .4H 19
Saffron Way KT6: Surb 5E 22
St Agatha's Dr. KT2: King T 3G 17
St Albans Av. TW13: Hanw 2C 14
W4 . . . . .1A 6
St Alban's Gdns. TW11: Tedd 2B 16
St Alban's Rd. KT2: King T 3F 17
SM1: Sutt 1J 31
St Albans Ter. W6 . . . . .3H 7
St Andrews Cl. KT7: T Ditt 5C 22
St Andrews Mans. W14 . . . . .3H 7
(off St Andrews Rd.)
St Andrew's Rd. KT6: Surb 3E 22
W14 .3H 7
St Andrew's Sq. KT6: Surb 3E 22
St Ann's Pas. SW13 . . . . .7B 6
St Ann's Rd. SW13 . . . . .6C 6
ST ANTHONY'S HOSPITAL 5G 25
St Aubyn's Av. SW19 . . . . .2J 19
TW3: Houn 2F 9
St Barnabas Gdns.
KT8: W Mole 2F 21
St Catherines Cl. KT9: Chess 3E 28
St Catherine's Ct. W4 . . . . .1B 6
St Cecilia's Cl. SM3: Sutt 5H 25
St Chads Cl. KT6: Surb 4D 22
St Christophers Ct.
KT12: Walt T 6B 20
(off Rydens Av.)
St Clair Dr. KT4: Wor Pk 7E 24
St Clare Bus. Pk.
TW12: Hamp H 3H 15
St Clements Mans. SW6 . . . . .3G 7
(off Lillie Rd.)
St Dionis Rd. SW6 . . . . .6J 7
ST DUNSTAN'S 3J 31
St Dunstan's Hill SM1: Sutt 1H 31
St Dunstan's Rd. W6 . . . . .2G 7
ST EBBA'S 5K 29
St Edith Cl. KT18: Eps 3K 33
St Edmund's La. TW2: Whit 4G 9
St Edmunds Sq. SW13 . . . . .3F 7
St Elizabeth Dr. KT18: Eps 3K 33
St George's Ct. SW15 . . . . .1J 13
St George's Gdns. KT6: Surb 6J 23
KT17: Eps 3C 34
St George's Ind. Est.
KT2: King T 2E 16
St George's Pl. TW1: Twick 5B 10
St Georges Rd. KT2: King T 4H 17
SW19 . . . . .4J 19
(not continuous)
TW1: Twick 2C 10
TW9: Rich 7G 5
TW13: Hanw 1C 14
St George's Sq. KT3: N Mald 7B 18
St Helens KT7: T Ditt 4A 22
St Helier's Av. TW3: Houn 2F 9
St Helier Station (Rail) 3K 25
St Hilda's Rd. SW13 . . . . .3E 6
St James Av. KT17: Ewe 7C 30
SM1: Sutt 2K 31
St James Cl. KT3: N Mald 2C 24
KT18: Eps 3B 34
St James Ct. KT21: Asht 6E 32
St James Rd. KT6: Surb 3E 22
SM1: Sutt 2K 31

St James's Av.—Sheen Wood

St James's Av.
TW12: Hamp H ... 2H 15
St James's Cotts. TW9: Rich ... 2E 10
St James's Ct.
KT1: King T ... 6C 36 (7F 17)
St James's Rd.
KT1: King T ... 4B 36 (6E 16)
TW12: Hamp H ... 2G 15
St James St. W6 ... 2F 7
ST JOHN'S AND AMYAND HOUSE
... 4B 10
St John's Av. KT17: Eps ... 1D 34
SW15 ... 2G 13
St John's Cl. SW6 ... 4K 7
St John's Ct. KT1: King T ... 7D 36
TW7: Isle ... 6A 4
W6 ... 1E 6
(off Glenthorne Rd.)
St John's Dr. KT12: Walt T ... 5B 20
St John's Gro. SW13 ... 6C 6
TW9: Rich ... 1F 11
St John's Pas. SW19 ... 3H 19
St John's Rd.
KT1: Hamp W ... 3A 36 (6D 16)
KT3: N Mald ... 7K 17
KT8: E Mos ... 1J 21
SM1: Sutt ... 6K 25
SW19 ... 4H 19
TW7: Isle ... 6A 4
TW9: Rich ... 1F 11
TW13: Hanw ... 1D 14
St John's Ter. *SW15 ... 7B 12*
(off Kingston Va.)
St Josephs Almshouses
W6 ... 1G 7
(off Brook Grn.)
St Joseph's Ho. *W6 ... 1G 7*
(off Brook Grn.)
St Lawrence Bus. Cen.
TW13: Felt ... 6A 8
St Leonards Ct. SW14 ... 7K 5
St Leonard's Rd. KT6: Surb ... 2E 22
KT7: T Ditt ... 3B 22
KT10: Clay ... 3A 28
KT18: Tatt C ... 7F 35
SW14 ... 7J 5
St Leonards Sq. KT6: Surb ... 2E 22
St Luke's Pas.
KT2: King T ... 1E 36 (5G 17)
St Margaret Dr. KT18: Eps ... 3K 33
ST MARGARETS ... 3C 10
St Margaret's Av.
SM3: Cheam ... 7H 25
St Margarets Bus. Cen.
TW1: Twick ... 3C 10
St Margarets Ct. SW15 ... 1E 12
St Margaret's Cres.
SW15 ... 2E 12
St Margaret's Dr. TW1: Twick ... 2C 10
St Margaret's Gro.
TW1: Twick ... 3B 10
St Margaret's La. W8 ... 1K 7
St Margarets Rd. TW1: Twick ... 3C 10
TW7: Isle ... 1C 10
ST MARGARETS RDBT. ... 3C 10
St Margarets Station (Rail) ... 3C 10
St Marks Cl. SW6 ... 5K 7
St Mark's Hill KT6: Surb ... 3F 23
St Mark's Pl. SW19 ... 3J 19
St Mark's Rd. KT18: Tatt C ... 7F 35
TW11: Tedd ... 4C 16
St Martin's Av. KT18: Eps ... 3B 34
St Martins Cl. KT17: Eps ... 2B 34
St Martins Dr. KT12: Walt T ... 7B 20
St Mary Abbot's Ct. *W14 ... 1J 7*
(off Warwick Gdns.)
St Mary Abbot's Pl. W8 ... 1J 7
St Mary Abbot's Ter. W14 ... 1J 7
St Mary's Av. TW11: Tedd ... 3A 16
St Mary's Cl. KT9: Chess ... 4G 29
KT17: Ewe ... 4C 30
St Mary's Copse
KT4: Wor Pk ... 6B 24
St Mary's Gro. SW13 ... 7E 6
TW9: Rich ... 1G 11
W4 ... 3J 5
St Marys M. TW10: Ham ... 6D 10
St Mary's Rd. KT4: Wor Pk ... 6B 24
KT6: Surb ... 4D 22
(St Chads Cl.)
KT6: Surb ... 3E 22
(Victoria Rd.)
KT8: E Mos ... 2J 21
SW19 ... 2H 19
St Mary's University College
Sports Cen. ... 1A 16
St Matthew's Av. KT6: Surb ... 5F 23
St Maur Rd. SW6 ... 5J 7
St Michael's Cl. KT4: Wor Pk ... 6C 24
KT12: Walt T ... 6B 20
St Nicholas Ct. KT1: King T ... 7C 36
St Nicholas M. KT7: T Ditt ... 3A 22
St Nicholas Rd. KT7: T Ditt ... 3A 22
St Normans Way KT17: Ewe ... 6D 30
St Olaf's Rd. SW6 ... 4H 7
St Oswalds Studios *SW6 ... 3K 7*
(off Sedlescombe Rd.)
St Paul's Cl. KT9: Chess ... 1E 28
St Paul's Rd. TW8: Bford ... 3E 4
TW9: Rich ... 7G 5
St Paul's Studios *W14 ... 2H 7*
(off Talgarth Rd.)
St Paul's Wlk. KT2: King T ... 4H 17
St Peters Ct. KT8: W Mole ... 1F 21
St Peter's Gro. W6 ... 1D 6
St Peter's Rd. KT1: King T ... 6H 17
KT8: W Mole ... 1F 21
TW1: Twick ... 2C 10
W6 ... 2D 6
St Peter's Sq. W6 ... 1C 6
St Peter's Ter. SW6 ... 4J 7
St Peter's Vs. W6 ... 1D 6
St Peter's Wharf W4 ... 2D 6
St Philip's Av. KT4: Wor Pk ... 6E 24
St Philip's Ga. KT4: Wor Pk ... 6E 24
St Philips Rd. KT6: Surb ... 3E 22
ST RAPHAEL'S HOSPICE ... 6G 25
St Simon's Av. SW15 ... 2F 13
St Stephen's Av. KT21: Asht ... 5F 33
St Stephen's Gdns.
SW15 ... 2J 13
TW1: Twick ... 3D 10
St Stephen's Pas.
TW1: Twick ... 3D 10
St Stephen's Rd. TW3: Houn ... 3F 9
St Theresa Cl. KT18: Eps ... 3K 33
St Thomas Cl. KT6: Surb ... 5G 23
St Thomas Rd. W4 ... 3K 5
St Thomas's Way SW6 ... 4J 7
St Vincent Rd. KT12: Walt T ... 7A 20
TW2: Whit ... 3H 9
St Winifred's Rd.
TW11: Tedd ... 3C 16
Salamander Cl. KT2: King T ... 2D 16
Salamander Quay
KT1: Hamp W ... 2A 36 (5E 16)
Salcombe Dr. SM4: Mord ... 5G 25
Salcombe Vs. TW10: Rich ... 2F 11
Salisbury Av. SM1: Sutt ... 3J 31
Salisbury Cl. KT4: Wor Pk ... 7C 24
Salisbury Gdns. SW19 ... 4H 19
Salisbury M. SW6 ... 4J 7
Salisbury Pas. *SW6 ... 4J 7*
(off Dawes Rd.)
Salisbury Pavement *SW6 ... 4J 7*
(off Dawes Rd.)
Salisbury Rd. KT3: N Mald ... 7A 18
KT4: Wor Pk ... 7A 24
SW19 ... 4H 19
TW4: Houn ... 1B 8
TW9: Rich ... 1F 11
TW13: Felt ... 5B 8
Salix Cl. TW16: Sun ... 4A 14
Salliesfield TW2: Whit ... 3J 9
Salmons Rd. KT9: Chess ... 3F 29
Saltash Cl. SM1: Sutt ... 1J 31
Salvin Rd. SW15 ... 7G 7
Samels Ct. W6 ... 2D 6
Samuel Gray Gdns.
KT2: King T ... 1B 36 (5E 16)
Samuel Lewis Trust Dwellings
SW6 ... 4K 7
(off Vanston Pl.)
W14 ... 1J 7
(off Lisgar Ter.)
Samuel Richardson Ho.
W14 ... 1J 7
(off Nth. End Cres.)
Samuel's Cl. W6 ... 1F 7
Sanctuary, The SM4: Mord ... 3K 25
Sandal Rd. KT3: N Mald ... 2A 24
Sandalwood Mans. *W8 ... 1K 7*
(off Stone Hall Gdns.)
Sandalwood Rd. TW13: Felt ... 7A 8
Sandbourne Av. SW19 ... 6K 19
Sanders Cl. TW12: Hamp H ... 2H 15
Sandersfield Gdns.
SM7: Bans ... 4K 35
Sandersfield Rd. SM7: Bans ... 4K 35
Sandes Pl. KT22: Lea ... 7B 32
Sandhurst Av. KT5: Surb ... 4J 23
Sandiford Rd. SM3: Sutt ... 6J 25
Sandon Cl. KT10: Esh ... 4J 21
Sandown Av. KT10: Esh ... 2H 27
Sandown Ct. SM2: Sutt ... 4K 31
Sandown Ga. KT10: Esh ... 7J 21
Sandown Lodge KT18: Eps ... 3A 34
Sandown Pk. Racecourse ... 7H 21
Sandown Rd. KT10: Esh ... 7H 21
Sandown Ski Cen. ... 7G 21
Sandpiper Rd. SM1: Sutt ... 2J 31
Sandpits Rd. TW10: Ham ... 6E 10
Sandra Cl. TW3: Houn ... 2G 9
Sandra Ho. KT8: E Mos ... 2J 21
Sandringham Av. SW20 ... 5H 19
Sandringham Cl. SW19 ... 5G 13
Sandringham Ct.
KT2: King T ... 1C 36
(off Skerne Wlk.)
SM2: Sutt ... 5K 31
Sandringham Gdns.
KT8: W Mole ... 1F 21
Sandringham Ho. *W14 ... 1H 7*
(off Windsor Way)
Sandringham M.
TW12: Hamp ... 5E 14
Sandringham Pk.
KT11: Cobh ... 7F 27
Sandringham Rd.
KT4: Wor Pk ... 7D 24
Sandycombe Rd.
TW9: Kew, Rich ... 7G 5
TW14: Felt ... 5A 8
Sandycombe Rd.
TW1: Twick ... 3D 10
Sandy Ct. KT11: Cobh ... 7E 26
Sandy Cft. KT17: Ewe ... 6F 31
Sandy Dr. KT11: Cobh ... 7F 27
Sandy La. KT1: Hamp W ... 4B 16
KT12: Walt T ... 3A 20
KT22: Oxs ... 7E 26
SM2: Cheam ... 4H 31
TW10: Ham ... 6D 10
TW11: Tedd ... 4B 16
Sandy Mead KT19: Eps ... 6H 29
Sandy Way KT11: Cobh ... 7F 27
Sanger Av. KT9: Chess ... 2F 29
Santos Rd. SW18 ... 2K 13
Sarjant Path *SW19 ... 6G 13*
(off Blincoe Cl.)
Satis Ct. KT17: Ewe ... 7C 30
Savery Dr. KT6: Surb ... 4D 22
Savile Cl. KT3: N Mald ... 2B 24
KT7: T Ditt ... 5A 22
Saville Rd. TW1: Twick ... 5A 10
Savill Gdns. SW20 ... 7D 18
Savona Cl. SW19 ... 4G 19
Sawkins Cl. SW19 ... 6H 13
Sawyer's Hill TW10: Rich ... 4G 11
Saxon Av. TW13: Hanw ... 6D 8
Saxonbury Av. TW16: Sun ... 7A 14
Saxonbury Gdns. KT6: Surb ... 5D 22
Saxon Cl. KT6: Surb ... 3E 22
Saxon Ho. TW13: Hanw ... 6E 8
Saxon Rd.
KT2: King T ... 1C 36 (5F 17)
KT12: Walt T ... 7C 20
Sayer's Wlk. TW10: Rich ... 4G 11
Scarborough Cl. SM2: Cheam ... 7J 31
Scarsdale Studios *W8 ... 1K 7*
(off Stratford Rd.)
Scarsdale Vs. W8 ... 1K 7
Scarth Rd. SW13 ... 7C 6
School All. TW1: Twick ... 5B 10
School Ho. La. TW11: Tedd ... 4C 16
School La.
KT1: Hamp W ... 2A 36 (5D 16)
KT6: Surb ... 5H 23
School Pas. KT1: King T ... 6G 17
School Rd. KT1: Hamp W ... 5D 16
KT8: E Mos ... 1J 21
TW12: Hamp H ... 3H 15
School Rd. Av.
TW12: Hamp H ... 3H 15
Schubert Rd. SW15 ... 2J 13
SCILLY ISLES ... 6K 21
Scope Way
KT1: King T ... 7D 36 (1F 23)
Scotsdale Cl. SM3: Cheam ... 4H 31
Scott Cl. KT19: Ewe ... 2K 29
Scott Farm Cl. KT7: T Ditt ... 5C 22
Scotts Dr. TW12: Hamp ... 4G 15
Scotts Farm Rd. KT19: Ewe ... 3K 29
Scotts La. KT12: Hers ... 1C 26
Seaforth Av. KT3: N Mald ... 2E 24
Seaforth Gdns. KT19: Ewe ... 7C 24
Seagrave Lodge *SW6 ... 3K 7*
(off Seagrave Rd.)
Seagrave Rd. SW6 ... 3K 7
Seaton Cl. SW15 ... 5E 12
TW2: Whit ... 3J 9
Seaton Rd. TW2: Whit ... 3H 9
Secombe Theatre ... 2K 31
Second Av. KT12: Walt T ... 3A 20
SW14 ... 7B 6
Second Cl. KT8: W Mole ... 1H 21
Second Cross Rd. TW2: Twick ... 6K 9
Sedleigh Rd. SW18 ... 3J 13
Sedlescombe Rd. SW6 ... 3K 7
SEETHING WELLS ... 3D 22
Seething Wells La.
KT6: Surb ... 3D 22
Sefton Rd. KT19: Ewe ... 6A 30
Sefton St. SW15 ... 7F 7
Sekhon Ter. TW13: Hanw ... 7F 9
Selborne Rd. KT3: N Mald ... 6B 18
Selbourne Av. KT6: Surb ... 6G 23
Selby Cl. KT9: Chess ... 4F 29
Selhurst Cl. SW19 ... 5G 13
Selkirk Rd. TW2: Twick ... 6H 9
Selsdon Cl. KT6: Surb ... 2F 23
Selwood Rd. KT9: Chess ... 1E 28
SM3: Sutt ... 5J 25
Selwyn Av. TW9: Rich ... 7F 5
Selwyn Cl. TW4: Houn ... 1D 8
Selwyn Rd. KT3: N Mald ... 2A 24
Senhouse Rd. SM3: Cheam ... 7G 25
Sergeant Ind. Est.
SW18 ... 3K 13
Servite Ho. *KT4: Wor Pk ... 6C 24*
(off Avenue, The)
Servius Ct. TW8: Bford ... 4E 4
Settrington Rd. SW6 ... 6K 7
Seven Kings Way
KT2: King T ... 1C 36 (5F 17)
Sevenoaks Cl. SM2: Sutt ... 6K 31
Severn Ct.
KT2: King T ... 1B 36 (5E 16)
Severn Dr. KT10: Hin W ... 6B 22
KT12: Walt T ... 6C 20
Seymour Av. KT17: Ewe ... 5E 30
SM4: Mord ... 4G 25
Seymour Cl. KT8: E Mos ... 2H 21
Seymour Ct. KT19: Ewe ... 5B 30
Seymour Gdns. KT5: Surb ... 2G 23
TW1: Twick ... 4C 10
TW13: Hanw ... 1B 14
Seymour M. KT17: Ewe ... 6D 30
Seymour Rd.
KT1: Hamp W ... 2A 36 (5E 16)
KT8: W Mole ... 2H 21
SW18 ... 4J 13
SW19 ... 7G 13
TW12: Hamp H ... 2H 15
W4 ... 1K 5
Shacklegate La. TW11: Tedd ... 1K 15
Shadbolt Cl. KT4: Wor Pk ... 6C 24
Shaef Way TW11: Tedd ... 4B 16
Shaftesbury Av. TW14: Felt ... 3A 8
Shaftesbury M. *W8 ... 1K 7*
(off Stratford Rd.)
Shaftesbury Pl. *W14 ... 1J 7*
(off Warwick Rd.)
Shaftesbury Rd. TW9: Rich ... 7F 5
Shaftesbury Way TW2: Twick ... 7J 9
Shakespeare Way
TW13: Hanw ... 1B 14
Shalden Ho. SW15 ... 3C 12
Shaldon Dr. SM4: Mord ... 2H 25
Shaldon Way KT12: Walt T ... 7B 20
Shalstone Rd. SW14 ... 7J 5
Shalston Vs. KT6: Surb ... 3G 23
Shannon Commercial Cen.
KT3: N Mald ... 1D 24
SHANNON CORNER ... 1D 24
Shannon Cnr. Retail Pk.
KT3: N Mald ... 1D 24
Shanti Ct. SW18 ... 5K 13
Sharnbrook Ho. W14 ... 3K 7
Sharon Cl. KT6: Surb ... 5D 22
KT19: Eps ... 2K 33
Sharon Rd. W4 ... 2A 6
Sharp Ho. TW1: Twick ... 3E 10
Shaw Cl. KT17: Ewe ... 7C 30
Shaw Dr. KT12: Walt T ... 4B 20
Shawford Ct. SW15 ... 4D 12
Shawford Rd. KT19: Ewe ... 3A 30
Shawley Cres. KT18: Tatt C ... 7F 35
Shawley Way KT18: Tatt C ... 7E 34
Shaws Path *KT1: Hamp W ... 5D 16*
(off Bennett Cl.)
Sheaf Cotts. *KT7: T Ditt ... 5K 21*
(off Weston Grn.)
Shearwater Rd. SM1: Sutt ... 2J 31
Sheath Cotts. *KT7: T Ditt ... 3C 22*
(off Ferry Rd.)
Sheen Comn. Dr.
TW10: Rich ... 1H 11
Sheen Ct. TW10: Rich ... 1H 11
Sheen Ct. Rd. TW10: Rich ... 1H 11
Sheendale Rd. TW9: Rich ... 1G 11
Sheen Ga. Gdns. SW14 ... 1K 11
Sheengate Mans. SW14 ... 1A 12
Sheen La. SW14 ... 2K 11
Sheen Pk. TW9: Rich ... 1G 11
Sheen Rd. TW9: Rich ... 2F 11
TW10: Rich ... 2F 11
Sheen Sports & Fitness Cen.
... 1B 12
Sheen Wood SW14 ... 2K 11

Sheephouse Way—Stapleford Cl.

Sheephouse Way
KT3: N Mald 5A 24
Sheep Wlk. M. SW19 3G 19
Shelburne Dr. TW4: Houn 3F 9
Shelford KT1: King T 6H 17
Shelley Cl. SM7: Bans 4G 35
Shelton Rd. SW19 5K 19
Shepherd Cl. TW13: Hanw 1D 14
Shepherd's Bush Rd. W6 1F 7
Sheppard Cl.
KT1: King T 7D 36 (1F 23)
Sheraton Dr. KT19: Eps 2K 33
Sherborne Cl. KT18: Tatt C 6F 35
Sherborne Rd. KT9: Chess 2F 29
SM3: Sutt 6K 25
Sherbrooke Rd. SW6 4H 7
Sherbrooke Ter. *SW6* 4H 7
(off Sherbrook Rd.)
Sherbrooke Way
KT4: Wor Pk 4E 24
Shere Av. SM2: Cheam 6F 31
Shere Cl. KT9: Chess 2E 28
Sherfield Cl. KT3: N Mald 1J 23
Sherfield Gdns. SW15 3C 12
Sheridan Ct. TW4: Houn 2D 8
Sheridan Pl. SW13 7C 6
TW12: Hamp 5G 15
Sheridan Rd. SW19 5J 19
TW10: Ham 7D 10
Sheringham Av. TW2: Whit 5E 8
Sherland Rd. TW1: Twick 5A 10
Sherwood Cl. SW13 7E 6
Sherwood Pk. Rd. SM1: Sutt 2K 31
Sherwood Rd. SW19 4J 19
TW12: Hamp H 2H 15
Shield Dr. TW8: Bford 3B 4
Shillingstone Ho. *W14* 1H 7
(off Russell Rd.)
Ship All. W4 3H 5
Ship La. SW14 7K 5
Shire Ct. KT17: Ewe 4C 30
Shire Horse Way TW7: Isle 7A 4
Shire M. TW2: Whit 3H 9
Shire Pl. TW8: Bford 4D 4
Shires, The TW10: Ham 1F 17
Shires Cl. KT21: Asht 7E 32
Shirley Av. SM2: Cheam 5J 31
Shirley Cl. TW3: Houn 2H 9
Shirley Dr. TW3: Houn 2H 9
SHOOTING STAR HOUSE
CHILDREN'S HOSPICE 3E 14
Shore Cl. TW12: Hamp 3D 14
Shore Gro. TW13: Hanw 6E 8
Shorrold's Rd. SW6 4J 7
Shortcroft Rd. KT17: Ewe 4C 30
Shortlands W6 1G 7
Shortlands Rd. KT2: King T 4G 17
Short Rd. W4 3B 6
Short Way TW2: Whit 4H 9
Shottendane Rd. SW6 5K 7
Shottfield Av. SW14 1B 12
Shrewsbury Av. SW14 1K 11
Shrewsbury Cl. KT6: Surb 6F 23
Shrewsbury Wlk. TW7: Isle 7B 4
Shrubbery, The KT6: Surb 5F 23
Shrubland Gro. KT4: Wor Pk 7F 25
Shrubland Rd. SM7: Bans 5J 35
Shuters Sq. W14 2J 7
Sidbury St. SW6 5H 7
Sidney Gdns. TW8: Bford 3E 4
Sidney Rd. KT12: Walt T 4A 20
TW1: Twick 3B 10
Sigrist Sq.
KT2: King T 2D 36 (5F 17)
Silver Cres. W4 1J 5
Silverdale Cl. SM1: Sutt 1J 31
Silverdale Dr. TW16: Sun 6A 14
Silvergate KT19: Ewe 2K 29
Silverglade Bus. Pk.
KT9: Chess 1D 32
Silverhall St. TW7: Isle 7B 4
Silverton Rd. W6 3G 7
Simmil Rd. KT10: Clay 2K 27
Simmons Cl. KT9: Chess 3D 28
Simmons Ga. KT10: Esh 2H 27
Simpson Rd. TW4: Houn 3E 8
TW10: Ham 1D 16
Simpson Way KT6: Surb 3D 22
Simrose Ct. SW18 2K 13
Sinclair Dr. SM2: Sutt 5K 31
Sinclair Rd. W14 1H 7
Sion Ct. TW1: Twick 5C 10
Sion Rd. TW1: Twick 5C 10
Sir Abraham Dawes Cotts.
SW15 1H 13
Sir Cyril Black Way
SW19 4K 19
Sir Oswald Stoll Foundation, The
SW6 4K 7
(off Fulham Rd.)
Sir Oswald Stoll Mans.
SW6 4K 7
(off Fulham Rd.)
Sir William Atkins Ho.
KT18: Eps 2A 34
Sir William Powell's Almshouses
SW6 6H 7
Sispara Gdns. SW18 3J 13
Sixth Cross Rd. TW2: Twick 7H 9
Skeena Hill SW18 4H 13
Skelgill Rd. SW15 1J 13
Skelwith Rd. W6 3F 7
Skerne Rd.
KT2: King T 2B 36 (5E 16)
Skerne Wlk.
KT2: King T 1B 36 (5E 16)
Skinners La. KT21: Asht 7E 32
Slade Ho. TW4: Houn 3E 8
Slattery Rd. TW13: Felt 5C 8
Smallberry Av. TW7: Isle 6A 4
Smeaton Cl. KT9: Chess 3E 28
Smeaton Rd. SW18 4K 13
Smith Hill TW8: Bford 3F 5
Smith St. KT5: Surb 3G 23
Smithwood Cl. SW19 5H 13
Smoothfield TW3: Houn 1F 9
Snakey La. TW13: Felt 1A 14
Snellings Rd. KT12: Hers 2B 26
Snowdrop Cl. TW12: Hamp 3F 15
Snowy Fielder Waye
TW7: Isle 6C 4
Soames Wlk. KT3: N Mald 5B 18
Soaphouse La. TW8: Bford 4F 5
Sobraon Ho. KT2: King T 1E 36
Solna Av. SW15 2F 13
Sombourne Ho. *SW15* 4D 12
(off Fontley Way)
Somer Ct. *SW6* 3K 7
(off Anselm Rd.)
Somerfield Cl. KT20: Tad 7H 35
Somerset Av. KT9: Chess 1E 28
SW20 6E 18
Somerset Cl. KT3: N Mald 3B 24
KT12: Hers 2A 26
KT19: Ewe 5A 30
Somerset Gdns. TW11: Tedd 2K 15
Somerset Ho. SW19 7G 13
Somerset Lodge TW8: Bford 3E 4
Somerset Rd. KT1: King T 6G 17
SW19 7G 13
TW8: Bford 3D 4
TW11: Tedd 2K 15
Somerton Av. TW9: Rich 7J 5
Somerville Av. SW13 3E 6
Sonning Gdns. TW12: Hamp 3D 14
Sontan Ct. TW2: Twick 5J 9
Sophia Ho. *W6* 2F 7
(off Queen Caroline St.)
Sopwith Av. KT9: Chess 2F 29
Sopwith Cl. KT2: King T 2G 17
Sopwith Way
KT2: King T 2C 36 (5F 17)
Sorrento Rd. SM1: Sutt 7K 25
Souldern Rd. W14 1G 7
South Av. TW9: Kew 6H 5
South Bank KT6: Surb 3F 23
Southbank KT7: T Ditt 4C 22
Sth. Bank Ter. KT6: Surb 3F 23
Sth. Black Lion La. W6 2D 6
SOUTHBOROUGH 5F 23
Southborough Cl. KT6: Surb 5E 22
Southborough Rd. KT6: Surb 5F 23
Sth. CC Smallholdings Rd.
KT17: Eps 3F 35
(not continuous)
Sth. Circular Rd. SW15 1D 12
South Cl. SM4: Mord 3K 25
TW2: Twick 7F 9
Southcombe St. W14 1H 7
Southcote Av. KT5: Surb 4J 23
Southdean Gdns. SW19 6J 13
Southdown Av. W7 1B 4
Southdown Dr. SW20 4G 19
Southdown Rd. KT12: Hers 7D 20
SW20 5G 19
South Dr. SM2: Cheam 6H 31
Sth. Ealing Rd. W5 1E 4
Sth. Edwardes Sq. W8 1J 7
Southerton Rd. W6 1F 7
Southey Rd. SW19 4K 19
Southfield Gdns. TW1: Twick 1A 16
SOUTHFIELDS 5J 13
Southfields KT8: E Mos 3K 21
Southfields Ct. SM1: Sutt 6K 25
Southfields M. SW18 3K 13
Southfields Pas. SW18 3K 13
Southfields Rd. SW18 3K 13
Southfields Station (Tube) 5J 13
Southlands Dr. SW19 6G 13
Southland Way TW3: Houn 2J 9
South La.
KT1: King T 6B 36 (7E 16)
(not continuous)
KT3: N Mald 1A 24
South La. W. KT3: N Mald 1A 24
South Lodge TW2: Whit 3H 9
Sth. Lodge Rd. KT12: Hers 5A 26
South Mall SW18 3K 13
South Mead KT19: Ewe 4C 30
Southmead Rd. SW19 5H 13
South Merton Station (Rail) 7J 19
Southmont Rd. KT10: Hin W 6K 21
South Pde. W4 1A 6
South Pk. Gro. KT3: N Mald 1K 23
South Pk. Rd. SW19 3K 19
South Pl. KT5: Surb 4G 23
Southridge Pl. SW20 4G 19
South Rd. TW2: Twick 7J 9
TW12: Hamp 3D 14
TW13: Hanw 2C 14
W5 1E 4
Southsea Rd.
KT1: King T 7C 36 (1F 23)
South Side W6 1C 6
Southside Comn. SW19 3F 19
Southside House 3F 19
Southside Shop. Cen.
SW18 3K 13
South St. KT18: Eps 2A 34
TW7: Isle 7B 4
South Ter. KT6: Surb 3F 23
South Vw. KT19: Eps 6H 29
SW19 3G 19
South Vw. Rd. KT21: Asht 7E 32
Southville Cl. KT19: Ewe 5A 30
Southville Rd. KT7: T Ditt 4B 22
Southway SW20 2F 25
Sth. Western Rd.
TW1: Twick 3B 10
South W. Middlesex Crematorium
TW13: Felt 5D 8
SOUTH WIMBLEDON 3K 19
Southwood Av. KT2: King T 5K 17
Southwood Cl. KT4: Wor Pk 5G 25
Southwood Dr. KT5: Surb 4K 23
Southwood Gdns.
KT10: Hin W 7B 22
Sth. Worple Av. SW14 7B 6
Sth. Worple Way SW14 7A 6
Sovereign Ct. KT8: W Mole 1E 20
TW3: Houn 1F 9
Space Waye TW14: Felt 2A 8
Spa Dr. KT18: Eps 3H 33
Sparks Cl. TW12: Hamp 3D 14
Sparrow Cl. TW12: Hamp 3D 14
Sparrow Farm Dr. TW14: Felt 4B 8
(not continuous)
Sparrow Farm Rd.
KT17: Ewe 1D 30
Spear M. SW5 1K 7
Speer Rd. KT7: T Ditt 3A 22
Speirs Cl. KT3: N Mald 3C 24
Spencer Ct. SW20 5E 18
Spencer Gdns. SW14 2K 11
Spencer Hill SW19 3H 19
Spencer Hill Rd. SW19 4H 19
Spencer Mans. *W14* 3H 7
(off Queen's Club Gdns.)
Spencer M. W6 3H 7
Spencer Pk. KT8: E Mos 2H 21
Spencer Rd. KT8: E Mos 1H 21
SW20 5E 18
TW2: Twick 7K 9
W4 4K 5
Spencer Wlk. SW15 1G 13
Spicer Cl. KT12: Walt T 3B 20
Spinnaker Ct. KT1: Hamp W 2A 36
Spinney, The KT18: Tatt C 7E 34
KT22: Oxs 7H 27
SM3: Cheam 1F 31
SW13 4E 6
TW16: Sun 5A 14
Spinney Cl. KT3: N Mald 2B 24
KT4: Wor Pk 6C 24
KT11: Cobh 7F 27
Spray La. TW2: Whit 3K 9
Spread Eagle Wlk.
KT19: Eps 2A 34
Spreighton Rd. KT8: W Mole 1G 21
Springclose La. SM3: Cheam 3H 31
Spring Cotts. KT6: Surb 2E 22
Spring Ct. KT17: Ewe 5C 30
Springfield Av. SW20 7J 19
TW12: Hamp 3G 15
Springfield Ct. KT1: King T 6C 36
Springfield Pl. KT3: N Mald 1K 23
Springfield Rd.
KT1: King T 6D 36 (7F 17)
KT17: Ewe 6F 31
SW19 2J 19
Springfield Rd. TW2: Whit 5F 9
TW11: Tedd 2B 16
Spring Gdns. KT8: W Mole 2G 21
SPRING GROVE 5A 4
Spring Gro. TW12: Hamp 5G 15
W4 2H 5
Spring Gro. Rd. TW10: Rich 2G 11
Spring Health Leisure Club 1E 10
(in Pools on the Pk.)
Spring M. KT17: Ewe 5C 30
Spring Pas. SW15 7G 7
Spring St. KT17: Ewe 5C 30
Spring Ter. TW9: Rich 2F 11
Springvale Av. TW8: Bford 2E 4
Spurfield KT8: W Mole 7G 15
Spur Rd. TW7: Isle 4B 4
TW14: Felt 1A 8
Square, The TW9: Rich 2E 10
W6 2F 7
Squires Ct. SW19 1K 19
Squirrels Ct. *KT4: Wor Pk* 6C 24
(off Avenue, The)
Squirrels Grn. KT4: Wor Pk 6C 24
Squirrels Way KT18: Eps 3A 34
Stable Cl. KT2: King T 3G 17
Stables Yd. SW18 3K 13
Stable Yd. SW15 7F 7
Stafford Cl. SM3: Cheam 3H 31
Stafford Cripps Ho. *SW6* 3J 7
(off Clem Attlee Ct.)
Stafford Mans. *W14* 1G 7
(off Haarlem Rd.)
Stafford Pl. TW10: Rich 4G 11
Stafford Rd. KT3: N Mald 7K 17
Stag Ct. *KT2: King T* 5H 17
(off Coombe Rd.)
STAG LANE 6C 12
Stag La. SW15 7C 12
Stags Way TW7: Isle 3A 4
Staines Av. SM3: Cheam 6G 25
Staines Rd. TW2: Twick 7F 9
TW3: Houn 3A 8
TW4: Houn 3A 8
TW14: Felt 3A 8
(not continuous)
Staines Rd. E. TW16: Sun 4A 14
Stamford Bridge 4K 7
Stamford Brook Arches
W6 1D 6
Stamford Brook Av. W6 1C 6
Stamford Brook Gdns.
W6 1C 6
Stamford Brook Mans.
W6 1C 6
(off Goldhawk Rd.)
Stamford Brook Rd. W6 1C 6
Stamford Brook Station (Tube) 1C 6
Stamford Ct. W6 1D 6
STAMFORD GREEN 2J 33
Stamford Grn. Rd. KT18: Eps 2J 33
Stamford Rd. KT12: Walt T 7C 20
Stanborough Cl.
TW12: Hamp 3E 14
Stanbridge Rd. SW15 7F 7
Standard Rd. TW4: Houn 1D 8
Standen Rd. SW18 4J 13
Standish Ho. *W6* 1D 6
(off St Peter's Gro.)
Standish Rd. W6 1D 6
Stane Way KT17: Ewe 6D 30
Stanford Cl. TW12: Hamp 3E 14
Stanfords, The *KT17: Eps* 1C 34
(off East St.)
Stanhope Ter. TW2: Twick 4A 10
Stanier Cl. W14 2J 7
Stanley Av. KT3: N Mald 2D 24
Stanley Ct. SM2: Sutt 4K 31
Stanley Gdns. KT12: Hers 3B 26
Stanley Gdns. Rd.
TW11: Tedd 2K 15
Stanley Picker Gallery 6D 36
(off College Wlk.)
Stanley Rd. SM2: Sutt 3K 31
SM4: Mord 1K 25
SW14 1J 11
SW19 3K 19
TW2: Twick 7J 9
TW3: Houn 1H 9
TW11: Tedd 1K 15
Stanmore Gdns. TW9: Rich 7G 5
Stanmore Rd. TW9: Rich 7G 5
Stanstead Mnr. SM1: Sutt 3K 31
Stanton Av. TW11: Tedd 3K 15
Stanton Cl. KT4: Wor Pk 5G 25
KT19: Ewe 2J 29
Stanton Rd. SW13 6C 6
SW20 5G 19
Stanwick Rd. W14 1J 7
Stapleford Cl. KT1: King T 6H 17
SW19 4H 13

Star & Garter Hill—Teddington Bus. Pk.

Star & Garter Hill
TW10: Rich 5F **11**
Starling Wlk. TW12: Hamp 2D **14**
Star Rd. W14 3J **7**
Staten Gdns. TW1: Twick 5A **10**
Station App. KT1: King T 5H **17**
KT4: Wor Pk 5D **24**
KT10: Hin W 7A **22**
KT17: Ewe 6E **30**
(Cheam Rd.)
KT17: Ewe 5C **30**
(Fennells Mead)
KT19: Eps 2A **34**
KT19: Ewe 2D **30**
SM2: Cheam 4H **31**
SM2: Sutt 6K **31**
SW6 7H **7**
SW14 7K **5**
TW8: Bford 3D 4
(off Sidney Gdns.)
TW9: Kew 5H **5**
TW12: Hamp 5F **15**
Station App. Rd. W4 4K **5**
Station Av. KT3: N Mald 7B **18**
KT19: Ewe 5B **30**
TW9: Kew 5H **5**
Station Bldgs. KT1: King T 3C **36**
Station Cl. TW12: Hamp 5G **15**
Station Est. Rd. TW14: Felt 5A **8**
Station Gdns. W4 4K **5**
Station Pde. TW9: Kew 5H **5**
TW14: Felt 5A **8**
W4 4K **5**
Station Path SW6 7J **7**
Station Rd.
KT1: Hamp W 1A **36** (5D **16**)
KT2: King T 5H **17**
KT3: N Mald 2E **24**
KT7: T Ditt 4A **22**
KT9: Chess 2F **29**
KT10: Clay 3K **27**
KT10: Esh 6J **21**
SM2: Sutt 6K **31**
SW13 6C **6**
TW1: Twick 5A **10**
TW3: Houn 1G **9**
TW11: Tedd 3B **16**
TW12: Hamp 5F **15**
Station Way KT10: Clay 3K **27**
KT19: Eps 2A **34**
SM3: Cheam 3H **31**
Station Yd. TW1: Twick 4B **10**
Staunton Rd. KT2: King T 3F **17**
Staveley Gdns. W4 5A **6**
Staveley Rd. W4 3K **5**
Stayton Rd. SM1: Sutt 7K **25**
Steadfast Rd.
KT1: King T 2B **36** (5E **16**)
Steele Rd. TW7: Isle 1B **10**
Steeple Cl. SW6 6H **7**
SW19 2H **19**
Stephen Fox Ho. *W4 2B 6*
(off Chiswick La.)
Stephenson Ct. *SM2: Cheam 4H 31*
(off Station App.)
Stephenson Rd. TW2: Whit 4F **9**
Sterling Pl. W5 1F **5**
Sterndale Rd. W14 1G **7**
Sterry Dr. KT7: T Ditt 3K **21**
KT19: Ewe 7B **24**
Steve Biko Way TW3: Houn 1F **9**
Stevenage Rd. SW6 4G **7**
Stevens Cl. KT17: Eps 1B **34**
TW12: Hamp 2D **14**
Stevens La. KT10: Clay 4B **28**
Stewart Cl. TW12: Hamp 3D **14**
Steyning Way TW4: Houn 1B **8**
Stile Hall Gdns. W4 2H **5**
Stile Hall Pde. W4: Bford 2H **5**
Stile Path TW16: Sun 7A **14**
Stillingfleet Rd. SW13 3D **6**
Stirling Cl. SM7: Bans 6J **35**
Stirling Rd. TW2: Whit 4F **9**
W3 1J **5**
Stirling Wlk. KT5: Surb 3J **23**
Stockfield Rd. KT10: Clay 2K **27**
Stockhurst Cl. SW15 6F **7**
Stoford Cl. SW19 4H **13**
Stokenchurch St. SW6 5K **7**
Stoke Rd. KT2: King T 4K **17**
KT12: Walt T 7B **20**
Stokesby Rd. KT9: Chess 3G **29**
Stokesheath Rd. KT22: Oxs 7H **27**
Stonecot Cl. SM3: Sutt 5H **25**
Stonecot Hill SM3: Sutt 5H **25**
Stone Hall Gdns. W8 3K **7**
Stonehill Cl. SW14 2A **12**
Stone Hill Rd. W4 2H **5**
Stonehill Rd. SW14 2K **11**
STONELEIGH **2D 30**
Stoneleigh Av. KT4: Wor Pk 1D **30**
Stoneleigh B'way.
KT17: Ewe 2D **30**
Stoneleigh Cres. KT19: Ewe 2C **30**
Stoneleigh Pk. Rd.
KT19: Ewe 3C **30**
Stoneleigh Station (Rail) **2D 30**
Stone Pl. KT4: Wor Pk 6D **24**
Stone's Rd. KT17: Eps 1B **34**
Stoneydeep TW11: Tedd 1B **16**
Stonny Cft. KT21: Asht 6G **33**
Stonor Rd. W14 1J **7**
Stony Hill KT10: Esh 4E **26**
Stoop Memorial Ground **4K 9**
Stormont Way KT9: Chess 2D **28**
Stoughton Av. SM3: Cheam 2G **31**
Stoughton Cl. SW15 5D **12**
Stourhead Cl. SW19 4G **13**
Stourhead Gdns. SW20 7D **18**
Stourton Av. TW13: Hanw 1E **14**
Strachan Pl. SW19 3F **19**
Strafford Rd. TW1: Twick 4B **10**
TW3: Houn 1E **8**
STRAND ON THE GREEN **3H 5**
Strand on the Grn. W4 3H **5**
Stratford Ct. KT3: N Mald 1A **24**
Stratford Gro. SW15 1G **13**
Stratford Rd. W8 1K **7**
Stratford Studios W8 1K **7**
Strathan Cl. SW18 3H **13**
Strathearn Av. TW2: Whit 5G **9**
Strathearn Rd. SM1: Sutt 2K **31**
SW19 2K **19**
Strathmore Rd. SW19 7K **13**
TW11: Tedd 1K **15**
Strathville Rd. SW18 6K **13**
(not continuous)
Stratton Cl. KT12: Walt T 5B **20**
SW19 6K **19**
Stratton Rd. SW19 6K **19**
STRAWBERRY HILL **7A 10**
Strawberry Hill TW1: Twick 7A **10**
Strawberry Hill Cl.
TW1: Twick 7A **10**
Strawberry Hill House *7A 10*
(off Strawberry Va.)
Strawberry Hill Rd.
TW1: Twick 7A **10**
Strawberry Hill Station (Rail) **7A 10**
Strawberry Va. TW1: Twick 7B **10**
(not continuous)
Street, The KT21: Asht 7F **33**
Stretton Rd. TW10: Ham 6D **10**
Strode Rd. SW6 4H **7**
Stroud Cres. SW15 7D **12**
Stroudes Cl. KT4: Wor Pk 4B **24**
Stroud Rd. SW19 7K **13**
Stuart Av. KT12: Walt T 5A **20**
Stuart Gro. TW11: Tedd 2K **15**
Stuart Ho. *W14 1H 7*
(off Windsor Way)
Stuart Lodge KT18: Eps 2A **34**
Stuart Rd. SW19 7K **13**
TW10: Ham 6C **10**
Stubbs Ct. *W4 2J 5*
(off Chaseley Dr.)
Studdridge St. SW6 6K **7**
(not continuous)
Studland Rd. KT2: King T 3F **17**
Studland St. W6 1E **6**
Sudbrook Gdns. TW10: Ham 7E **10**
Sudbrook La. TW10: Ham 5F **11**
Sudbury Ho. SW18 2K **13**
Sudlow Rd. SW18 2K **13**
Suffolk Rd. KT4: Wor Pk 6C **24**
SW13 4C **6**
Sugden Rd. KT7: T Ditt 5C **22**
Sulivan Ct. SW6 6K **7**
Sulivan Ent. Cen. SW6 7K **7**
Sulivan Rd. SW6 7K **7**
Sullivan Cl. KT8: W Mole 7G **15**
Summer Av. KT8: E Mos 2K **21**
Summer Crossing
KT7: E Mos 2K **21**
Summerfield KT21: Asht 7E **32**
Summerfield La. KT6: Surb 6E **22**
Summer Gdns. KT8: E Mos 2K **21**
Summer Rd. KT7: T Ditt 2A **22**
KT8: E Mos 2K **21**
(not continuous)
Summers Cl. SM2: Sutt 4K **31**
Summer Trees TW16: Sun 5A **14**
Summerville Gdns.
SM1: Sutt 3J **31**
Summerwood Rd. TW7: Isle 2A **10**
Summit Bus. Pk. TW16: Sun 4A **14**
Sun All. TW9: Rich 1F **11**
SUNBURY **7B 14**
Sunbury Av. SW14 1A **12**
Sunbury Av. Pas. SW14 1B **12**
Sunbury Cl. KT12: Walt T 3A **20**
Sunbury Ct. Island
TW16: Sun 7C **14**
Sunbury Ct. M. TW16: Sun 6C **14**
Sunbury Ct. Rd. TW16: Sun 6B **14**
Sunbury La. KT12: Walt T 3A **20**
Sunburylock Ait KT12: Sun 1A **20**
Sunbury Pk. Walled Garden **7A 14**
Sunbury Rd. SM3: Cheam 7G **25**
Sunbury Way TW13: Hanw 2B **14**
Sun Life Trad. Est. TW14: Felt 1A **8**
Sunna Gdns. TW16: Sun 6A **14**
Sunningdale Av. TW13: Hanw 6D **8**
Sunningdale Cl. KT6: Surb 6F **23**
Sunningdale Ct. *TW7: Isle 3J 9*
(off Whitton Dene)
Sunningdale Gdns. *W8 1K 7*
(off Stratford Rd.)
Sunningdale Rd. SM1: Sutt 7J **25**
Sunnybank KT18: Eps 5K **33**
Sunnyhurst Cl. SM1: Sutt 7K **25**
Sunnymead Rd. SW15 2E **12**
Sunnymede Av. KT19: Ewe 5B **30**
Sunnyside KT12: Walt T 2B **20**
SW19 3H **19**
Sunnyside Pas. SW19 3H **19**
Sunnyside Pl. SW19 3H **19**
Sunnyside Rd. TW11: Tedd 1J **15**
Sunray Av. KT5: Surb 6J **23**
Sunrise Cl. TW13: Hanw 7E **8**
Sun Rd. W14 2J **7**
Sunset Rd. SW19 2E **18**
SURBITON **3E 22**
Surbiton Ct. KT6: Surb 3D **22**
Surbiton Cres.
KT1: King T 7C **36** (1F **23**)
Surbiton Hall Cl. KT1: King T 1F **23**
Surbiton Hill Pk. KT5: Surb 2G **23**
Surbiton Hill Rd. KT6: Surb 1F **23**
SURBITON HOSPITAL **3F 23**
Surbiton Pde. KT6: Surb 3F **23**
Surbiton Rd.
KT1: King T 7B **36** (1E **22**)
Surbiton Station (Rail) **3F 23**
Surrey Cres. W4 2H **5**
Surrey Institute of Art & Design, The
3B **34**
Surrey Lodge *KT12: Hers 2A 26*
(off Queens Rd.)
Sury Basin
KT2: King T 1C **36** (5F **17**)
Sussex Av. TW7: Isle 1K **9**
Sussex Cl. KT3: N Mald 1B **24**
TW1: Twick 3C **10**
Sussex Gdns. KT9: Chess 3E **28**
Sussex Pl. KT3: N Mald 1B **24**
W6 2F **7**
Sussex Rd. KT3: N Mald 1B **24**
Sutherland Gdns.
KT4: Wor Pk 5E **24**
SW14 7B **6**
Sutherland Gro. SW18 3H **13**
TW11: Tedd 2K **15**
Sutherland Ho. W8 1K **7**
Sutherland Rd. W4 3B **6**
Sutton Comn. Rd. SM1: Sutt 6K **25**
SM3: Sutt 4J **25**
Sutton Common Station (Rail)
6K 25
Sutton Ct. KT8: W Mole 2E **20**
W4 3K **5**
Sutton Ct. Rd. W4 4K **5**
Sutton La. Nth. W4 2K **5**
Sutton La. Sth. W4 3K **5**
Sutton United FC **1K 31**
Swail Ho. *KT18: Eps 2A 34*
(off Ashley Rd.)
Swallow Pk. Cvn. Site
KT6: Surb 7G **23**
Swan Cl. TW13: Hanw 1D **14**
Swan Ct. *SW6 4K 7*
(off Fulham Rd.)
TW7: Isle 7C 4
(off Swan St.)
Swan M. SW6 5J **7**
Swann Ct. *TW7: Isle 7B 4*
(off South St.)
Swan Pl. SW13 6C **6**
Swan Rd. TW13: Hanw 2D **14**
Swanscombe Rd. W4 2B **6**
Swan St. TW7: Isle 7C **4**
Swanton Gdns. SW19 5G **13**
Swanwick Cl. SW15 4C **12**
Swathling Ho. *SW15 3C 12*
(off Tunworth Cres.)
Sweet Briar La. KT18: Eps 3A **34**
Swift Rd. TW13: Hanw 7D **8**
Swift St. SW6 5J **7**
Swinburne Rd. SW15 1D **12**
Swinfield Cl. TW13: Hanw 7D **8**
Swyncombe Av. W5 1C **4**
Sybil Thorndike Casson Ho.
SW5 2K 7
(off Kramer M.)
Sycamore Cl. TW13: Felt 7A **8**
Sycamore Ct. KT3: N Mald 7B **18**
TW4: Houn 1D **8**
Sycamore Gro. KT3: N Mald 7A **18**
Sycamore Ri. SM7: Bans 3G **35**
Sycamore Rd. SW19 3F **19**
Sycamore Way TW11: Tedd 3D **16**
Sydney Rd. SM1: Sutt 1K **31**
SW20 6G **19**
TW9: Rich 1F **11**
TW11: Tedd 2A **16**
Sydney Ter. *KT10: Clay 3A 28*
(off Green, The)
Sylvan Gdns. KT6: Surb 4E **22**
Sylvestrus Cl. KT1: King T 5H **17**
Syon Ga. Way TW8: Bford 4B **4**
Syon House **5D 4**
Syon La. TW7: Isle 3A **4**
Syon Lane Station (Rail) **4B 4**
Syon Pk. **5C 4**
Syon Pk. Gdns. TW7: Isle 4A **4**

T

Tabarin Way KT17: Eps D 5F **35**
Tabor Ct. SM3: Cheam 3H **31**
Tabor Gdns. SM3: Cheam 3J **31**
Tabor Gro. SW19 4J **19**
Tabor Rd. W6 1E **6**
Tadlow *KT1: King T 7H 17*
(off Washington Rd.)
Tadworth Av. KT3: N Mald 1C **24**
Taggs Ho. *KT1: King T 4B 36*
(off Wadbrook St.)
Talbot Lodge KT10: Esh 2F **27**
Talbot Rd. TW2: Twick 5K **9**
TW7: Isle 1B **10**
Talgarth Mans. *W14 2H 7*
(off Talgarth Rd.)
Talgarth Rd. W6 2G **7**
W14 2G **7**
Talisman Way KT17: Eps D 5F **35**
Tallow Rd. TW8: Bford 3D **4**
Tall Pines KT17: Eps 7C **30**
Talma Gdns. TW2: Twick 3K **9**
Tamarind Ct. *W8 1K 7*
(off Stone Hall Gdns.)
Tamesis Gdns. KT4: Wor Pk 6B **24**
Tamian Ind. Est. TW4: Houn 1B **8**
Tamian Way TW4: Houn 1B **8**
Tamworth St. SW6 3K **7**
Tangier Rd. TW10: Rich 1H **11**
Tangier Way KT20: Tad 6H **35**
Tangier Wood KT20: Tad 7H **35**
Tanglewood Way TW13: Felt 7A **8**
Tangley Gro. SW15 3C **12**
Tangley Pk. Rd.
TW12: Hamp 2E **14**
Tangmere Gro. KT2: King T 2E **16**
Tankerton Rd. KT6: Surb 6G **23**
Tanners Cl. KT12: Walt T 3A **20**
Tanyard Ho. *TW8: Bford 4D 4*
(off High St.)
Tasso Rd. W6 3H **7**
Tasso Yd. *W6 3H 7*
(off Tasso Rd.)
Tatchbury Ho. *SW15 3C 12*
(off Tunworth Cres.)
Tate Rd. SM1: Sutt 2K **31**
TATTENHAM CORNER **7E 34**
Tattenham Cnr. Rd.
KT18: Eps D, Tatt C 6C **34**
Tattenham Corner Station (Rail)
7E 34
Tattenham Cres. KT18: Tatt C 7D **34**
Tattenham Gro. KT18: Tatt C 7E **34**
Tattenham Way KT20: Tad 7G **35**
Taunton Av. SW20 6E **18**
Taunton Cl. SM3: Sutt 5K **25**
Tawny Cl. TW13: Felt 7A **8**
Tayben Av. TW2: Twick 3K **9**
Tayles Hill Dr. KT17: Ewe 6C **30**
Taylor Av. TW9: Kew 6J **5**
Taylor Cl. KT19: Eps 7H **29**
TW12: Hamp H 2H **15**
Taylor Rd. KT21: Asht 6E **32**
Tealing Dr. KT19: Ewe 1A **30**
Teal Pl. SM1: Sutt 2J **31**
Teazlewood Pk. KT22: Lea 6B **32**
Teck Cl. TW7: Isle 6B **4**
Tedder Cl. KT9: Chess 2D **28**
TEDDINGTON **2B 16**
Teddington Bus. Pk.
TW11: Tedd 3A 16
(off Station Rd.)

Teddington Cl.—Vale Rd.

Teddington Cl. KT19: Eps 6A 30
Teddington Pk.
TW11: Tedd 2A 16
TEDDINGTON MEMORIAL HOSPITAL
. . . . .3K 15
Teddington Pk. Rd.
TW11: Tedd 1A 16
Teddington Pool & Fitness Cen.
. . . . .2B 16
Teddington Station (Rail) 3B 16
Teesdale Av. TW7: Isle 5B 4
Teesdale Gdns. TW7: Isle 5B 4
Telegraph La. KT10: Clay 2A 28
Telegraph Rd. SW15 . . . . .4E 12
Telephone Pl. SW6 . . . . .3J 7
Telford Dr. KT12: Walt T 4B 20
Telford Rd. TW2: Whit 4F 9
Tellisford KT10: Esh 7G 21
Temeraire Pl. TW8: Bford 2G 5
Templar Pl. TW12: Hamp 4F 15
Temple Cl. KT19: Eps 1A 34
Templecombe Way
SM4: Mord 2H 25
Temple Ct. KT19: Eps 1A 34
Temple Rd. KT19: Eps 1A 34
TW3: Houn 1G 9
TW9: Rich 6G 5
W4 . . . . .1K 5
W5 . . . . .1E 4
Temple Sheen SW14 . . . . .1K 11
Temple Sheen Rd.
SW14 . . . . .1J 11
Templeton Pl. SW5 . . . . .1K 7
Tennis Ct. La. KT8: E Mos 7A 16
Tennyson Av. KT3: N Mald 2E 24
TW1: Twick 5A 10
Tennyson Mans. W14 . . . . .3J 7
(off Queen's Club Gdns.)
Terrace, The SW13 . . . . .6B 6
Terrace Gdns. SW13 . . . . .6C 6
Terrace La. TW10: Rich 3F 11
Terrace Rd. KT12: Walt T 4A 20
Terrano Ho. TW9: Kew 4J 5
Tersha St. TW9: Rich 1G 11
Thackeray Cl. SW19 . . . . .4G 19
TW7: Isle 6B 4
Thackeray Ct. W14 . . . . .1H 7
(off Blythe Rd.)
Thames Bank SW14 . . . . .6K 5
Thames Cl. TW12: Hamp 6G 15
Thames Cotts. KT7: T Ditt 3C 22
Thames Ct. KT8: W Mole 6G 15
Thames Cres. W4 . . . . .4B 6
THAMES DITTON 3B 22
Thames Ditton Miniature Railway
. . . . .5B 22
Thames Ditton Station (Rail)
. . . . .4A 22
Thames Eyot TW1: Twick 5B 10
Thamesgate Cl. TW10: Ham 1C 16
Thames Haven KT6: Surb 2E 22
Thames Ho. KT1: King T 7B 36
Thameside KT8: W Mole 7G 15
TW11: Tedd 4E 16
Thameside Cen. TW8: Bford 3G 5
Thameside Pl.
KT1: Hamp W 5E 16
Thames Lock KT12: Walt T 7B 14
Thames Mead KT12: Walt T 4A 20
Thames Mdw. KT8: W Mole 6F 15
Thames Pl. SW15 . . . . .7G 7
(not continuous)
Thamespoint TW11: Tedd 4E 16
Thames Reach W6 . . . . .3F 7
(off Rainville Rd.)
Thames Rd. W4 . . . . .3H 5
Thames Side
KT1: King T 2B 36 (5E 16)
KT7: T Ditt 3C 22
Thames St.
KT1: King T 3B 36 (6E 16)
(not continuous)
TW12: Hamp 5G 15
TW16: Sun 1A 20
Thames Village W4 . . . . .5K 5
Thames Wharf Studios
W6 . . . . .3F 7
(off Rainville Rd.)
Thatchers Way TW7: Isle 2J 9
Thaxted Pl. SW20 . . . . .4G 19
Thaxton Rd. W14 . . . . .3J 7
Theatre Ct. KT18: Eps 2A 34
Thelma Gro. TW11: Tedd 3B 16
Theresa Rd. W6 . . . . .1D 6
Thetford Rd. KT3: N Mald 3A 24
Thetis Ter. TW9: Kew 3H 5
Third Cl. KT8: W Mole 1H 21
Third Cross Rd. TW2: Twick 6J 9
Thistlecroft Rd. KT12: Hers 1B 26
Thistledene KT7: T Ditt 3K 21
Thistleworth Marina
TW7: Isle 1C 10
(off Railshead Rd.)
Thomas Wall Cl. SM1: Sutt 2K 31
Thompson Av. TW9: Rich 7H 5
Thompson Cl. SM3: Sutt 5K 25
Thompson Rd. TW3: Houn 1G 9
Thorkhill Gdns. KT7: T Ditt 5B 22
Thorkhill Rd. KT7: T Ditt 5B 22
Thorncroft Rd. SM1: Sutt 2K 31
Thorndon Gdns. KT19: Ewe 2B 30
Thorne Ho. KT10: Clay 4C 28
Thorne Pas. SW13 . . . . .6B 6
Thorne St. SW13 . . . . .7B 6
Thorneycroft Cl.
KT12: Walt T 3B 20
Thorney Hedge Rd. W4 . . . . .1J 5
Thornfield Rd. SM7: Bans 6K 35
Thornhill Av. KT6: Surb 6F 23
Thornhill Ho. W4 . . . . .2B 6
(off Wood St.)
Thornhill Rd. KT6: Surb 6F 23
Thornton Av. W4 . . . . .1B 6
Thornton Hill SW19 . . . . .4H 19
Thornton Rd. SW14 . . . . .1A 12
SW19 . . . . .3G 19
Thornton Rd. E. SW19 . . . . .3G 19
Thornycroft Ho. W4 . . . . .2B 6
(off Fraser St.)
Thorpe Rd. KT2: King T 4F 17
Thrigby Rd. KT9: Chess 3G 29
Thrupp's Av. KT12: Hers 2C 26
Thrupp's La. KT12: Hers 2C 26
Thurleston Av. SM4: Mord 2H 25
Thurnby Ct. TW2: Twick 7K 9
Thursley Gdns. SW19 . . . . .6G 13
Thurstan Rd. SW20 . . . . .4E 18
Tibbet's Cl. SW19 . . . . .5G 13
TIBBET'S CORNER 4G 13
Tibbet's Ride SW15 . . . . .4G 13
Tichmarsh KT19: Eps 6K 29
Tideswell Rd. SW15 . . . . .1F 13
Tideway Cl. TW10: Ham 1C 16
Tiffany Hgts. SW18 . . . . .4K 13
Tiffin School Sports Hall
. . . . .3E 36 (6G 17)
Tildesley Rd. SW15 . . . . .3F 13
Tilehurst Rd. SM3: Cheam 2H 31
Tilford Gdns. SW19 . . . . .5G 13
Tilia Cl. SM1: Sutt 2J 31
Tilley Rd. TW13: Felt 5A 8
Tilton St. SW6 . . . . .3H 7
Timbercroft KT19: Ewe 1B 30
Timberhill KT21: Asht 7F 33
Timbers, The SM3: Cheam 3H 31
Timsbury Wlk. SW15 . . . . .5D 12
Tinderbox All. SW14 . . . . .7A 6
Tinefields KT20: Tad 7H 35
Tintagel Cl. KT17: Eps 3C 34
Tintern Cl. SW15 . . . . .2H 13
Titan Ct. TW8: Bford 2G 5
Tithe Barn Cl.
KT2: King T 2E 36 (5G 17)
Tithe Cl. KT12: Walt T 3A 20
Tiverton Way KT9: Chess 2E 28
Tivoli Rd. TW4: Houn 1D 8
Toad La. TW4: Houn 1E 8
Toby Way KT5: Surb 6J 23
Token Yd. SW15 . . . . .1H 13
Toland Sq. SW15 . . . . .2D 12
Tolson Rd. TW7: Isle 7B 4
Tolverne Rd. SW20 . . . . .5F 19
TOLWORTH 6J 23
Tolworth B'way. KT6: Surb 5J 23
Tolworth Cl. KT6: Surb 5J 23
TOLWORTH HOSPITAL 6H 23
TOLWORTH JUNC. (TOBY JUG)
. . . . .6J 23
Tolworth Pk. Rd. KT6: Surb 6G 23
Tolworth Recreation Cen. 7G 23
Tolworth Ri. Nth. KT5: Surb 5J 23
Tolworth Ri. Sth. KT5: Surb 6J 23
Tolworth Rd. KT6: Surb 6F 23
Tolworth Station (Rail) 6J 23
Tolworth Twr. KT6: Surb 6J 23
Tomlin Cl. KT19: Eps 7A 30
Tomlin Ct. KT19: Eps 7A 30
Tomlins All. TW1: Twick 5B 10
Tomlinson Cl. W4 . . . . .2J 5
Tom Williams Ho. SW6 . . . . .3J 7
(off Clem Attlee Ct.)
Tonbridge Rd. KT8: W Mole 1E 20
Tonfield Rd. SM3: Sutt 5J 25
Tonstall Rd. KT19: Eps 6A 30
Topiary Sq. TW9: Rich 7G 5
Tormead Cl. SM1: Sutt 3K 31
Torrington Cl. KT10: Clay 3K 27
Torrington Rd. KT10: Clay 3K 27
Torrington Way SM4: Mord 3K 25
Torwood Rd. SW15 . . . . .2D 12
Tourist Info. Cen.
Hounslow 1G 9
Kingston upon Thames
. . . . .4B 36 (6E 16)
Richmond upon Thames
. . . . .2E 10
Twickenham 5C 10
Tournay Rd. SW6 . . . . .4J 7
Tower Gdns. KT10: Clay 4C 28
Tower Ri. TW9: Rich 7F 5
Tower Rd. TW1: Twick 7A 10
Towers Pl. TW9: Rich 2F 11
Tower Yd. TW10: Rich 2G 11
Towfield Ct. TW13: Hanw 6E 8
Towfield Rd. TW13: Hanw 6E 8
Town End Pde. KT1: King T 5B 36
Town Fld. Way TW7: Isle 6B 4
Town Hall Av. W4 . . . . .2A 6
Town Mdw. TW8: Bford 3E 4
Town Mdw. Rd. TW8: Bford 4E 4
Townmead Rd. TW9: Rich 6J 5
Townshend Rd. TW9: Rich 1G 11
Townshend Ter. TW9: Rich 1G 11
Town Sq. TW7: Isle 7C 4
(off Swan St.)
Town Wharf TW7: Isle 7C 4
Toynbee Rd. SW20 . . . . .5H 19
Trafalgar Av. KT4: Wor Pk 5G 25
Trafalgar Dr. KT12: Walt T 7A 20
Trafalgar Rd. TW2: Twick 6J 9
Traherne Lodge TW11: Tedd 2A 16
Tranmere Rd. TW2: Whit 4G 9
Transport Av. TW8: Bford 2B 4
Traps La. KT3: N Mald 5B 18
Treadwell Rd. KT18: Eps 5B 34
Treaty Cen. TW3: Houn 1G 9
Trebovir Rd. SW5 . . . . .2K 7
Tree Cl. TW10: Ham 5E 10
Treemount Ct. KT17: Eps 2B 34
Treen Av. SW13 . . . . .7C 6
Tregaron Gdns. KT3: N Mald 1B 24
Trehern Rd. SW14 . . . . .7A 6
Trematon Pl. TW11: Tedd 4D 16
Trenchard Cl. KT12: Hers 2B 26
Trenchard Ct. SM4: Mord 3K 25
Trentham St. SW18 . . . . .5K 13
Trent Ho.
KT2: King T 1B 36 (5E 16)
Trent Way KT4: Wor Pk 7F 25
Trevanion Rd. W14 . . . . .1H 7
Treville St. SW15 . . . . .4E 12
Trevor Cl. TW7: Isle 2A 10
Trevor Rd. SW19 . . . . .4H 19
Trewenna Dr. KT9: Chess 2E 28
Trewince Rd. SW20 . . . . .5F 19
Triangle, The KT1: King T 6J 17
Trigo Ct. KT19: Eps 7A 30
Trimmer Wlk. TW8: Bford 3F 5
Trinder M. TW11: Tedd 2B 16
Tring Ct. TW1: Twick 1B 16
Trinity Chu. Pas. SW13 . . . . .3E 6
Trinity Chu. Rd. SW13 . . . . .3E 6
Trinity Cl. TW4: Houn 1D 8
Trinity Cotts. TW9: Rich 7G 5
Trinity Rd. SW19 . . . . .3K 19
TW9: Rich 7G 5
Trotter Way KT19: Eps 1J 33
Trowlock Av. TW11: Tedd 3D 16
Trowlock Way TW11: Tedd 3E 16
Trussley Rd. W6 . . . . .1F 7
Trystings Cl. KT10: Clay 3B 28
Tucklow Wlk. SW15 . . . . .4C 12
Tudor Av. KT4: Wor Pk 7E 24
TW12: Hamp 3F 15
Tudor Cl. KT9: Chess 2F 29
KT17: Ewe 6C 30
SM3: Cheam 2G 31
SM7: Bans 4H 35
TW12: Hamp H 2H 15
Tudor Ct. TW11: Tedd 3A 16
TW13: Hanw 1B 14
Tudor Dr. KT2: King T 2E 16
KT12: Walt T 5C 20
SM4: Mord 3G 25
Tudor Gdns. SW13 . . . . .7B 6
TW1: Twick 5A 10
Tudor Ho. W14 . . . . .1G 7
(off Windsor Way)
Tudor Rd. KT2: King T 4H 17
TW3: Houn 1J 9
TW12: Hamp 4F 15
Tufton Gdns. KT8: W Mole 6G 15
Tulip Cl. TW12: Hamp 3E 14
Tulip Tree Ct. SM2: Sutt 7K 31
Tumblewood Rd. SM7: Bans 5H 35
Tunstall Wlk. TW8: Bford 3F 5
Tunworth Cres. SW15 . . . . .3C 12
Turner Av. TW2: Twick 7H 9
Turner Ho. TW1: Twick 3E 10
(off Clevedon Rd.)
Turner M. SM2: Sutt 4K 31
Turner Rd. KT3: N Mald 4A 24
Turners La. KT12: Hers 3A 26
Turneville Rd. W14 . . . . .3J 7
TURNHAM GREEN 1B 6
Turnham Green Station (Tube) . . .1B 6
Turnham Grn. Ter. W4 . . . . .1B 6
Turnham Grn. Ter. M. W4 . . . . .1B 6
Turnpike Way TW7: Isle 5B 4
TWICKENHAM 5B 10
Twickenham Baths 5B 10
Twickenham Bri. TW1: Twick 2D 10
TW9: Rich 2D 10
Twickenham Pl. KT7: T Ditt 6A 22
(off Woodfield Rd.)
Twickenham Rd. TW7: Isle 2B 10
TW9: Rich 1D 10
TW11: Tedd 1B 16
(not continuous)
TW13: Hanw 7E 8
Twickenham Rugby Union
Football Ground 3K 9
Twickenham Station (Rail) 4B 10
Twickenham Trad. Est.
TW1: Twick 3A 10
Twining Av. TW2: Twick 7H 9
Tybenham Rd. SW19 . . . . .7K 19
Tynamara KT1: King T 7B 36
Tyne Ho. KT2: King T 1B 36 (5E 16)
Tyrawley Rd. SW6 . . . . .5K 7

U

Udney Pk. Rd. TW11: Tedd 3B 16
UGC Cinema
Hammersmith 1E 6
Ullswater Cl. SW15 . . . . .1A 18
Ullswater Cres. SW15 . . . . .1A 18
Ullswater Rd. SW13 . . . . .4D 6
Ulva Rd. SW15 . . . . .2G 13
Umbria St. SW15 . . . . .3D 12
Underwood Ho. KT8: W Mole 2F 21
(off Approach Rd.)
Union Ct. TW9: Rich 2F 11
Union St.
KT1: King T 3B 36 (6E 16)
University of Surrey Roehampton
. . . . .3C 12
Unwin Mans. W14 . . . . .3J 7
(off Queen's Club Gdns.)
Unwin Rd. TW7: Isle 7A 4
Upham Pk. Rd. W4 . . . . .1B 6
Uplands Cl. SW14 . . . . .2J 11
Upland Way KT18: Tatt C 7F 35
Up. Brighton Rd. KT6: Surb 3E 22
Upper Butts TW8: Bford 3D 4
Upper Ct. Rd. KT19: Eps 7K 29
Upper Dunnymans
SM7: Bans 3J 35
Up. Farm Rd. KT8: W Mole 1E 20
Up. Grotto Rd. TW1: Twick 6A 10
Up. Ham Rd. TW10: Ham 1E 16
Up. High St. KT17: Eps 2B 34
Upper Mall W6 . . . . .2D 6
(not continuous)
Up. Mulgrave Rd.
SM2: Cheam 4H 31
Upper Pk. Rd. KT2: King T 3H 17
Up. Richmond Rd.
SW15 . . . . .1C 12
Up. Richmond Rd. W.
SW14 . . . . .1J 11
TW10, Rich 1H 11
Up. Sawleywood SM7: Bans 3J 35
Upper Sq. TW7: Isle 7B 4
Up. Sunbury Rd.
TW12: Hamp 5D 14
Up. Teddington Rd.
KT1: Hamp W 4D 16
Upton Rd. TW3: Houn 1F 9
Urmston Dr. SW19 . . . . .5H 13
Uxbridge Ct. KT1: King T 2E 22
(off Uxbridge Rd.)
Uxbridge Rd. KT1: King T 1E 22
TW12: Hamp, Hamp H 1F 15
TW13: Felt 6B 8

V

Vale, The TW14: Felt 3A 8
TW16: Sun 3A 14
Vale Cl. TW1: Twick 7B 10
Vale Cotts. SW15 . . . . .7B 12
Vale Cres. SW15 . . . . .1B 18
Vale Cft. KT10: Clay 5A 28
Vale Pde. SW15 . . . . .7B 12
Vale Rd. KT4: Wor Pk 7C 24
KT10: Clay 5K 27

A-Z Richmond & Kingston 65

Vale Rd. KT19: Ewe 7C **24**
SM1: Sutt 7K **25**
Vale Rd. Nth. KT6: Surb 6F **23**
Vale Rd. Sth. KT6: Surb 6F **23**
Valery Pl. TW12: Hamp 4F **15**
Valley M. TW1: Twick 6A **10**
Vallis Way KT9: Chess 1E **28**
Valonia Gdns. SW18 3J **13**
Vanbrugh Dr. KT12: Walt T 4B **20**
Vanbrugh M. KT12: Walt T 4B **20**
Vancouver Cl. KT19: Eps 7K **29**
Vancouver Rd. TW10: Ham 1D **16**
Van Dyck Av. KT3: N Mald 4A **24**
Vandyke Cl. SW15 4G **13**
Van Gogh Cl. TW7: Isle 7B **4**
Vanneck Sq. SW15 2D **12**
Vanston Pl. SW6 4K **7**
Vantage Pl. W8 1K **7**
Vantage W. W3 1G **5**
Varna Rd. SW6 4H **7**
TW12: Hamp 5G **15**
Varsity Dr. TW1: Twick 2K **9**
Varsity Row SW14 6K **5**
Vaughan Av. W6 1C **6**
Vaughan Cl. TW12: Hamp 3D **14**
Vaughan Rd. KT7: T Ditt 4C **22**
Vaux Cres. KT12: Hers 3A **26**
Vencourt Pl. W6 1D **6**
Vera Rd. SW6 5H **7**
Verbena Gdns. W6 2D **6**
Verdun Rd. SW13 3D **6**
Vereker Dr. TW16: Sun 7A **14**
Vereker Rd. W14 2H **7**
Vermont Rd. SM1: Sutt 7K **25**
Vernon Av. SW20 6G **19**
Vernon Cl. KT19: Ewe 3K **29**
Vernon M. W14 1H **7**
Vernon Rd. SW14 7A **6**
Vernon St. W14 1H **7**
Verona Ct. W4 2B **6**
Verona Dr. KT6: Surb 6F **23**
Vicarage Cl. KT4: Wor Pk 5B **24**
Vicarage Dr. SW14 2A **12**
Vicarage Flds. KT12: Walt T 3B **20**
Vicarage Gdns. SW14 2K **11**
Vicarage Ho. *KT1: King T 6G 17*
(off Cambridge Rd.)
Vicarage La. KT17: Ewe 5D **30**
(not continuous)
Vicarage Rd. KT1: Hamp W 5D **16**
KT1: King T 3B **36** (6E **16**)
SM1: Sutt 7K **25**
SW14 2K **11**
TW2: Twick 6K **9**
TW2: Whit 3H **9**
TW11: Tedd 2B **16**
Vickers Way TW4: Houn 2D **8**
Victoria Av. KT6: Surb 3E **22**
KT8: W Mole 7G **15**
TW3: Houn 2F **9**
Victoria Cl. KT8: W Mole 7F **15**
Victoria Cotts. TW9: Kew 5G **5**
Victoria Cres. SW19 4J **19**
Victoria Dr. SW19 4G **13**
Victoria Pde. *TW9: Kew 5H 5*
(off Sandycombe Rd.)
Victoria Pl. *KT10: Esh 1G 27*
(off Esher Pk. Av.)
KT17: Eps 1B **34**
TW9: Rich 2E **10**
Victoria Rd.
KT1: King T 4E **36** (6G **17**)
KT6: Surb 3E **22**
SW14 7A **6**
TW1: Twick 4C **10**
TW11: Tedd 3B **16**
TW13: Felt 5A **8**
Victoria Vs. TW9: Rich 7G **5**
Victor Rd. TW11: Tedd 1K **15**
Victors Dr. TW12: Hamp 3D **14**
Victory Bus. Cen. TW7: Isle 1A **10**
Vidler Cl. KT9: Chess 3D **28**
Viewfield Rd. SW18 3J **13**
Viking Ct. SW6 3K **7**
Village Gdns. KT17: Ewe 6C **30**
Village Row SM2: Sutt 4K **31**
Villiers Av.
KT5: Surb 7E **36** (2G **23**)
TW2: Whit 5E **8**
Villiers Cl. KT5: Surb 1G **23**
Villiers Gro. SM2: Cheam 5G **31**
Villiers Path KT6: Surb 2F **23**
Villiers Rd.
KT1: King T 7E **36** (1G **23**)
Vincam Cl. TW2: Whit 4F **9**
Vincent Av. KT5: Surb 6K **23**
Vincent Cl. KT10: Esh 7G **21**
Vincent Rd. KT1: King T 7H **17**
Vincent Row TW12: Hamp H 3H **15**
Vine Cl. KT5: Surb 3G **23**
Vine Ct. KT12: Hers 3B **26**
Vine Pl. TW3: Houn 1G **9**
Viner Cl. KT12: Walt T 3B **20**
Vine Rd. KT8: E Mos 1H **21**
SW13 7C **6**
Vine Sq. *W14 2J 7*
(off Star Rd.)
Vineyard, The TW10: Rich 2F **11**
Vineyard Cl.
KT1: King T 5E **36** (7G **17**)
Vineyard Hill Rd.
SW19 1J **19**
Vineyard M. TW10: Rich 2F **11**
Vineyard Pas. TW10: Rich 2F **11**
Vineyard Path SW14 7A **6**
Vineyard Row KT1: Hamp W 5D **16**
Vineyards, The TW16: Sun 7A **14**
Viola Av. TW14: Felt 3B **8**
Violet Cl. SM3: Sutt 5H **25**
Virginia Cl. KT3: N Mald 1K **23**
KT21: Asht 7E **32**
Virginia Ho. TW11: Tedd 2C **16**
Viscount Point SW19 4K **19**
Vitae Apartments W6 1D **6**
Vivien Cl. KT9: Chess 4F **29**
Vivienne Cl. TW1: Twick 3E **10**
Voewood Cl. KT3: N Mald 3C **24**
Vue Cinema
Fulham Broadway 4K 7

W

Wadbrook St.
KT1: King T 4B **36** (6E **16**)
Wades La. TW11: Tedd 2B **16**
Wadham Rd. SW15 1H **13**
Wadhurst Rd. W4 1A **6**
Wagner M. *KT6: Surb 2F 23*
(off Avenue Elmers)
Waight's Ct.
KT2: King T 1D **36** (5F **17**)
Wainford Cl. SW19 5G **13**
Wainwright Gro. TW7: Isle 1J **9**
Wakefield Rd. TW10: Rich 2E **10**
Waldeck Rd. SW14 7K **5**
W4 3H **5**
Waldeck Ter. *SW14 7K 5*
(off Waldeck Rd.)
Waldegrave Av. TW11: Tedd 2A **16**
Waldegrave Gdns.
TW1: Twick 6A **10**
Waldegrave Pk. TW1: Twick 1A **16**
Waldegrave Rd. TW1: Twick 1A **16**
TW11: Tedd 1A **16**
Waldemar Av. SW6 5H **7**
Waldemar Rd. SW19 2K **19**
WALHAM GREEN 5K **7**
Walham Grn. Ct. *SW6 4K 7*
(off Waterford Rd.)
Walham Gro. SW6 4K **7**
Walham Ri. SW19 3H **19**
Walham Yd. SW6 4K **7**
Walker Cl. TW12: Hamp 3E **14**
Walkers Pl. SW15 1H **13**
Walkfield Dr. KT18: Tatt C 6E **34**
Wallace Flds. KT17: Eps 2D **34**
Wallbrook Bus. Cen.
TW4: Houn 1A **8**
Wallgrave Rd. SW5 1K **7**
Wallorton Gdns. SW14 1A **12**
Walmer Ct. *KT5: Surb 2F 23*
(off Cranes Pk.)
Walnut Cl. KT18: Eps 4C **34**
Walnut Flds. KT17: Ewe 5C **30**
Walnut Gro. SM7: Bans 3G **35**
Walnut Tree Cl. SM7: Bans 1H **35**
SW13 5C **6**
Walnut Tree Cotts.
SW19 2H **19**
Walnut Tree Rd. TW8: Bford 3F **5**
Walpole Av. TW9: Kew 6G **5**
Walpole Ct. TW2: Twick 6K **9**
W14 1G 7
(off Blythe Rd.)
Walpole Cres. TW11: Tedd 2A **16**
Walpole Gdns. TW2: Twick 6K **9**
W4 2K **5**
Walpole Ho. *KT8: W Mole 2F 21*
(off Approach Rd.)
Walpole Pl. TW11: Tedd 2A **16**
Walpole Rd. KT6: Surb 4F **23**
TW2: Twick 6K **9**
TW11: Tedd 2A **16**
Walsham Rd. TW14: Felt 4A **8**
Walsingham Gdns.
KT19: Ewe 1B **30**
Walsingham Lodge
SW13 5D **6**
Walters Mead KT21: Asht 6F **33**
Walter St.
KT2: King T 2C **36** (5F **17**)
Walton Av. KT3: N Mald 1C **24**
SM3: Cheam 7J **25**
WALTON COMMUNITY HOSPITAL
6A 20
Walton-on-Thames Station (Rail)
7A **20**
Walton Pk. KT12: Walt T 6C **20**
Walton Pk. La. KT12: Walt T 6C **20**
Walton Rd.
KT8: W Mole, E Moss 1E **20**
KT12: Walt T 2B **20**
KT18: Eps D 6C **34**
Walton Swimming Pool 5A 20
Wanborough Dr. SW15 5E **12**
Wandle Ct. KT19: Ewe 1K **29**
Wandle Recreation Cen. 3K 13
Wandsdown Pl. SW6 4K **7**
WANDSWORTH 2K **13**
Wandsworth Bri. Rd.
SW6 5K **7**
WANDSWORTH GYRATORY 2K **13**
Wandsworth High St. SW18 2K **13**
Wandsworth Plain SW18 2K **13**
Warbank La. KT2: King T 4C **18**
Warboys App. KT2: King T 3J **17**
Warboys Rd. KT2: King T 3J **17**
Warburton Rd. TW2: Whit 5G **9**
Wardo Av. SW6 5H **7**
Wardrobe, The *TW9: Rich 2E 10*
(off Old Pal. Yd.)
Ware Ct. SM1: Sutt 1J **31**
Wareham Cl. TW3: Houn 1G **9**
Warfield Rd. TW12: Hamp 5G **15**
Warkworth Gdns. TW7: Isle 4B **4**
Warner Av. SM3: Cheam 6H **25**
Warner Cl. TW12: Hamp 2E **14**
Warners La. KT2: King T 1E **16**
Warnford Ho. *SW15 3B 12*
(off Tunworth Cres.)
Warren, The KT4: Wor Pk 7A **24**
Warren Av. SM2: Cheam 6J **31**
TW10: Rich 1J **11**
Warren Cl. KT10: Esh 7G **21**
Warren Cutting KT2: King T 4A **18**
Warren Dr. Nth. KT5: Surb 5J **23**
Warren Dr. Sth. KT5: Surb 5K **23**
Warren Footpath
TW1: Twick 5D **10**
Warren Hill KT18: Eps 5A **34**
Warren Ho. *W14 1J 7*
(off Beckford Cl.)
Warren La. KT22: Oxs 7H **27**
Warren Mead SM7: Bans 4F **35**
Warren Pk. KT2: King T 3K **17**
Warren Ri. KT3: N Mald 5A **18**
Warren Rd. KT2: King T 3K **17**
SM7: Bans 3F **35**
TW2: Whit 3H **9**
Warrington Rd. TW10: Rich 2E **10**
Warwick *W14 1J 7*
(off Kensington Village)
Warwick Cl. TW12: Hamp 4H **15**
Warwick Dr. SW15 7E **6**
Warwick Gdns. KT7: T Ditt 2A **22**
KT21: Asht 6D **32**
W14 1J **7**
Warwick Gro. KT5: Surb 4G **23**
Warwick Ho. KT2: King T 1D **36**
Warwick Lodge TW2: Twick 7G **9**
Warwick Pl. KT7: T Ditt 3B **22**
Warwick Rd. KT1: Hamp W 5D **16**
KT3: N Mald 7K **17**
KT7: T Ditt 2A **22**
SW5 1K **7**
TW2: Twick 5K **9**
W14 1J **7**
Washington Rd. KT1: King T 6H **17**
KT4: Wor Pk 6E **24**
SW13 4D **6**
Watchfield Ct. W4 2K **5**
Watcombe Cotts. TW9: Kew 3H **5**
Waterer Gdns. KT20: Tad 7G **35**
Waterford Cl. KT11: Cobh 7D **26**
Waterford Rd. SW6 4K **7**
(not continuous)
Watergardens, The
KT2: King T 3K **17**
Waterhouse Cl. W6 1G **7**
Water La.
KT1: King T 2B **36** (5E **16**)
TW1: Twick 5B **10**
TW9: Rich 2E **10**
Waterloo Pl. TW9: Kew 3H **5**
TW9: Rich 1F **11**
Waterloo Rd. KT19: Eps 1A **34**
Watermans Art Cen., Cinema &
Theatre 3F 5
Watermans Cl. KT2: King T 4F **17**
Watermans Ct. *TW8: Bford 3E 4*
(off High St.)
Waterman St. SW15 7G **7**
Watermill Cl. TW10: Ham 7D **10**
Water Mill Ho. TW13: Hanw 6F **9**
Watermill Way TW13: Hanw 6E **8**
Water's Edge *SW6 5F 7*
(off Palemead Cl.)
Watersedge KT19: Ewe 1K **29**
Waterside Bus. Cen.
TW7: Isle 1C **10**
Waterside Cl. KT6: Surb 6F **23**
Waterside Dr. KT12: Walt T 2A **20**
Waters Pl. SW15 6F **7**
Watersplash Cl.
KT1: King T 5C **36** (7F **17**)
Waters Rd. KT1: King T 6J **17**
Waters Sq. KT1: King T 7J **17**
Watery La. SW20 6J **19**
Watney Cotts. SW14 7K **5**
Watney Rd. SW14 7K **5**
Watson Av. SM3: Cheam 6H **25**
Watts La. TW11: Tedd 2B **16**
Watts Rd. KT7: T Ditt 4B **22**
Wavendon Av. W4 2A **6**
Waverley Av. KT5: Surb 3J **23**
TW2: Whit 5E **8**
Waverley Cl. KT8: W Mole 2F **21**
Waverley Rd. KT17: Ewe 2E **30**
Wayneflete Twr. Av.
KT10: Esh 7F **21**
Wayside SW14 2K **11**
Wayside Ct. TW1: Twick 3D **10**
Wealdstone Rd. SM3: Sutt 6J **25**
Weavers Cl. TW7: Isle 1K **9**
Weavers Ter. *SW6 3K 7*
(off Micklethwaite Rd.)
Webb Ho. TW13: Hanw 7D **8**
Weimar St. SW15 7H **7**
Weir Rd. KT12: Walt T 3A **20**
Weiss Rd. SW15 7G **7**
Welbeck Cl. KT3: N Mald 2C **24**
KT17: Ewe 4D **30**
Welbeck Ct. *W14 1J 7*
(off Addison Bri. Pl.)
Weldon Dr. KT8: W Mole 1E **20**
Welford Pl. SW19 1H **19**
Wellesford Cl. SM7: Bans 6J **35**
Wellesley Av. W6 1E **6**
Wellesley Ct. SM3: Sutt 5H **25**
Wellesley Cres. TW2: Twick 6K **9**
Wellesley Mans. *W14 2J 7*
(off Edith Vs.)
Wellesley Pde. TW2: Twick 7K **9**
Wellesley Rd. TW2: Twick 7J **9**
W4 2H **5**
Wellington Av. KT4: Wor Pk 7F **25**
TW3: Houn 2F **9**
Wellington Ct. TW12: Tedd 2J **15**
Wellington Cres.
KT3: N Mald 7K **17**
Wellington Gdns.
TW2: Twick 1J **15**
Wellington Rd. SW19 6K **13**
TW2: Twick 2J **15**
TW12: Hamp H 2J **15**
W5 1D **4**
Wellington Rd. Nth.
TW4: Houn 1E **8**
Wellington Rd. Sth.
TW4: Houn 1E **8**
Well La. SW14 2K **11**
Wellmeadow Rd. W7 1B **4**
WELLS, THE 3H **33**
Wells Ho. KT18: Eps 3H **33**
Wellside Gdns. SW14 1K **11**
Wells Rd. KT18: Eps 3H **33**
Well Way KT18: Eps 4H **33**
Welstead Way W4 1C **6**
Weltje Rd. W6 1D **6**
Wembley Rd. TW12: Hamp 5F **15**
Wendover Dr. KT3: N Mald 3C **24**
Wensleydale Gdns.
TW12: Hamp 4G **15**
Wensleydale Pas.
TW12: Hamp 5F **15**
Wensleydale Rd.
TW12: Hamp 3F **15**
Wentworth Cl. KT6: Surb 6E **22**
SM4: Mord 4K **25**
Wentworth Ct. *SW18 3K 13*
(off Garratt La.)
TW2: Twick 7K **9**
W6 3H 7
(off Paynes Wlk.)
Werter Rd. SW15 1H **13**
Wessex Av. SW19 7K **19**
Wessex Cl. KT1: King T 5J **17**
KT7: T Ditt 6A **22**
West Acres KT10: Esh 4E **26**